IMAGES
of America

Maine and the Nanticoke Valley

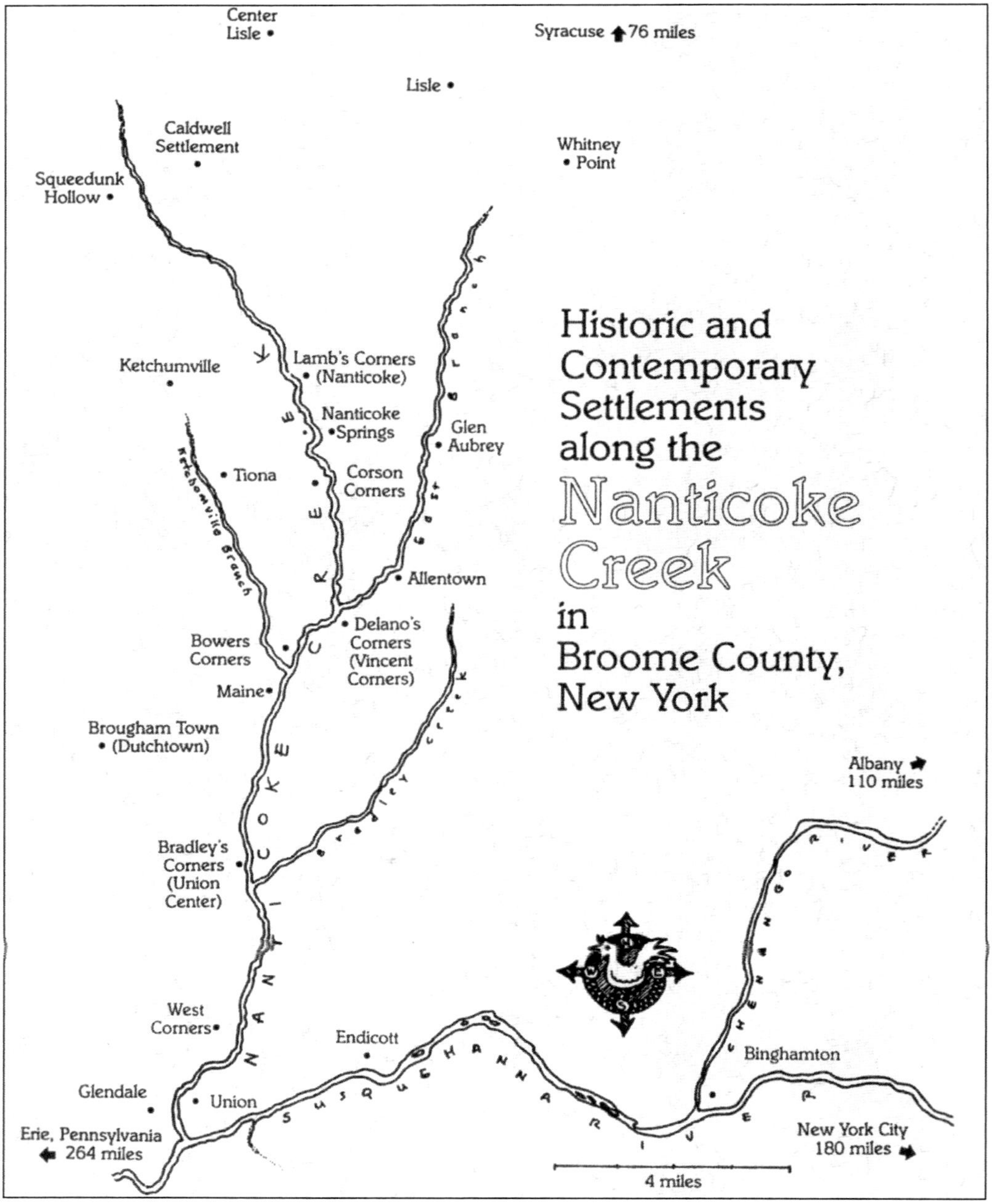

This map shows the location of the little hamlets and settlements along the Nanticoke Creek. Many of the names have changed, and some places have disappeared. Some of these names came from Native American tribes that lived in the Nanticoke Valley before settlers arrived, and some were named for prominent early families in the area. (Courtesy of the Nanticoke Valley Historical Society.)

On the Cover: This 1902 photograph shows the Pitcher twins, Inah and Inas, transporting milk to H.A. Niles Creamery in Maine Village. (Courtesy of the Nanticoke Valley Historical Society.)

IMAGES
of America

MAINE AND THE NANTICOKE VALLEY

Susan H. Lisk

ARCADIA
PUBLISHING

ISBN 978-0-7385-7686-2

Published by Arcadia Publishing
Charleston, South Carolina

Printed in the United States of America

Library of Congress Control Number: 2011936490

For all general information, please contact Arcadia Publishing:
Telephone 843-853-2070
Fax 843-853-0044
E-mail sales@arcadiapublishing.com
For customer service and orders:
Toll-Free 1-888-313-2665

Visit us on the Internet at www.arcadiapublishing.com

To Betsy Banks, my beloved sister, who is my model of strength, determination, and courage

Contents

ACKNOWLEDGMENTS

When an inexperienced volunteer undertakes a project of this magnitude, there are many people to thank for their help and support. First, I want to acknowledge those who are no longer living who did so much to preserve our local history in the Nanticoke Valley. This list includes Lee Loomis, who was fascinated with photography as a young man. Because of the volume of photographs he took, we have the opportunity to view life in the Nanticoke Valley around 1900.

Additionally, a special thanks to the founding and current members of the Nanticoke Valley Historical Society and all the past residents who kept diaries, photographs, and records that we still refer to today. It is these, along with generously donated artifacts, that insure the preservation of our community's history for future generations.

Thank you to Janet Bowers Bothwell and the Bowers Foundation for all they have done to preserve the history of the Nanticoke Valley. Also, thank you to Shirley and Gordon Woodward and Clark Gardner, who donated funds to buy the computer and scanner for use on this project and other future projects.

Thanks to a host of townspeople for their knowledge and willingness to share it with me: Marie Abbott, Nancy Berry, Philip Childs, Carol Egan, Marceil Hamill, Alice Hopkins, Joyce Jackson, Owen Loomis, Venley and Kathy McGregor, Janice McKitrick, Sally and Ron Meyers, Laura Riley, Sandy Rozek, Jane and Tom Scheibner, Richard and Anita Shipway, Chris Underwood, Betty Welch, and Jane Youngs. Special thanks go to Grey Osterud and Shirley Woodward for providing much-needed information. Unless otherwise noted, all of the images in this book are from the Nanticoke Valley Historical Society archives.

I am indeed indebted to my husband of 38 years, Stan Lisk, who has not only shared my enthusiasm for this project but, with his patience and technical expertise, guided me through the computer programs necessary for its completion. Thank you to Monica Lisk, Jim Lisk, and Betsy Banks for their unwavering encouragement and support.

And, finally, thank you to Sue Edelman for sending me my first Arcadia book!

INTRODUCTION

The towns of Maine and Nanticoke, both in New York, began as part of a 230,000-acre tract of land known as the Boston Purchase or the Massachusetts Ten Townships. This purchase was made in 1787 by 60 men from Berkshire County, Massachusetts, for 12.5¢ (333 Spanish dollars) per acre; in 1790, the United States signed the Treaty of New York with the local Native Americans.

The first settlers became aware of these lands when they traveled through them as soldiers in the Revolutionary War. Most of the pioneers came from Connecticut and Massachusetts. The Nanticoke Valley was hilly, with a narrow valley formed by the Nanticoke Creek. The hills were covered with hardwood and fir trees that could be harvested as logs, cut up in sawmills, and used to build local homes or barns or sent down the Susquehanna River for sale in cities to the south. The bark of the hemlock trees contained tannin, which was used in various tanneries in Glen Aubrey and the village of Maine. The gravelly loam soil was good for pastures, as well as dairy and sheep farming.

The first recorded settler in Maine was Benjamin Norton, who came from Stockbridge, Massachusetts, in 1794, and set up a homestead about a mile north of the hamlet. Russell and Alfred Gates arrived in 1795. Another man from Stockbridge, Jed Dudley, followed in 1796. Amos Howard was also an early settler. It was a difficult journey, cutting through the wilderness, and the forests were full of wolves, bears, and big cats.

The town of Maine was part of the town of Union until it split off to form a new township in 1848. Union is now to the south, Tioga County to the west, and the town of Nanticoke and village of Barker to the north of Maine. A small portion of Maine was split off to join the town of Chenango. Today, there are 45.8 square miles of land in the town of Maine.

The first town meetings in Maine were held in 1848 to elect the following officers: Andrew H. Arnold, supervisor; John W. Hunt, town clerk; Marshall Delano, superintendent of common schools; John T. Davis, collector; Cyrus Gates, four-year justice of the peace; John Blanchard, one-year justice of the peace; Hanan W. Moores, three-year justice of the peace; and others filling various positions.

The town of Maine had two small villages and various neighborhood settlements. Maine Village was called Graball by the first settlers. It was then changed to Maine, possibly because it was the main village between Whitney Point and Union Center. Another theory is that the surveyor general of New York State, Simeon De Witt, named the town "Maine Village" because it was the central location of many mills, shops, services, creameries, churches, and a school.

Union Center was the next-largest village in the town of Maine. Since the town of Maine was taken out of the town of Union, Union Center now straddles both towns. Once called Centerville, Union Center also had a number of mills, cheese factories, stores, services, churches, and schools. Other settlements in the town of Maine included Tiona, Gates, Arbutus, East Maine, Allentown, Delano's Corners, New Ireland, Brocket Hollow, Bowers' Corners, Norton's Corners, Oak Hill, Finch Hollow, and Broughamtown.

In 1848, the population of the town of Maine was 1,800. By 1870, it had grown to 2,305 (its apex), and then gradually dropped down to 1,360 by 1920. The population in 2012 was 5,377. In the past, people were subsidiary farmers who did other work on the side to make extra income, including smithing, running a mill, cabinet-making, wagon-making, shoemaking, and—in more recent years—working at the Endicott Johnson Corporation or IBM.

The town of Nanticoke was once part of the town of Lisle. It is bordered to the north by Lisle, to the east by Barker, to the south by Maine, and to the west by Tioga County. The first town meeting was held in March 1832 at the Philip Councilman home. The town covers 24.3 square miles of land. Nanticoke derives its name from the creek that has two branches flowing through the valley and was named for the Nanticoke Indians, who moved to the area from Maryland to be under the protection of the Iroquois Confederacy. There are two small villages—Glen Aubrey and Lamb's Corners—located in the town. Some of the early pioneers were John Beachtle, James Stoddard, John Ames, Jesse Lane, Stephen Japhet, and Horace Walter.

Glen Aubrey, the first part of Nanticoke to be settled, was located on the east branch of Nanticoke Creek. In the early days, Glen Aubrey was called Councilman's Settlement after Philip Councilman. The name was later changed to Glen Aubrey for Aubrey Smith, the wife of the town's first postmaster, George W. Smith, who also owned a tannery and the Octagon House. The little hamlet included stores, a creamery, sawmills, a blacksmith shop, and tanneries. The post office was established there on July 10, 1855. There were two churches, including the Baptist church, which is still attended. As soon as the trees were gone, the population declined—but the village is still there.

The other small village, on the west side of Nanticoke, was called Lamb's Corners for Isaac Lamb, who arrived there in 1804. The post office opened there in 1860 in a store run by Elijah Adams. The village's name was changed to Nanticoke in 1891. In 1872, George Littlewood opened a cheese factory. There was also a blacksmith shop run by Warren Gee and a fairground with a racetrack. The two beautiful churches, the Methodist Episcopal church and the Baptist church, were built in 1852 and 1853, respectively.

About a mile away was Nanticoke Springs. Nathan Cadwell owned two springs in the area and built a boardinghouse where visitors could come to take advantage of the healing properties of the waters by drinking and bathing. The house could hold up to 60 people. Visitors came from New York City and all over the country. For many years, a stage ran from Binghamton to the springs to accommodate visitors. Around 1865, the boardinghouse burned down.

Today, neither Maine nor Nanticoke supports much farming, but the Nanticoke Valley has become a charming bedroom community. It is a beautiful place to live with little commercial activity and no railroads or large, busy interstates passing through.

The Maine Community Band celebrated its 150th anniversary in 2011. The group started as a cornet band in 1861 and has continued on in one form or another up to today. In the 1860s and 1870s, stringed instruments were played by band members Charles Lincoln, A.D. Cummings, E.C. Johnson, and T.O. Smith.

In 1905 or 1906, the band ordered or purchased much-needed used instruments from a place in Philadelphia. They were given out among the band members, and conductors Frank Bean and Charles Lincoln taught them how to play. These days, the Maine Community Band contains more members from out of town than actual Maine residents. Sharing their love of music, they travel the county to play at parades, nursing homes, ice-cream socials, and other special events. They still practice on Tuesday nights at the Federated church in Maine and are always happy to have musicians join them, no matter their skill level.

It is quite unusual for a small town to have a large museum complex like the one belonging to the Nanticoke Valley Historical Society, but there is much history to see and discover in and around the area.

One
MAINE

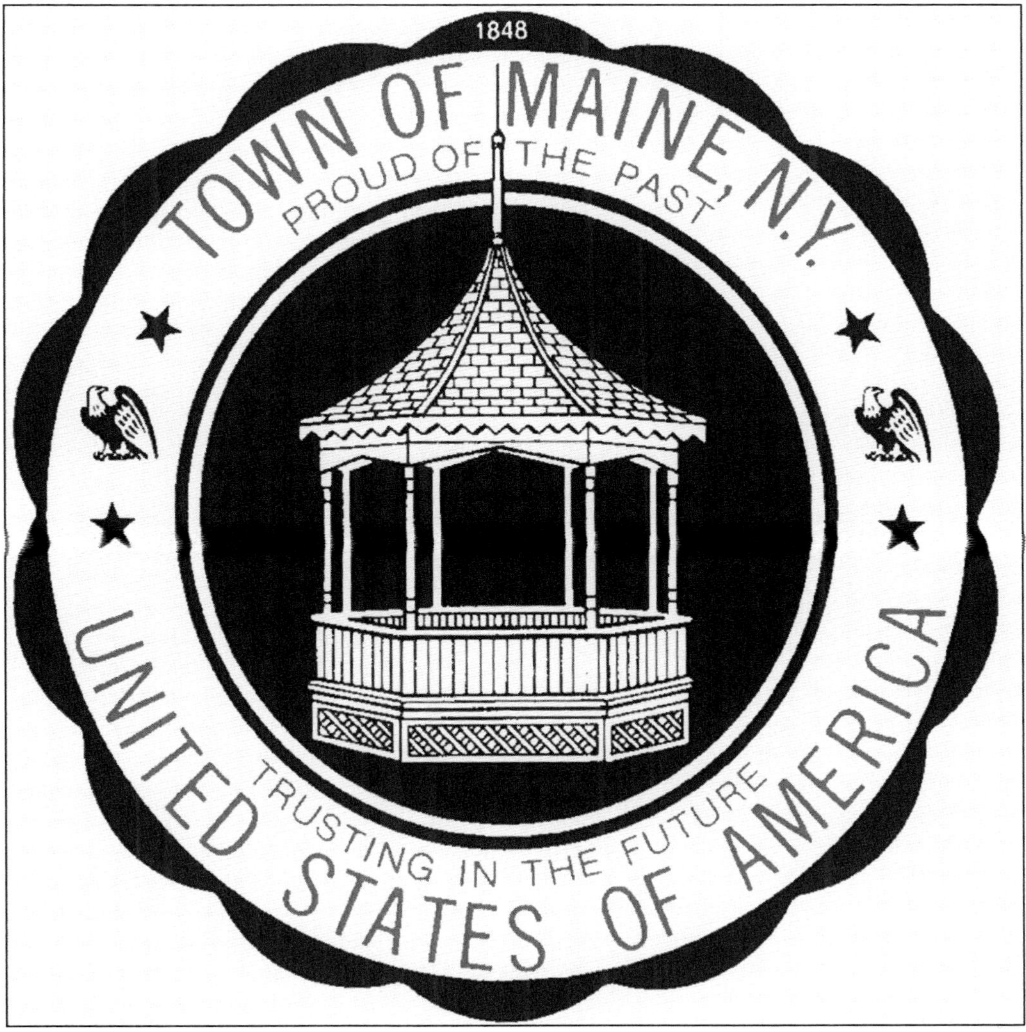

The Town of Maine seal was designed for the bicentennial in 1976 by 17-year-old student Douglas Guiles of Maine Village. Guiles based his design on the pagoda that once sat in the middle of Main Street. The seal has proudly represented Maine ever since. (Courtesy of the Town of Maine.)

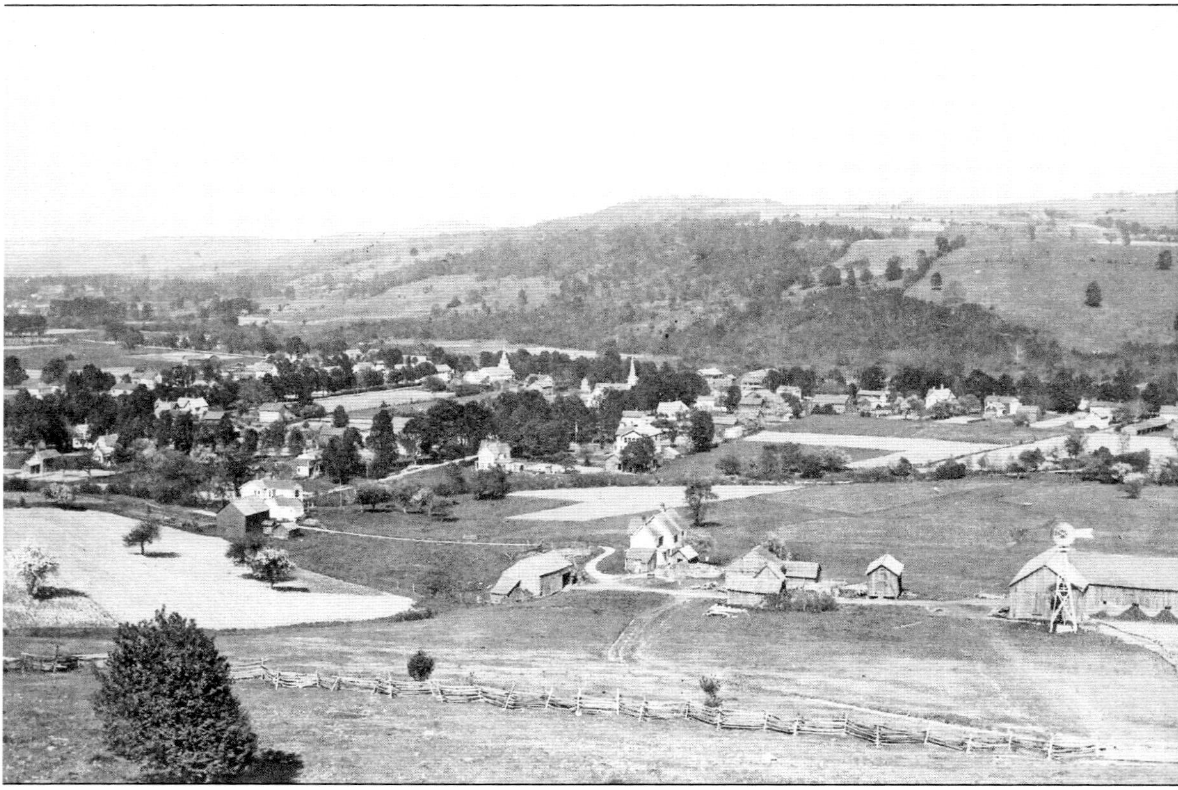

This c. 1908 view of the hamlet of Maine was taken from King Hill looking east. The spires of the three churches in town are visible; they are, from left to right, the Congregational church (on Main Street), the Baptist church (on Church Street), and the Methodist church (also on Main Street). This photograph also offers a clear view of the wide, flat valley and the beautiful hills.

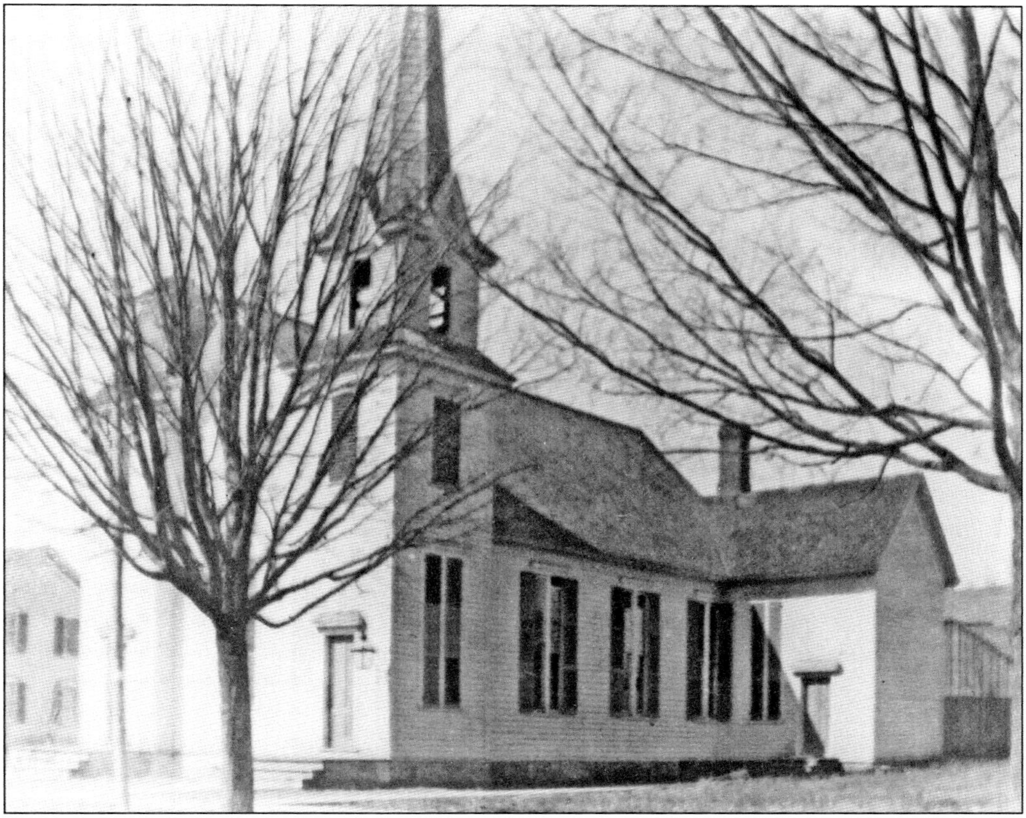

The first Methodist Episcopal church in Maine Village was incorporated in 1845. Earlier services were held in the Maine School on Church Street and the Curtis School, which was south of the village. In 1848, William Lincoln, a civic-minded merchant in Maine Village, donated the property and $100 toward building the church. The final cost was $2,000. It was dedicated on October 17, 1850, by Rev. J.M. Snyder. Note the horse sheds behind the church, which were necessary for the care of the horses of those attending the services. On May 9, 1928, this church burned down. The next day, the trustees and pastor of the Congregational Church of Maine invited the Methodists to meet with them, and the two groups have been united ever since. The image below shows a Christmas pageant in the Methodist church in the early 1900s. (Below, courtesy of Betty Welch.)

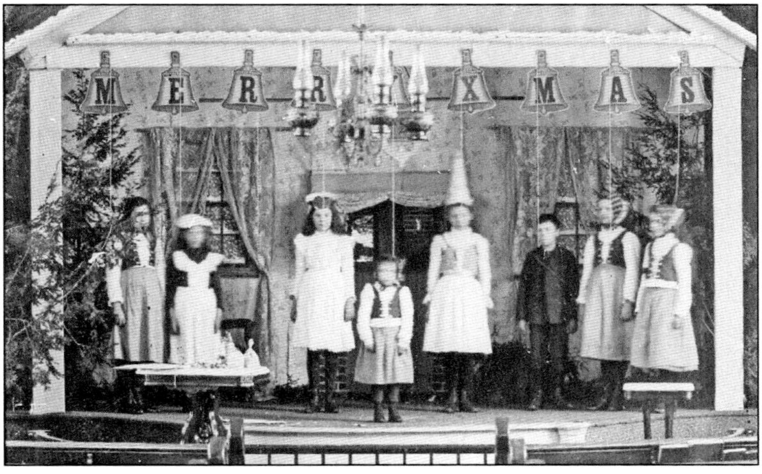

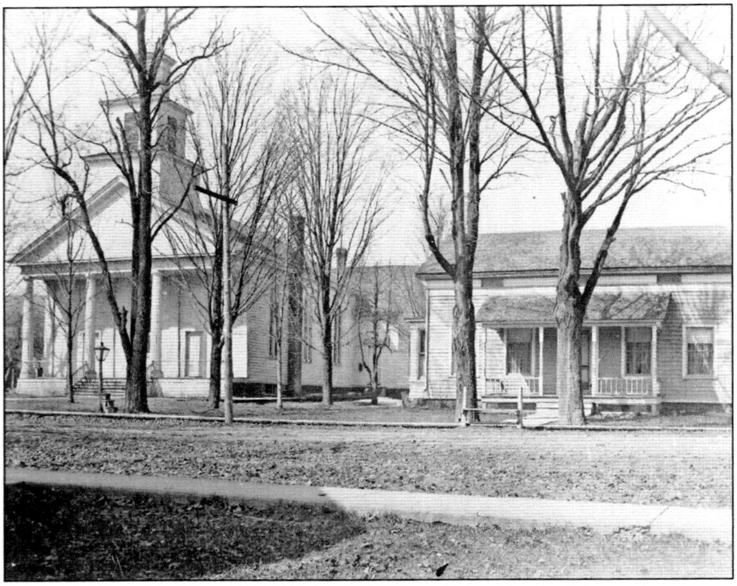

The Maine Congregational Church was founded in 1819 next to the Maine Cemetery. A new church was built on the corner of Church and Main Streets in Maine Village. In 1867, that church was moved by oxen teams through the backs of lots on Main Street to its present site. In 1928, it became the Federated church when the Methodists joined them.

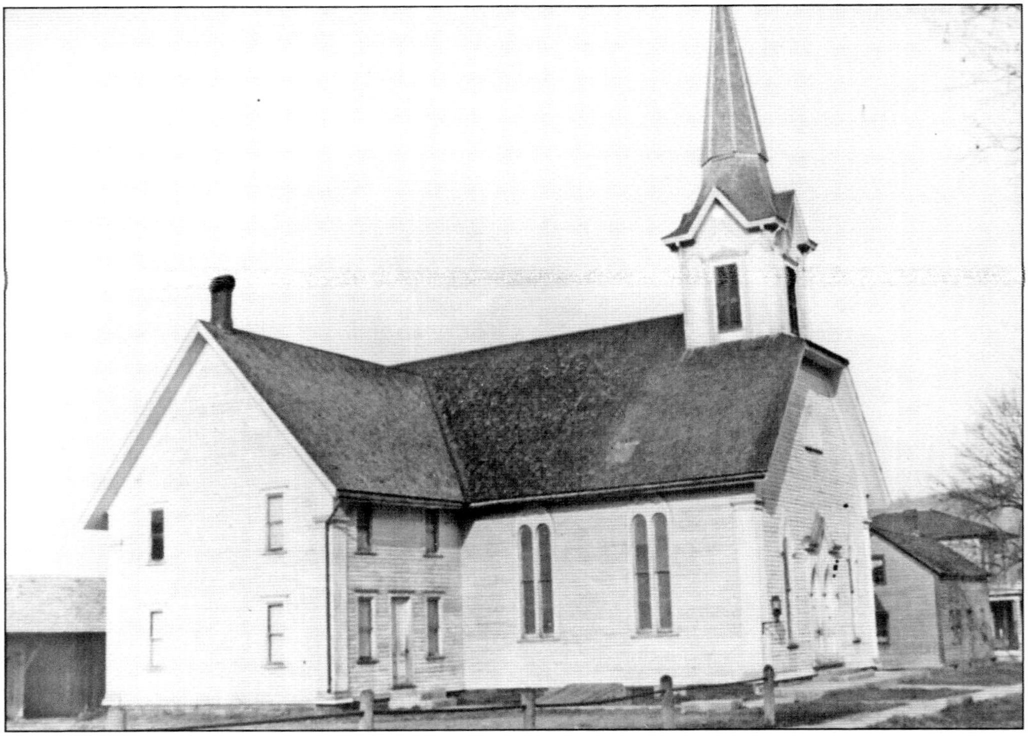

This 1910 photograph of the Maine Baptist Church was taken from a glass negative. The congregation formed in 1835 with 31 members. The church was built and dedicated in 1840. In 1980, this church was torn down and replaced with a larger one. Notice the horse barns in the back of the church, which were used before automobiles came on the scene.

The F.H. (Fred H.) Marean and Son store (pictured) was built in 1865 on the present-day site of the Most Holy Rosary parking lot. The post office was located inside the store. After Fred Marean died, his son, Henry, sold the store in 1900 and moved to Binghamton, where he opened a men's furnishings store. The store shown at right burned down in 1920.

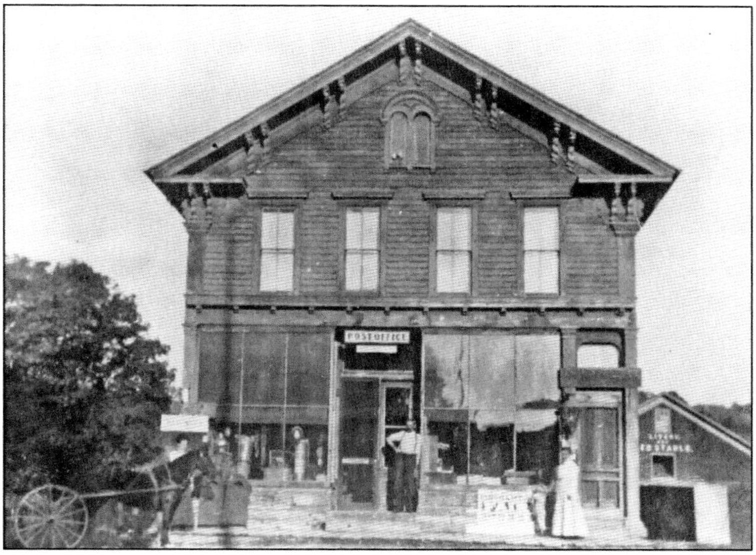

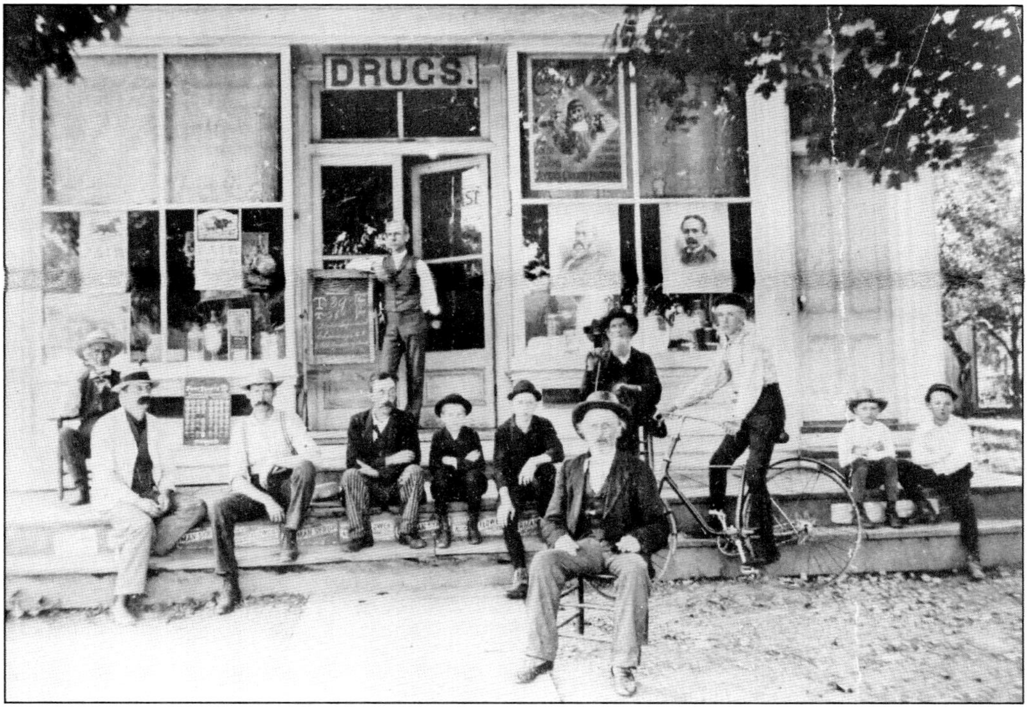

The drugstore owned by druggist LeRoy Bostwick was relocated to 7 McGregor Avenue in Maine Village after the previous store, which was on Main Street, burned down in 1893. The telephone exchange was moved to this building after its previous location, the Curtis store, burned in 1905. Pictured here are Jedidiah Dudley (front, sitting in chair), Bostwick (standing in doorway), Orlo Curlhair (on bicycle), and Morgan Leonard (second from left); the others are unidentified.

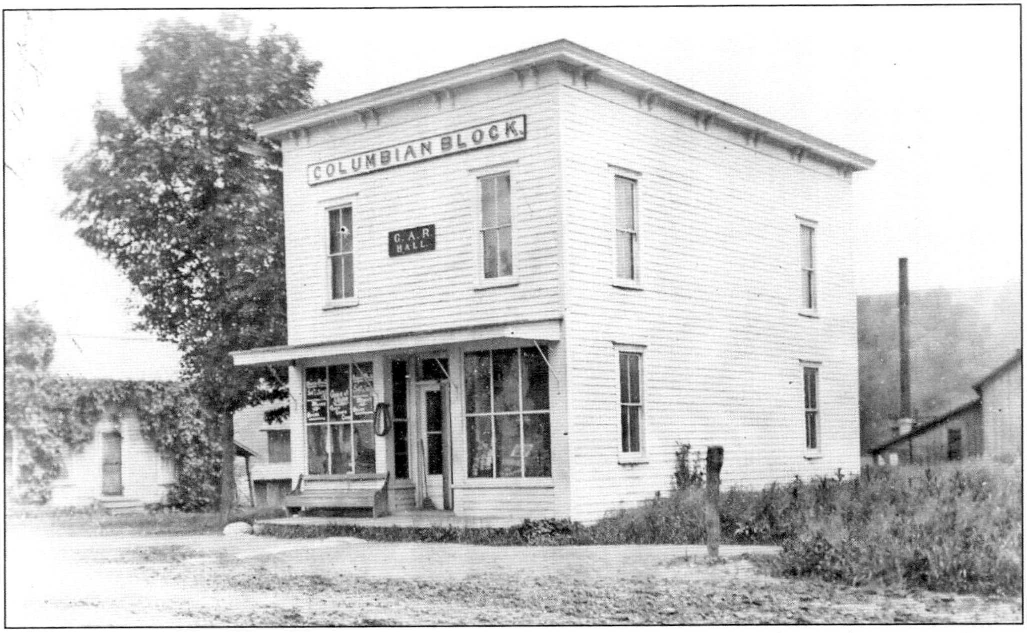

In the early 1900s, the Columbian Block, owned by F.C. Curlhair, was located next to what is now 2630 Main Street and housed the post office. The H.A. Niles Creamery is visible in the background at right. At the time of this photograph, the GAR Hall was located upstairs. In 1955, the Maine Masonic Lodge was built next door to the Columbian Block.

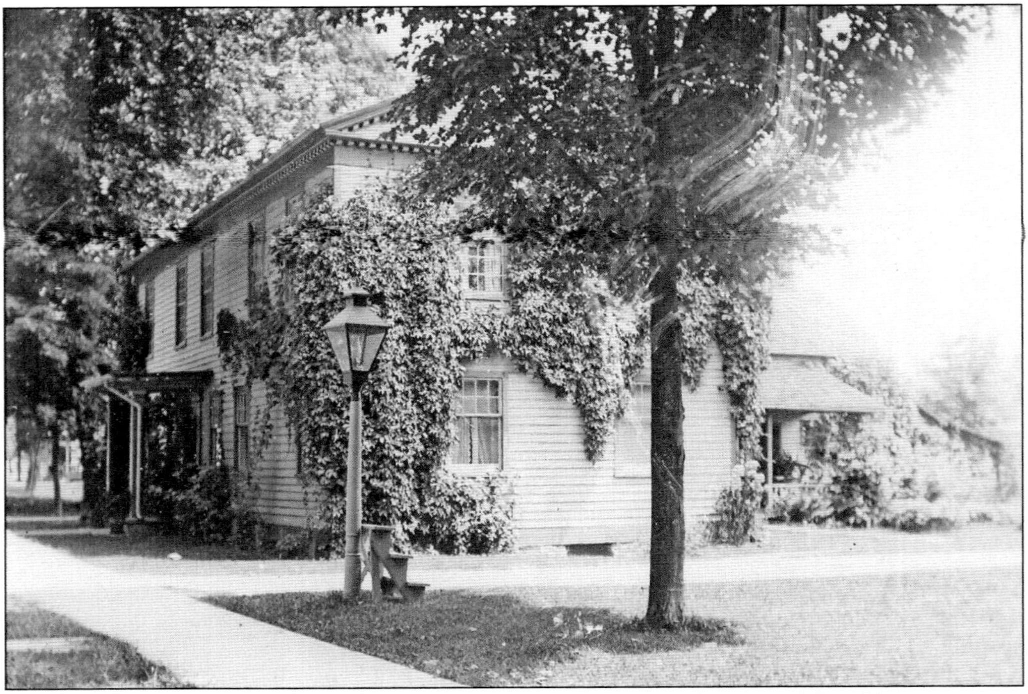

The Hathaway House was built by Oliver Whitcomb in 1815 and is one of the oldest structures in Maine Village. As an inn, it often accommodated cattle shippers from Whitney's Point, as it marked the halfway point in the journey to Binghamton. Later owned by David Hathaway, it featured a ballroom with a vaulted ceiling on the second floor.

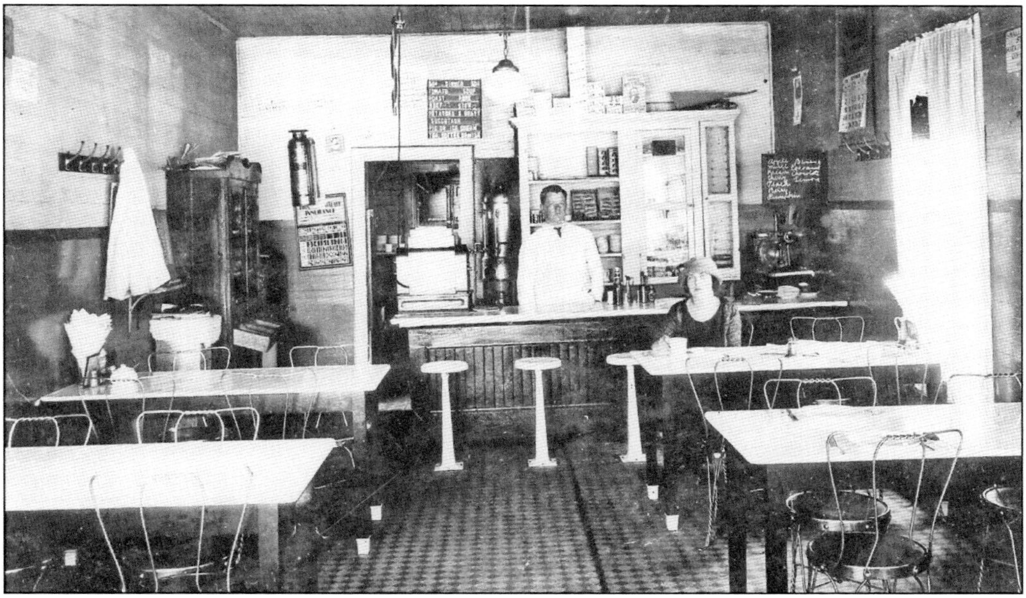

In 1920, Paddy's Ice Cream Parlor was next to the Tymeson Brothers store on Main Street in Maine Village. The Padbury family lived in the back. The clerk, Lester Padbury, was 18 when this photograph was taken; the woman is unidentified. Later, ice cream was sold on the front porch and groceries were sold inside.

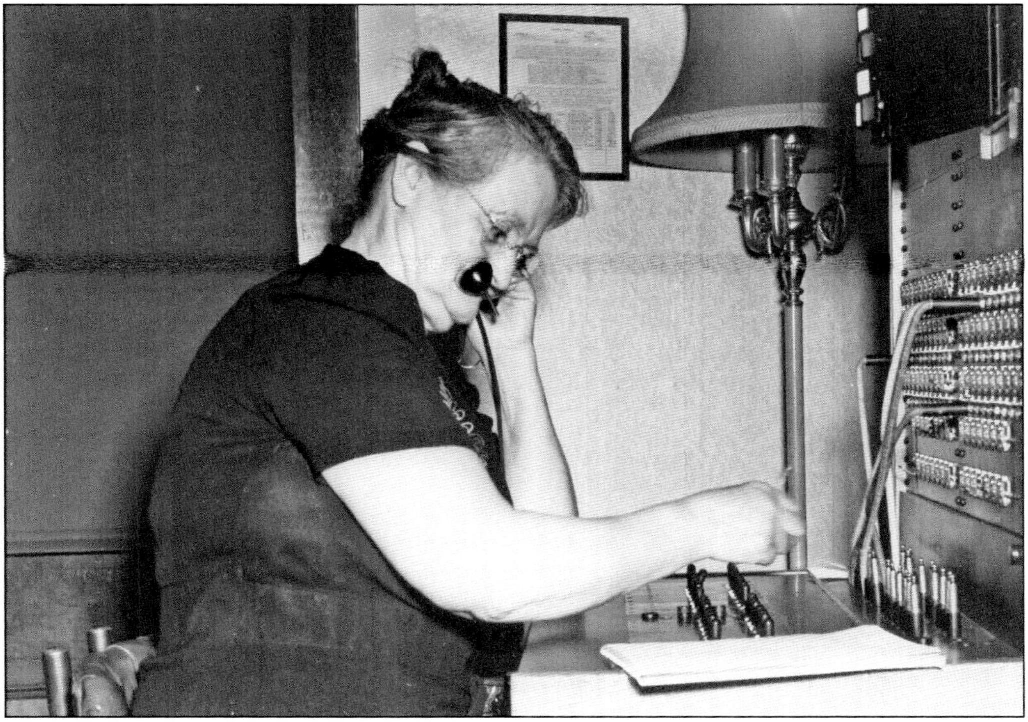

In the late 1800s, the Bell and York State Telephone companies set up in Maine. Eventually, Nel Gates (pictured) ran the central switchboard in her home on McGregor Avenue in Maine Village. On January 6, 1952, Ollie Ketchum made the last hand-crank call in Maine, which was the last community in New York State to convert to the dial telephone system.

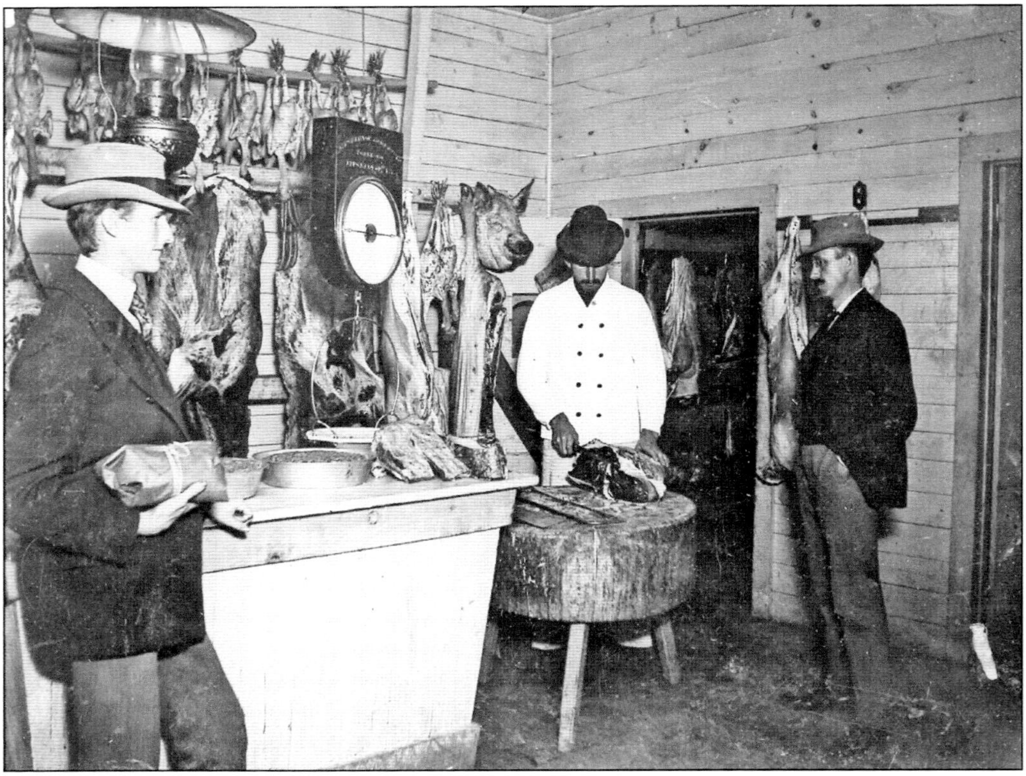

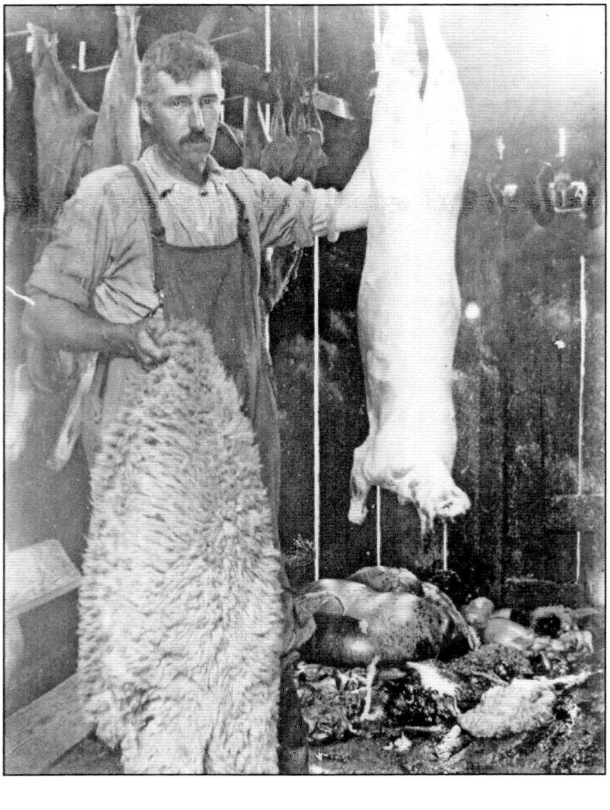

An article in the 1903 *Whitney Point Reporter* stated, "The meat trust has not so badly affected the meat markets as to cause them to close as G.B. Smith and H. Kattell are both doing a flourishing business." There was also an Ellis and Marean meat market behind the Sherwood store, which burned down in 1893. Earl Lewis also had a meat market in Maine Village and sold meat out of the back of his truck to outlying farm families. These photographs feature Herman Kattell—above, he is cutting meat for customers on the butcher block in his store (notice the pig head hanging on the wall), and at left, he holds a fleece next to a carcass.

The William O. Lincoln store was on the corner of Main and Church Streets. When the three-story building was constructed in 1856, it was the largest store in Maine Village. The Masonic lodge was on the third floor. It burned in 1893, but the Lincoln home, which was next door to the store, survives to this day. Lincoln was also a charter member of the town band in 1861.

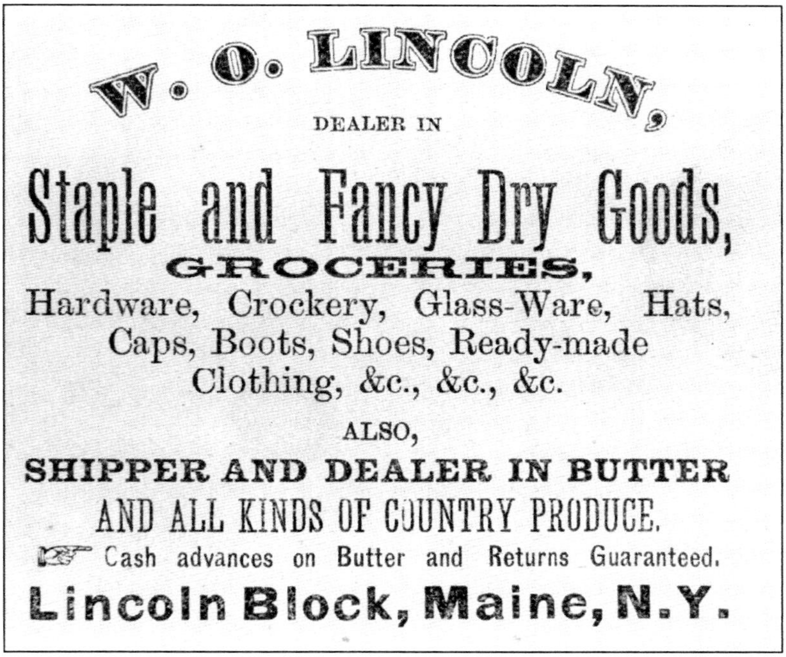
W. O. LINCOLN,
DEALER IN
Staple and Fancy Dry Goods,
GROCERIES,
Hardware, Crockery, Glass-Ware, Hats,
Caps, Boots, Shoes, Ready-made
Clothing, &c., &c., &c.
ALSO,
SHIPPER AND DEALER IN BUTTER
AND ALL KINDS OF COUNTRY PRODUCE.
☞ Cash advances on Butter and Returns Guaranteed.
Lincoln Block, Maine, N.Y.

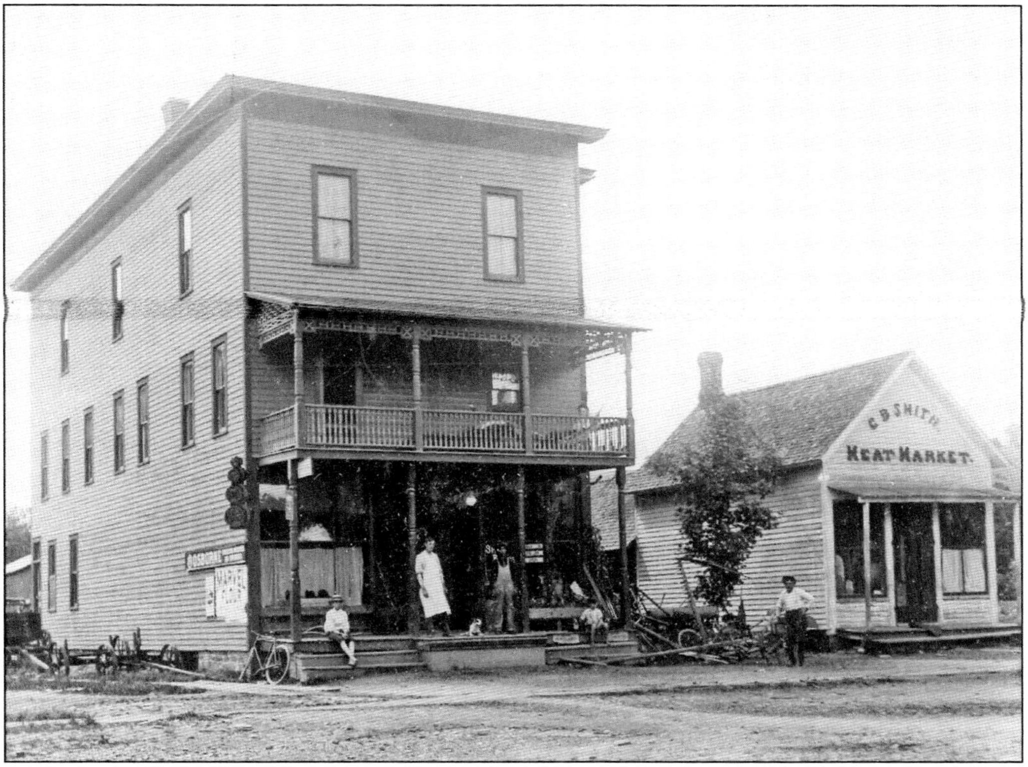

This store on the corner of Main and Church Streets was built after an 1893 fire destroyed the previous store and other surrounding buildings. In 1895, Leroy Brooks owned and operated it, and there was a Masonic lodge upstairs. The building was eventually purchased by the Tymeson family, who ran the Tymeson Brothers store there until 1945.

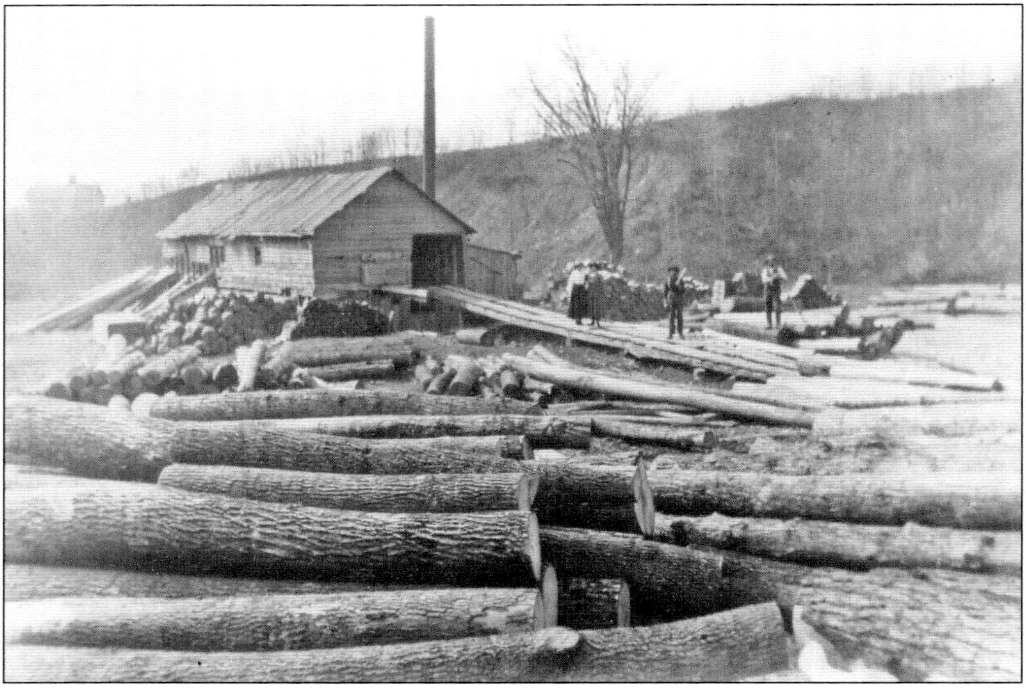

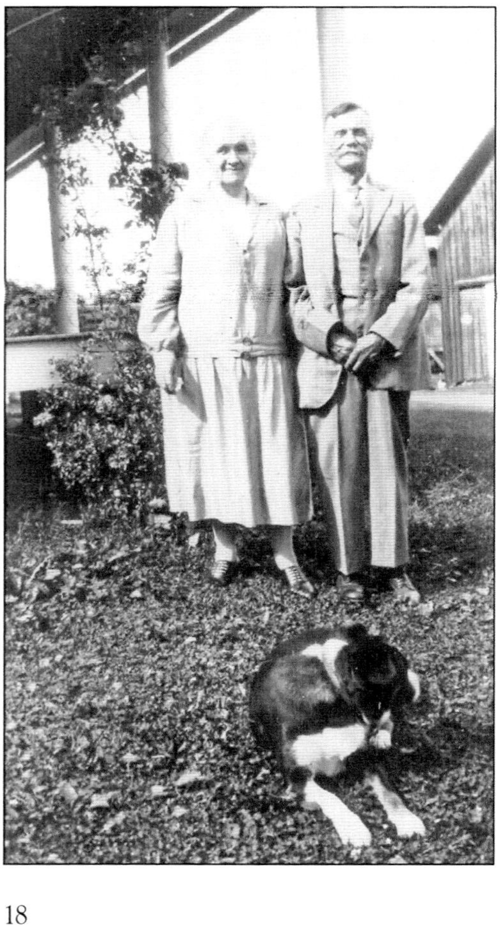

In 1878, Chauncey McIntyre built a sawmill (above) on Little Nanticoke Creek (also called Lewis Creek). The wooden rakes made there were sold and shipped as far away as Australia. The hay rakes were six feet long, with a two-foot beam holding 12 wooden teeth and braced by wire. The mill also made baseball bats and shingles. It closed in 1928.

Myrtie Durfee McIntyre and Chauncey F. McIntyre stand in front of their home on Lewis Street in 1927. Chauncey owned and operated the sawmill and rake factory pictured above (and visible in the background). Their grandson, Ralph Loomis, recalls that Myrtie helped assemble rakes at the factory. (Courtesy of Owen Loomis.)

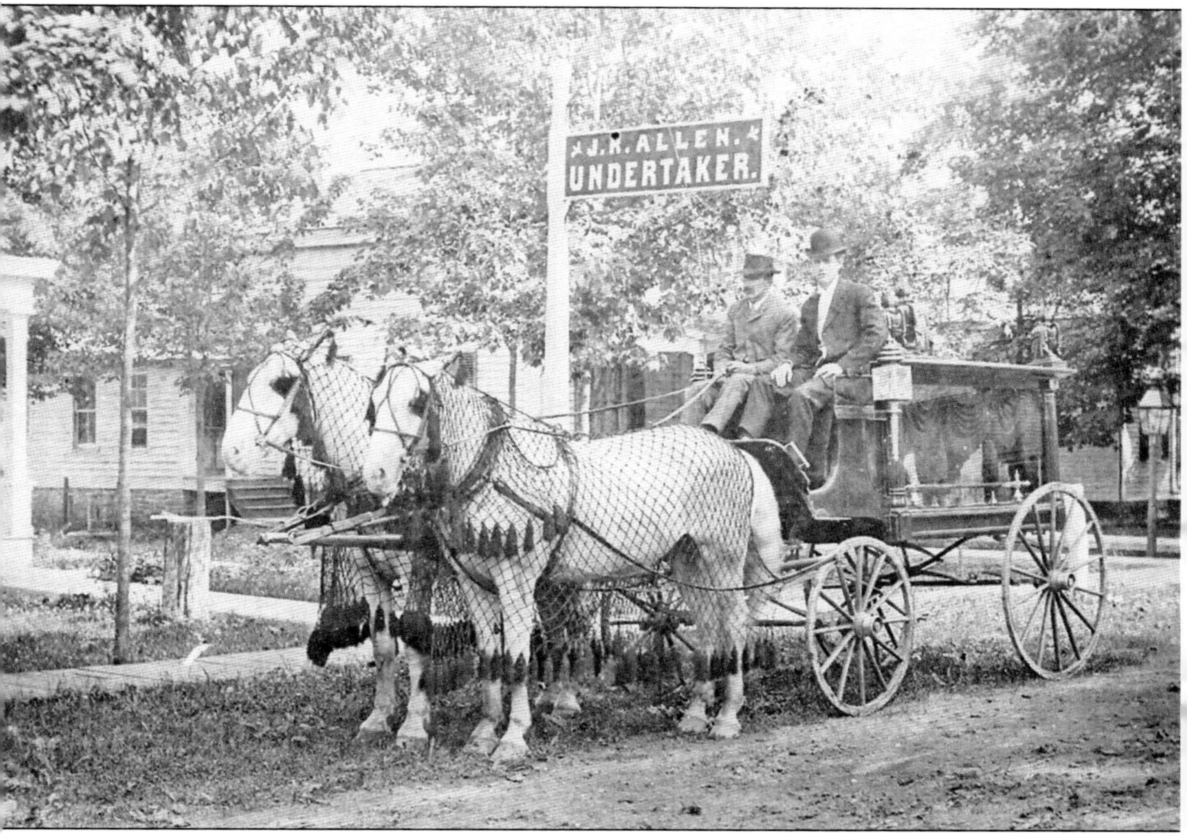

In this 1908 image, J.R. Allen (right) sits on the first hearse in Maine Village with driver Robert Taylor. The hearse is parked in front of Allen's home at what is now 2586 Main Street. The Allens started their undertaking business in Allentown, New York, near Flint Road on Route 26. When Allen was 14, he became an assistant to his father, John J. Allen, in the family's undertaking business. His family was well known for having beautiful singing voices. When the Allens started the business, common practice was for the undertaker to come to the home and set up the body in the parlor. While J.R. Allen had his business in Maine Village, he also worked at the Tymeson Brothers store and was a member of the town band, playing the bass drum. In 1915, the Allens moved their funeral business to Washington Avenue in Endicott.

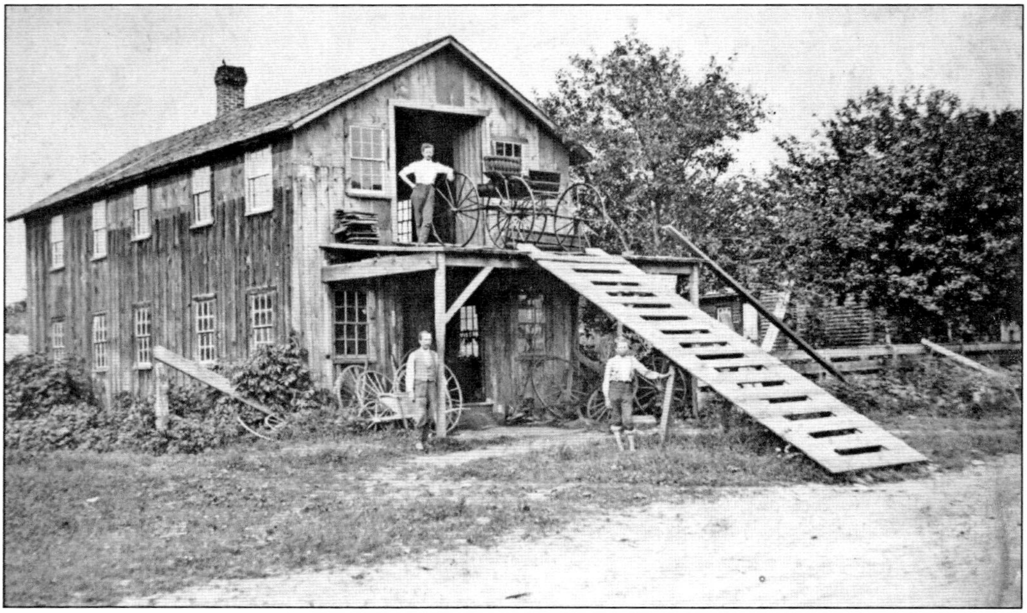

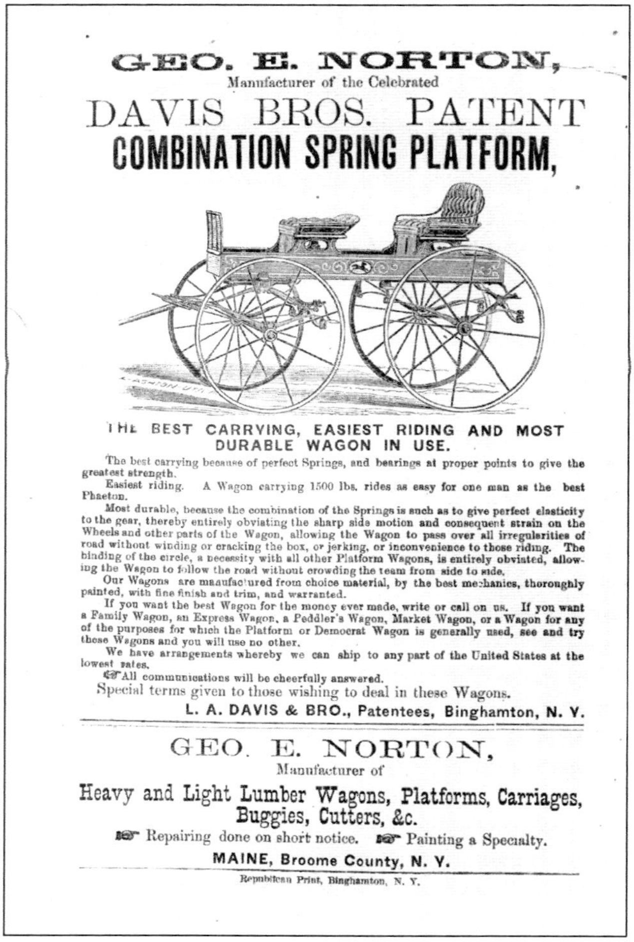

The George Norton Wagon Shop was located on Nanticoke Road, directly across from Tiona Road in Maine. The location along Nanticoke Creek is called Norton's Corners, which was directly across from Bowers' Corners. The shops were in operation from 1840 through 1929. William Henry Norton started the business making heavy or light wagons, carriages, buggies, cutters, guns, and caskets. He was also a blacksmith. After he retired, his son, George, continued to run the business, manufacturing furniture at one point. The shop and the men who worked there are pictured above. The ramp shows how they got carriages up to the second floor, where the painting studio was—it was located there because the second floor contained less dust, which could spoil paint jobs. Painting samples are still on the walls today. The advertisement at left is for the George Norton Wagon Shop.

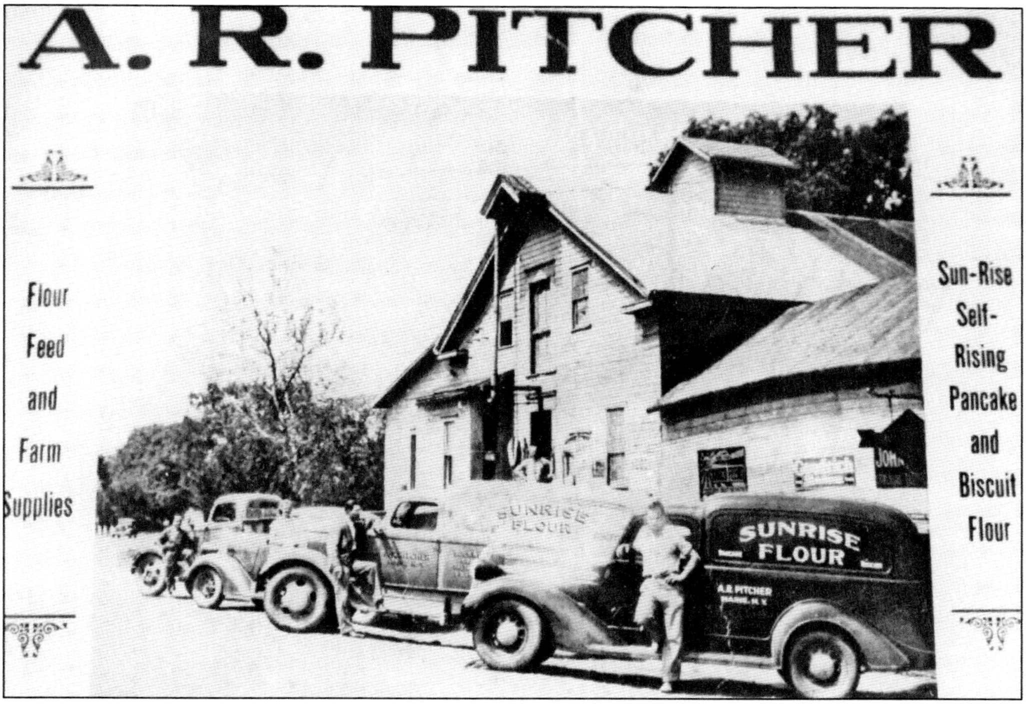

Pitcher's Mill has been located just outside Maine Village since 1830, when it was built by Belden and Daniel Slosson from hand-hewn red beech timbers. In 1848, it was enlarged and remodeled by Dr. William Butler and William Lincoln. From 1925 to 1941, the mill was owned and operated by Archie Pitcher. After 1941, the mill was converted to electric power. The Lainhart family owned the mill from 1945 to 1955. The image below shows the millrace. There is also a lovely house in the woods behind the mill where the miller and his family lived. Flour from this mill went west with those who left for the San Francisco Gold Rush in 1849. Much of the corn and grain grown on farms in the Nanticoke Valley was ground here.

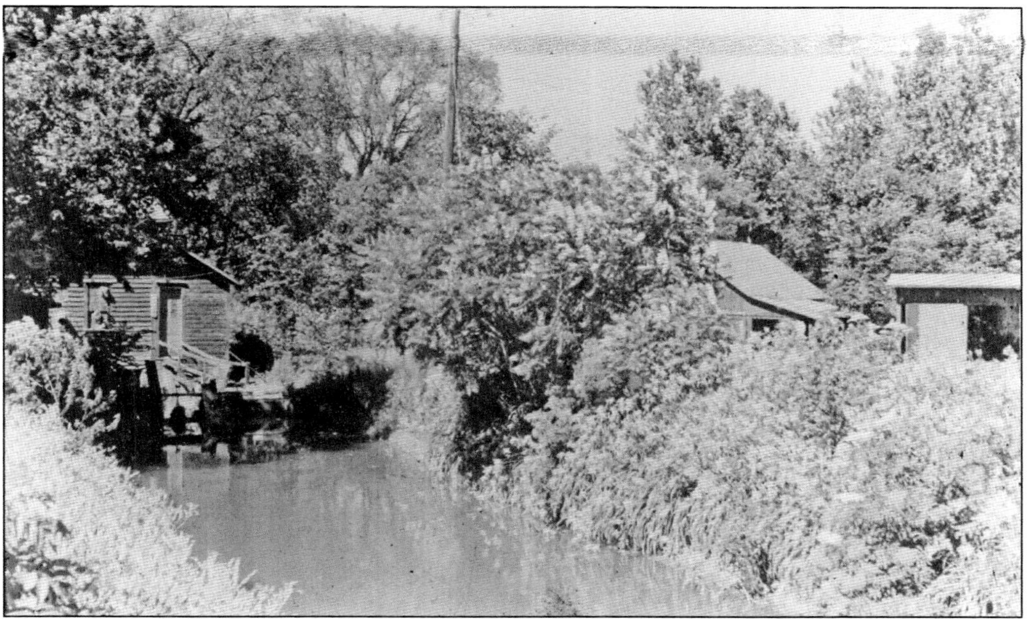

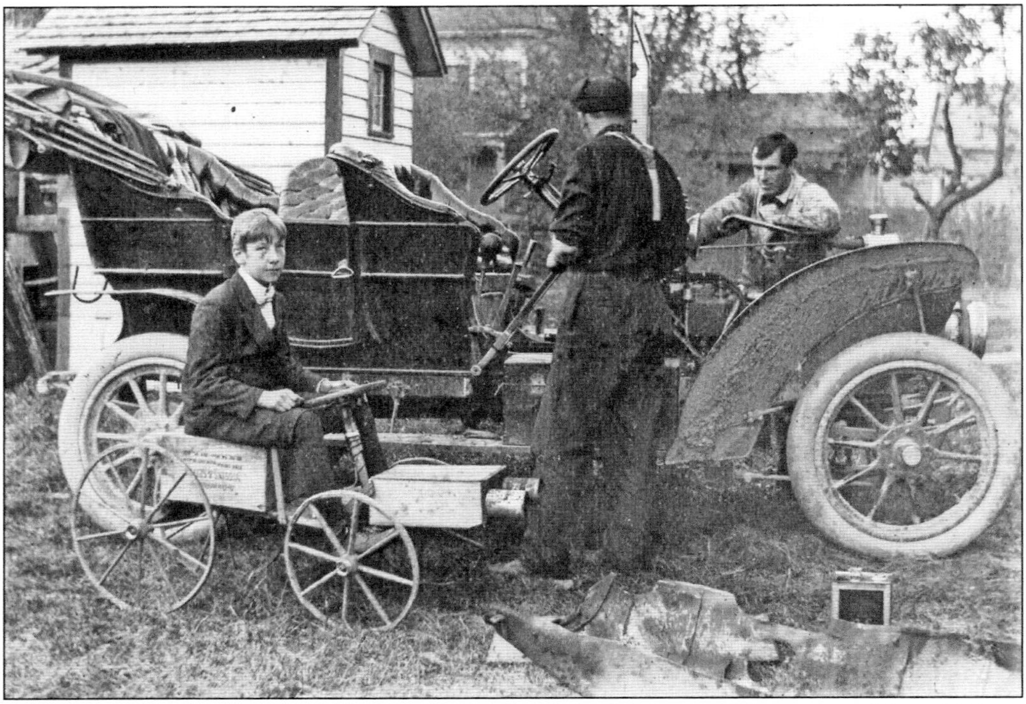

DeForest Watermen (center, with his back turned) ran the first automobile garage in Maine Village. This photograph was taken at the home of Olive Grey Vanderburg, which was at present-day 41 Lewis Street. With Watermen are Merle Lawton (left) and James McGregor Jr.

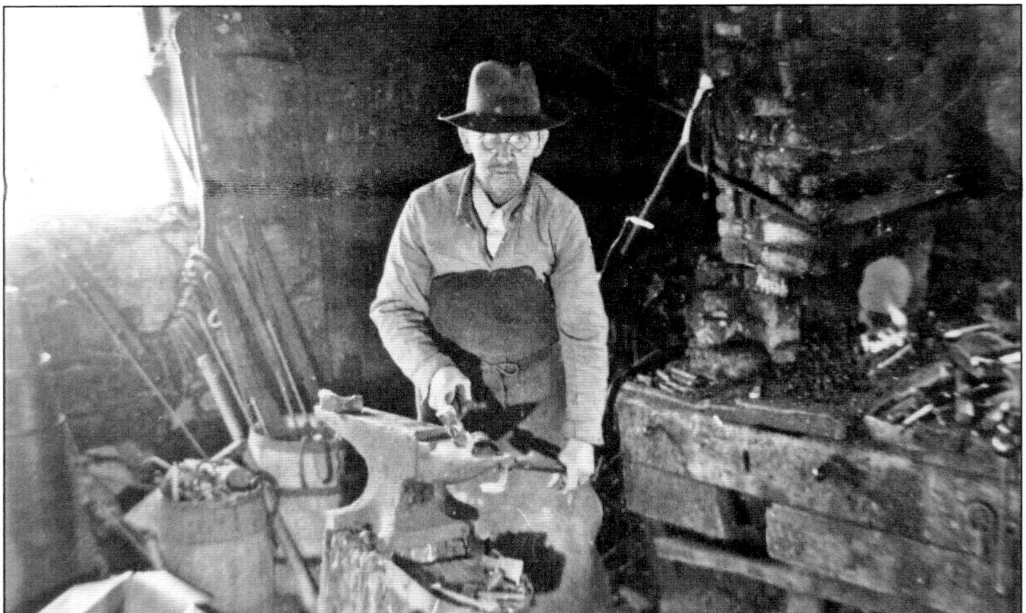

Moses Delano, Henry Hinaman, Burt Beals, George Page, and William, Fred, and Frank Bean—one of whom is pictured here—were all blacksmiths who worked in Maine. At first, blacksmiths were necessary to forge the parts for wagons, farm implements, and various hardware items, such as shoes for horses and oxen. Once the automobile arrived, smithing began to fade into the past.

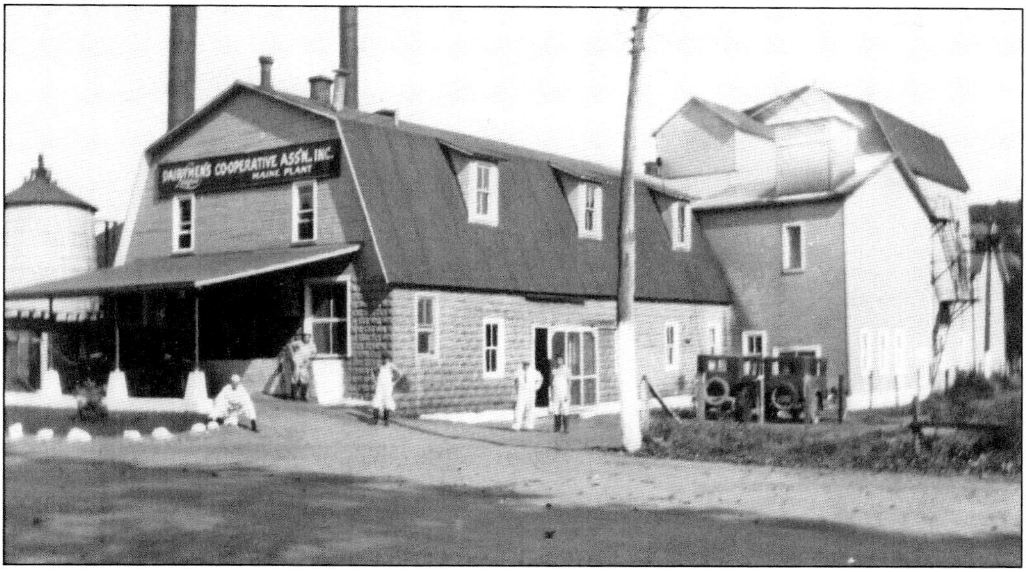

This 1927 image shows the Dairyman's League Cooperative Association's Maine plant. The milk-processing plant was on the northeast side of Main Street in Maine Village. In 1934, the V.C. McGregor and Sons Company bought the plant to house their egg and poultry business. It burned down on February 14, 1964.

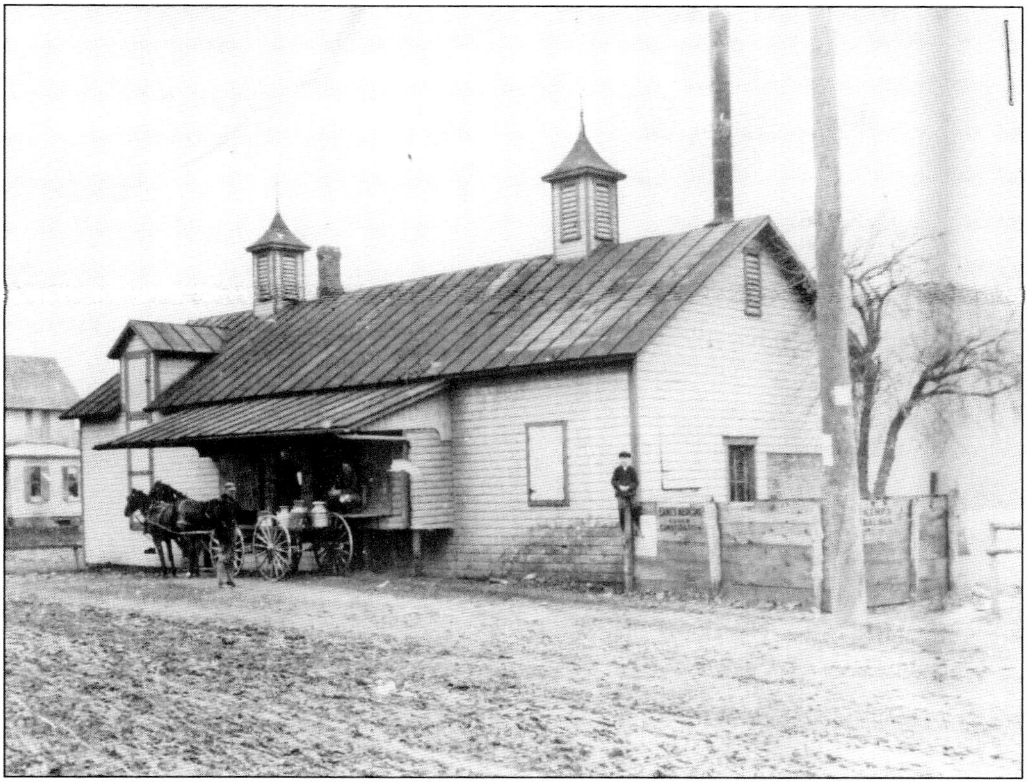

Doanes Creamery was located on the site of the old tannery east of Main Street in Maine Village. This creamery paid farmers per pound of butterfat and also bought cream from smaller creameries. They made and sold fresh cream, butter, cottage cheese, ice cream, and cream cheese.

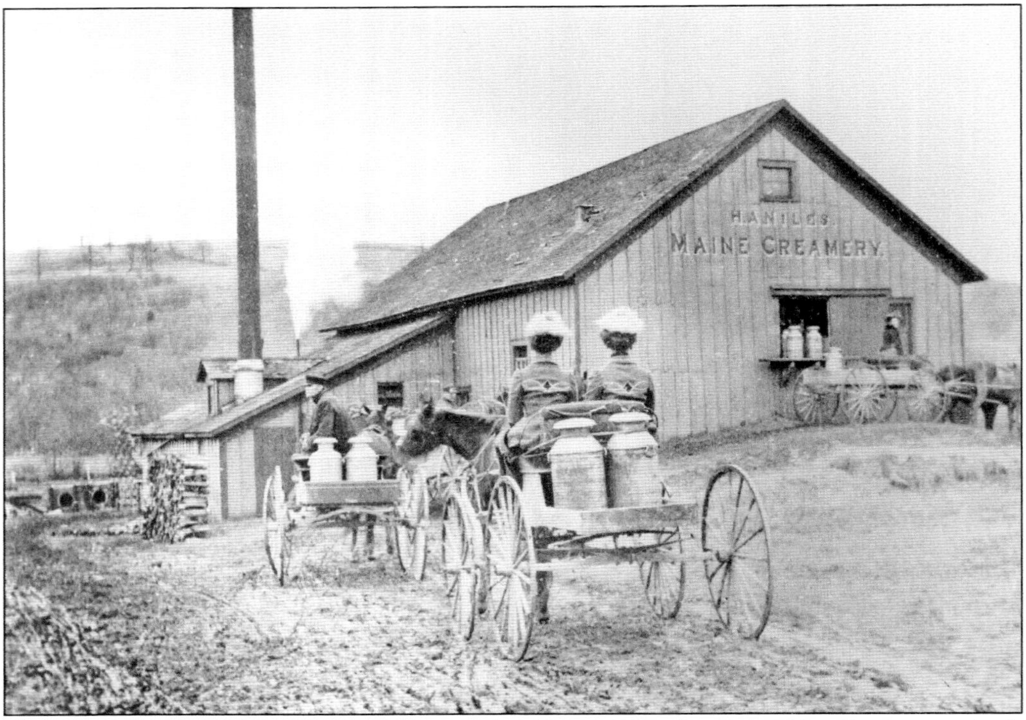

In 1902, the Pitcher twins, Inah and Inas, take their milk to the H.A. Niles Creamery, which was behind the Columbian block, east of Main Street. This creamery was listed in the New York State list of "butter and cheese factories, milk stations, and condenseries" as producing 26,828 pounds of butter in 1902. It was sold to Kinney Brothers of Binghamton in 1910.

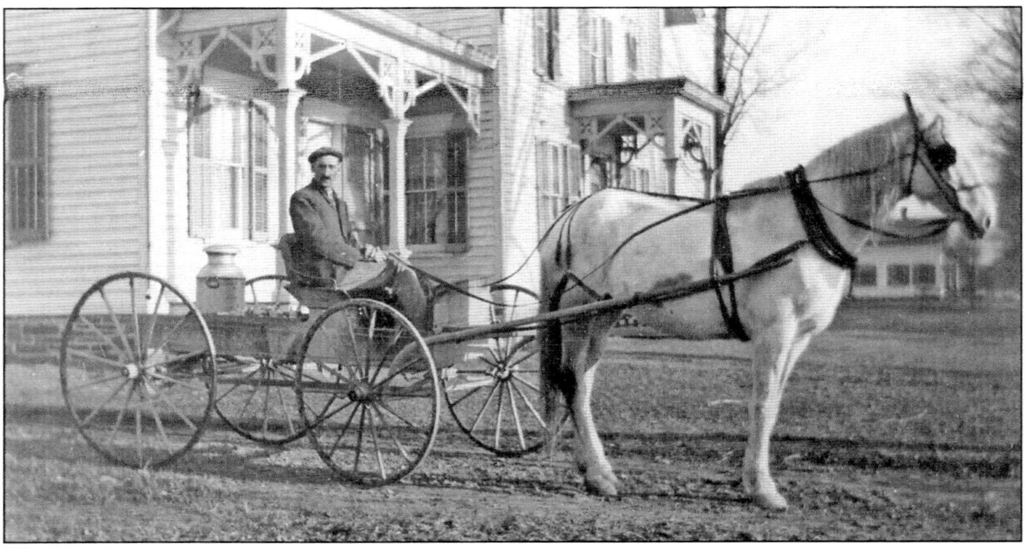

This 1905 image shows George L. Kenyon, a farmer and local milkman, posing with his horse and wagon in front of his home near Bowers' Corners. Kenyon bought this farm and house from Albert B. Dayton in January 1904. The McGregor family bought the house, and it now houses the Nanticoke Valley Historical Society Museum, who acquired the building on April 29, 1976.

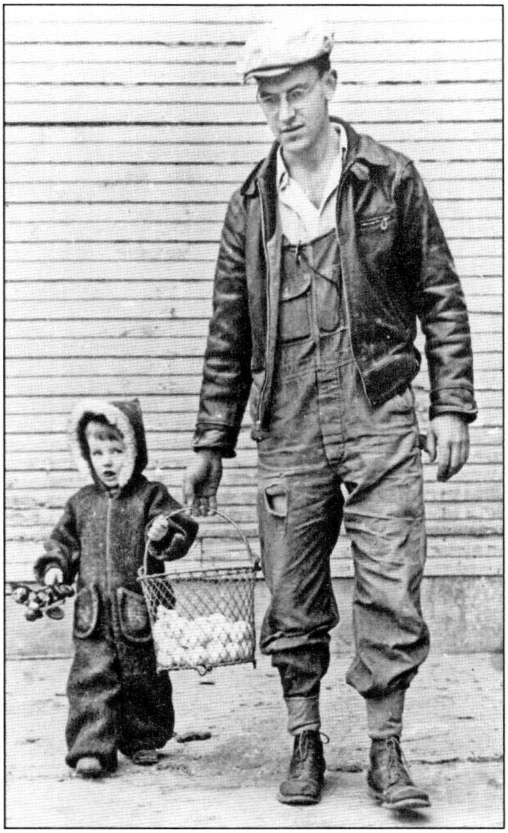

In 1907, James McGregor started a poultry business with 200 hens. His son, Venley, expanded the operation to 1,000 hens in 1914 with the help of his wife, Clara Durfee McGregor. Later, Venley's sons—Garth, Dane, and Warren—became a part of the family business. The business included the sale of eggs and chicks to other farms; they also sold dressed chickens. As the sons got older and became more involved, business continued to grow. Women were hired to candle-wash and grade the eggs. They also tended the incubator and brooders. Dane McGregor is pictured in both of these 1940 photographs; at right, he stands with his son Stan. (Courtesy of the McGregor family.)

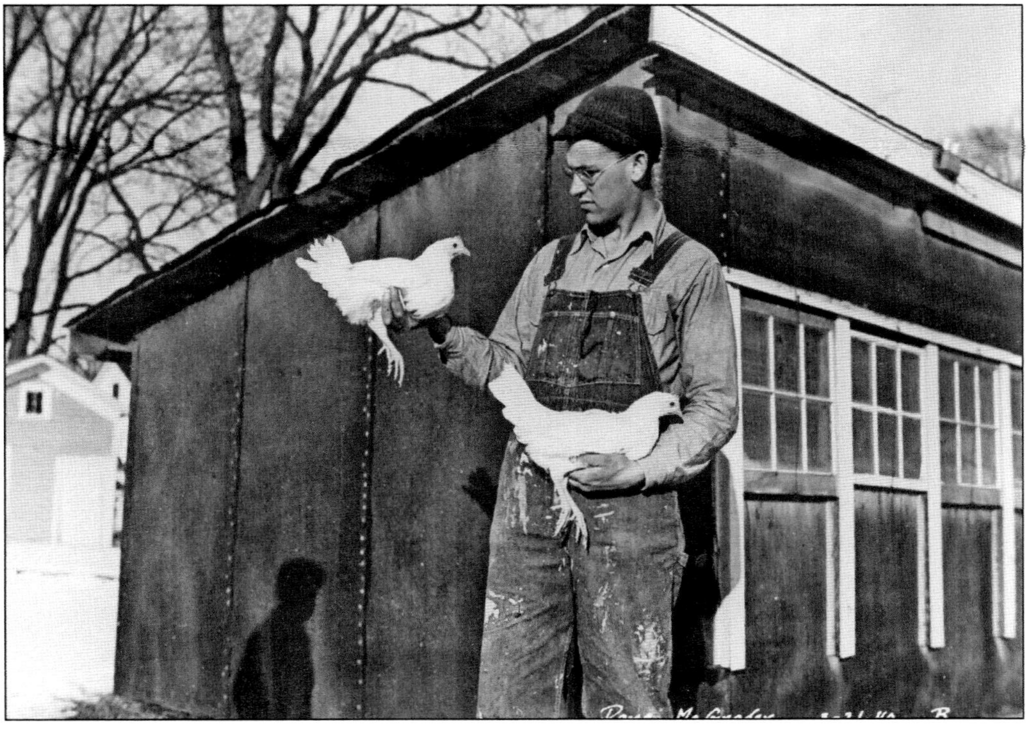

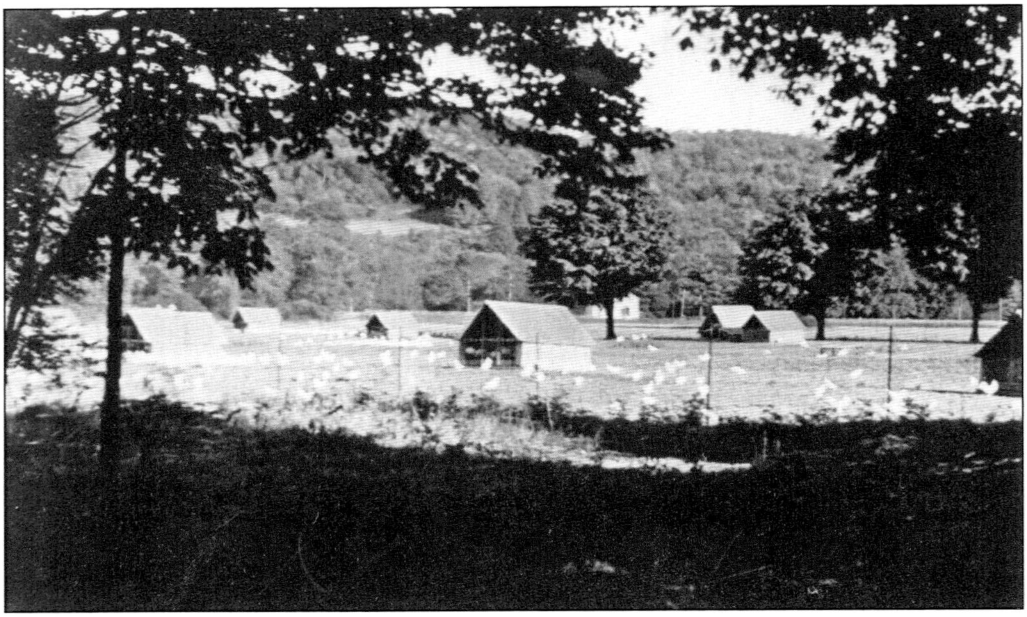

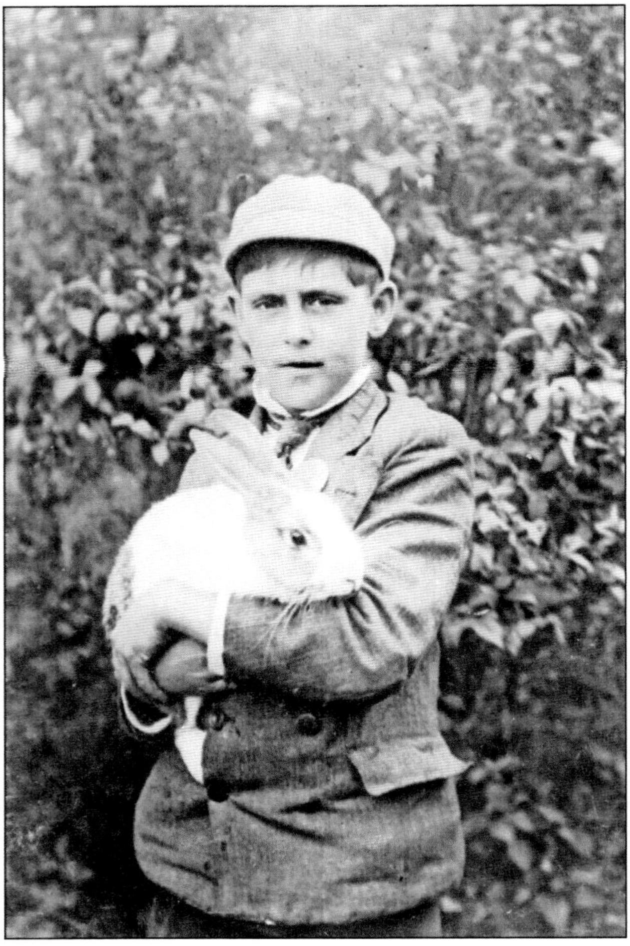

The McGregor poultry farm is shown above around 1940. The McGregors later expanded the business to the old creamery building (which once housed the Dairyman's League Cooperative Association–Maine Plant) on Main Street; the building burned down in 1964, killing 5,000 chickens and ruining feed and machinery. The cost of the fire was determined to be $25,000. (Courtesy of the McGregor family.)

In 1903, W.N. Mooers was the manager of the Maine Rabbitry. They specialized in breeding Belgian hares and had 60 to 75 of them in hutches. Rabbits were very much in demand at the time; some people bought them for pets, but many bought and raised them for food. The boy pictured at left is unidentified.

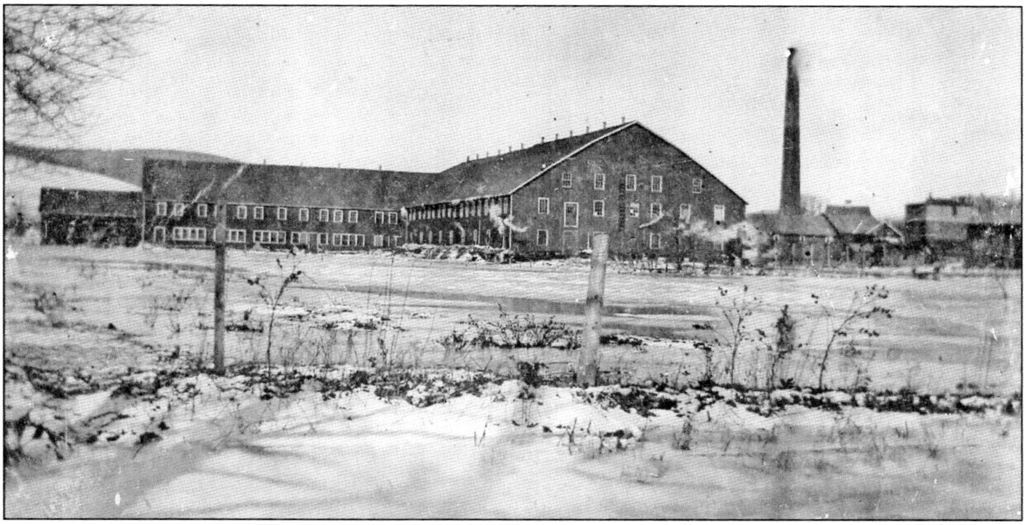

This tannery was built by E.H. Clark in 1832. In 1875, it was enlarged to employ 25 men, who put out 30,000 tanned hides per year. Because of the large quantity of hemlock trees in the Nanticoke Valley area, there was plenty of hemlock bark to provide tannin for the tanning process. LaMont Bowers recalls seeing 100 loads of hemlock bark pass his home in one day on the way to the tannery. When the trees were gone, the tannery closed in 1885.

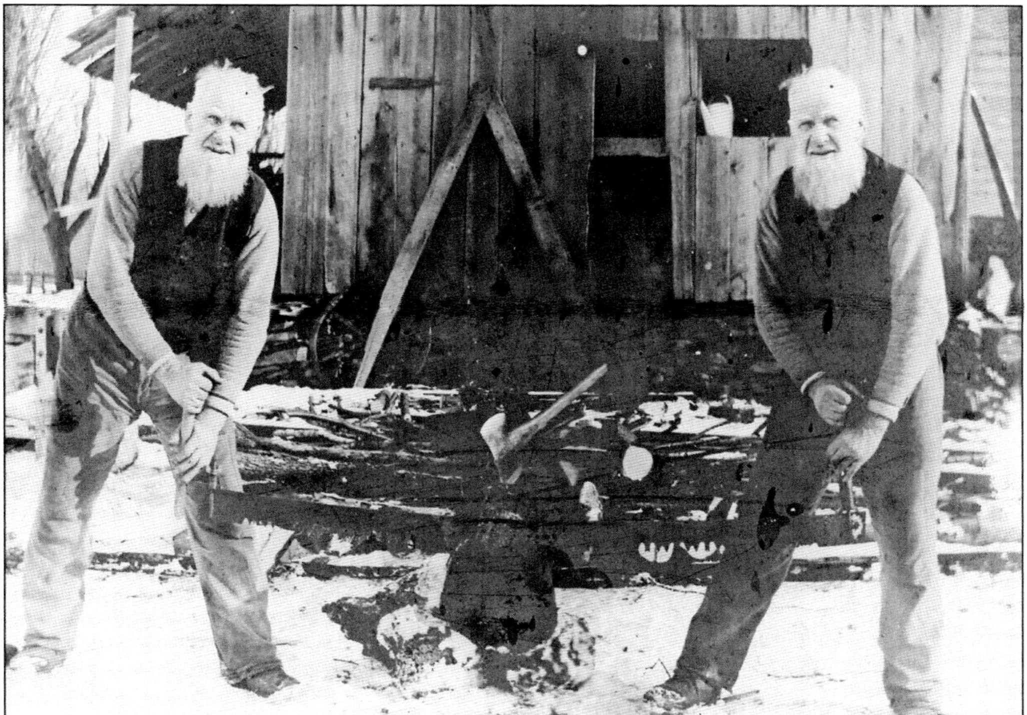

Belden Allen helps his mirror image saw through a log in this experimental photograph taken by Lee Loomis. Allen was born in 1837 and was the son of Ebinezer and Oladyne Allen, who moved to Allentown in Glen Aubrey a year earlier. Belden and his wife, Eliza Green Allen, lived in Allentown for their entire lives.

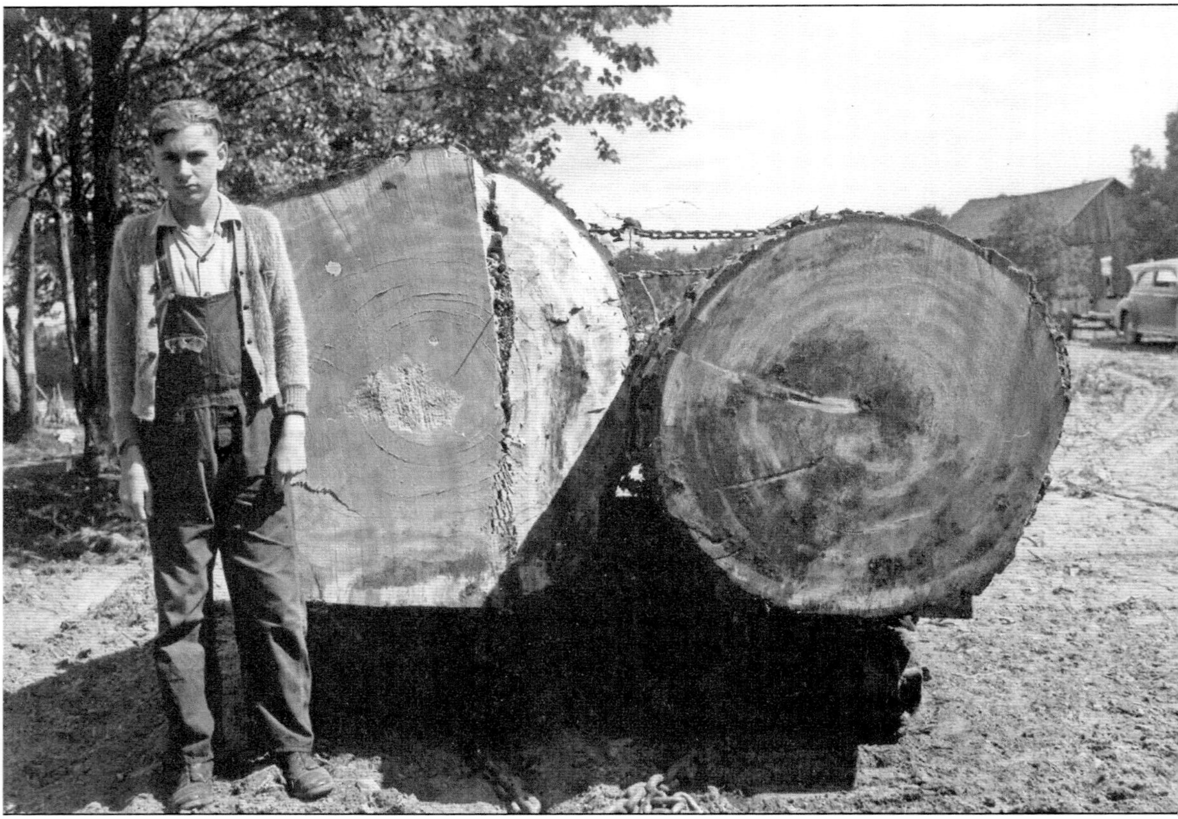

Robert Rozelle stands in front of large logs that were cut on the Ed Corson property. Corson was a local lumberman who had a portable sawmill that made it easier to process wood in areas that were not always easy to get to. The mill spent time on Nanticoke Road, on Ed Corson's farm, and also on Myers Road on occasion. Corson's sons—Joe, Ivan, and Bud—all worked in the sawmill. The size of these logs seems to identify them as old-growth trees, which were still growing in the Nanticoke Valley when this picture was taken in the 1930s but were not abundant.

Through the years, there have been two or three millinery shops in Maine Village, mostly run by single or widowed women. Women who came to the shops would choose an undecorated bonnet or hat from those in stock, and with the help of the milliner, would decide what to put on the hat. Many customers saved money by having old hats retrimmed instead of buying a new hat every time.

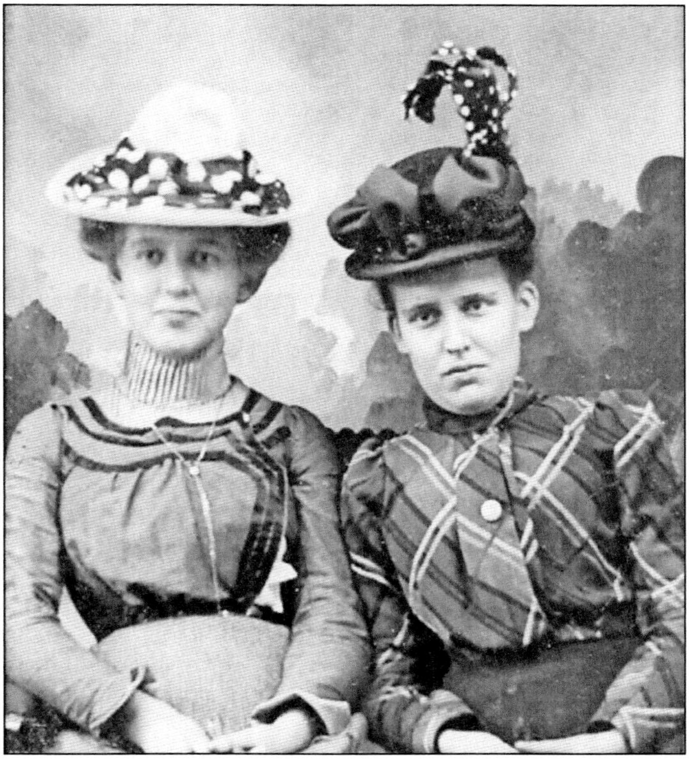

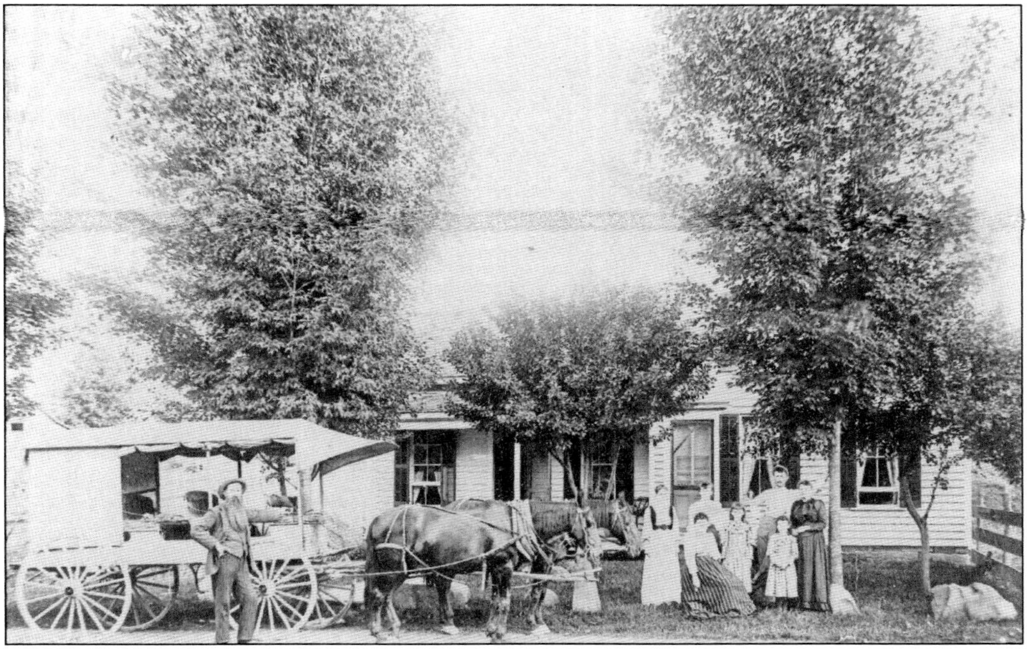

In 1878, Henry Curlhair started an express line between Maine and Binghamton for freight and passengers; the wagon left on Thursday and Saturday mornings. Curlhair lived in this house located between the J. Ralph Ingalls School and the Baptist parsonage. Here, Curlhair stands next to his stage at left. Posing in front of the house are, in no specified order, Eldora Brown; Ethel Steenberg; Henry's wife, Martha; Henry's son; and Henry's son's wife and two children.

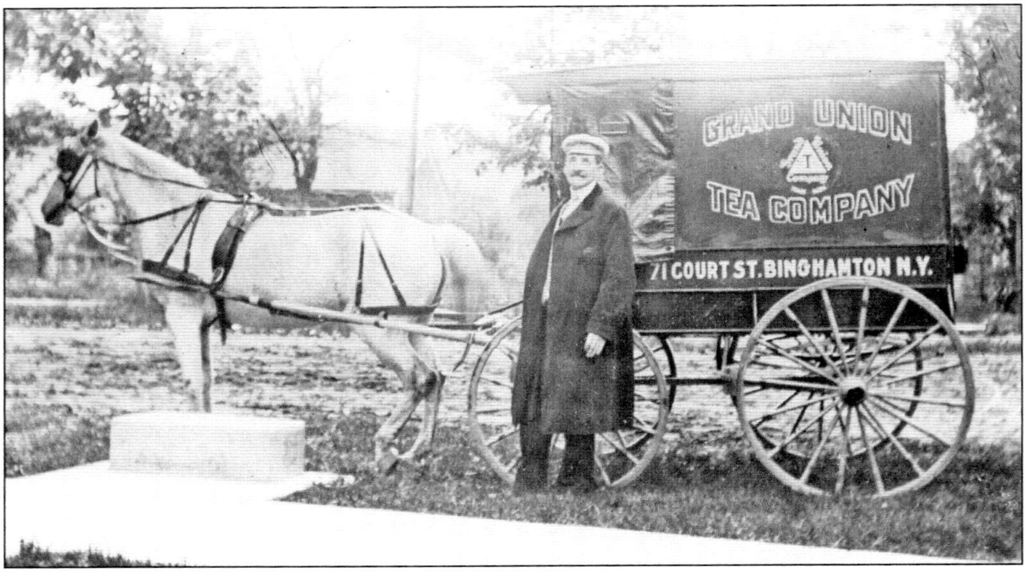

Before World War I, many peddlers in the Nanticoke Valley sold their wares by horse and wagon. Ray Lewis sold meat from the Maine Butcher Shop, Louis Drazen carried men's clothing, George Phipps was a tin peddler, and Mr. Treadwell (pictured above) from Glen Aubrey brought groceries and cloth in the Grand Union Tea Company wagon. These sellers brought goods directly to the farms, saving customers a trip to town.

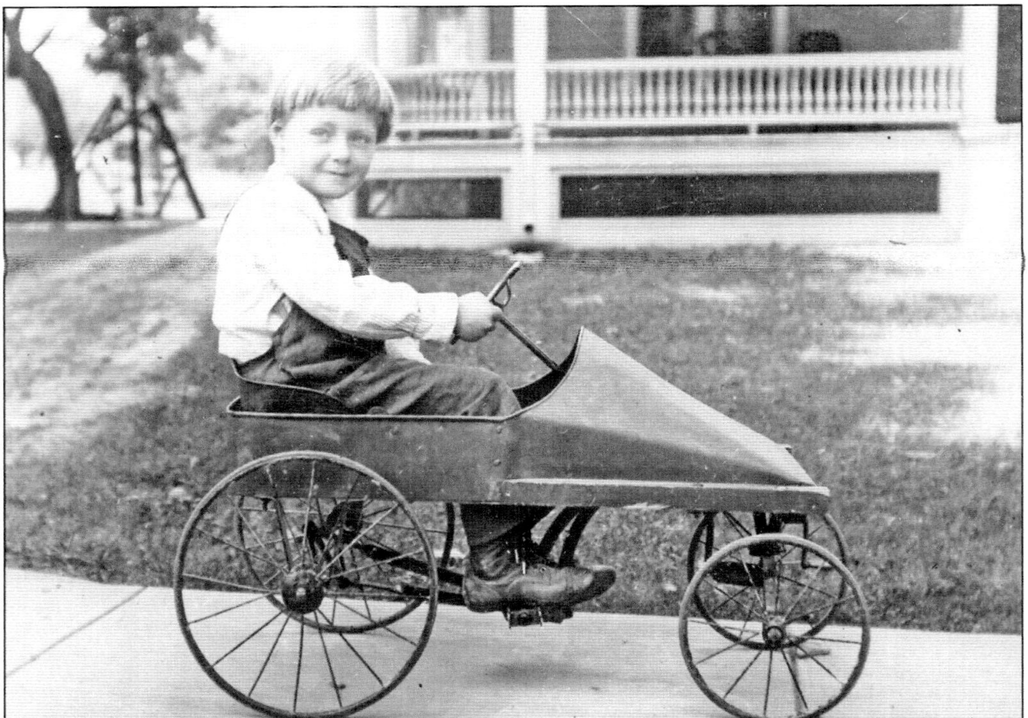

Audley Allen was born in 1907 to Jessie Dudley Allen and J. Rennie Allen. Here, he drives his pedal car in front of his house on Main Street. The Allens lived in several homes in Maine Village; this is the last one they owned before moving to Endicott and setting up their funeral parlor there.

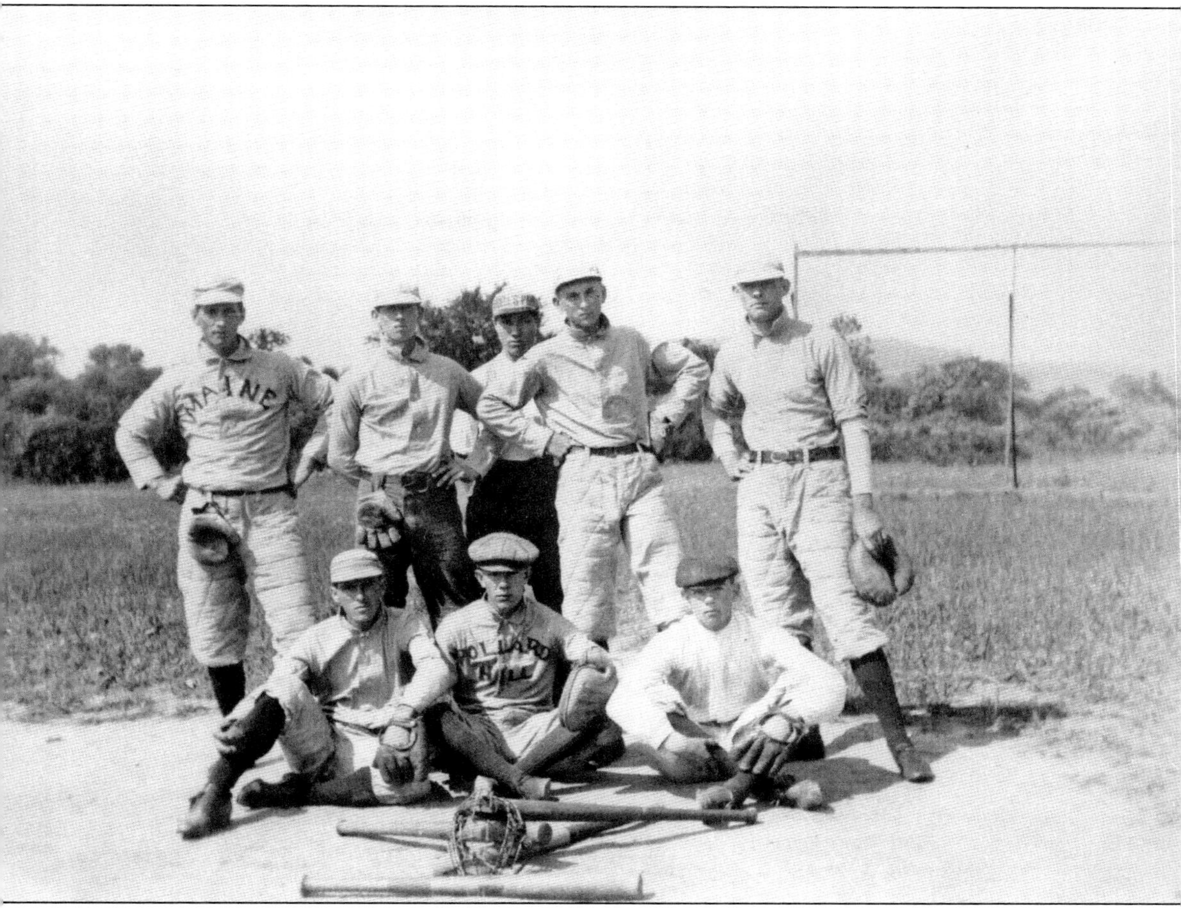

Maine and Glen Aubrey had local baseball teams as early as 1867. This 1906 Maine baseball team included, from left to right (first row) James McGregor, Jake Zimmer, and D. Guilford Dudley; (second row) Vernon Sweet, unidentified, unidentified, Vernon Vanderburg, and J.R. Allen. Daniel M. Casey, a professional pitcher for the Philadelphia Phillies, got his start on an East Maine team called New Ireland. Casey claimed that writer Ernest Thayer got his inspiration for his poem "Casey at the Bat" from Casey's strikeout in an 1887 game between the Phillies and the New York Giants; although Thayer stated that the poem was not based on a specific player, Casey said Thayer showed him the poem after the game. Casey left baseball in 1891 and went to work as a streetcar conductor in Binghamton.

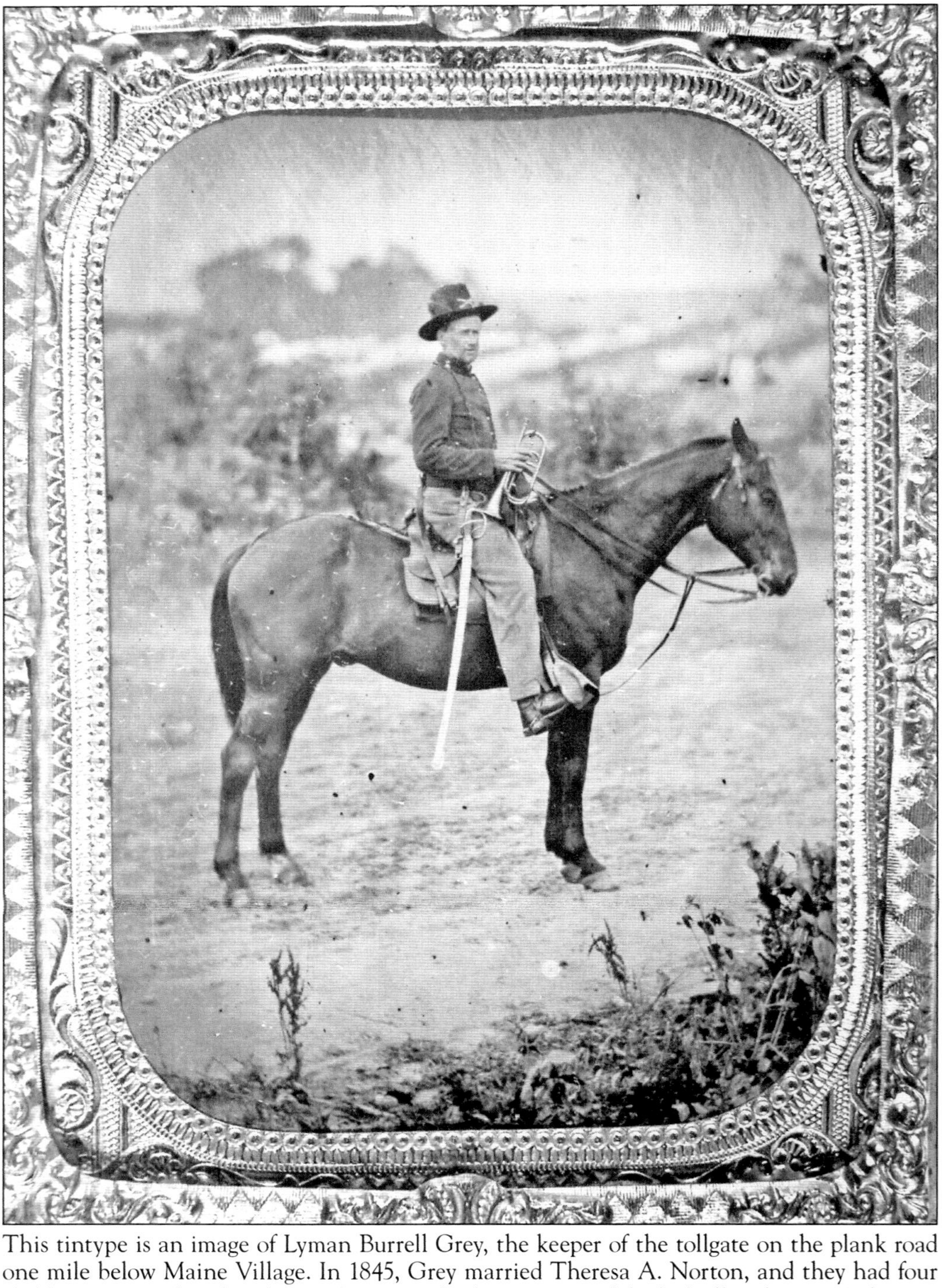

This tintype is an image of Lyman Burrell Grey, the keeper of the tollgate on the plank road one mile below Maine Village. In 1845, Grey married Theresa A. Norton, and they had four children. Grey enlisted in the Civil War as a bugler in 1861 and died of yellow fever at Yorktown, Virginia, in 1863.

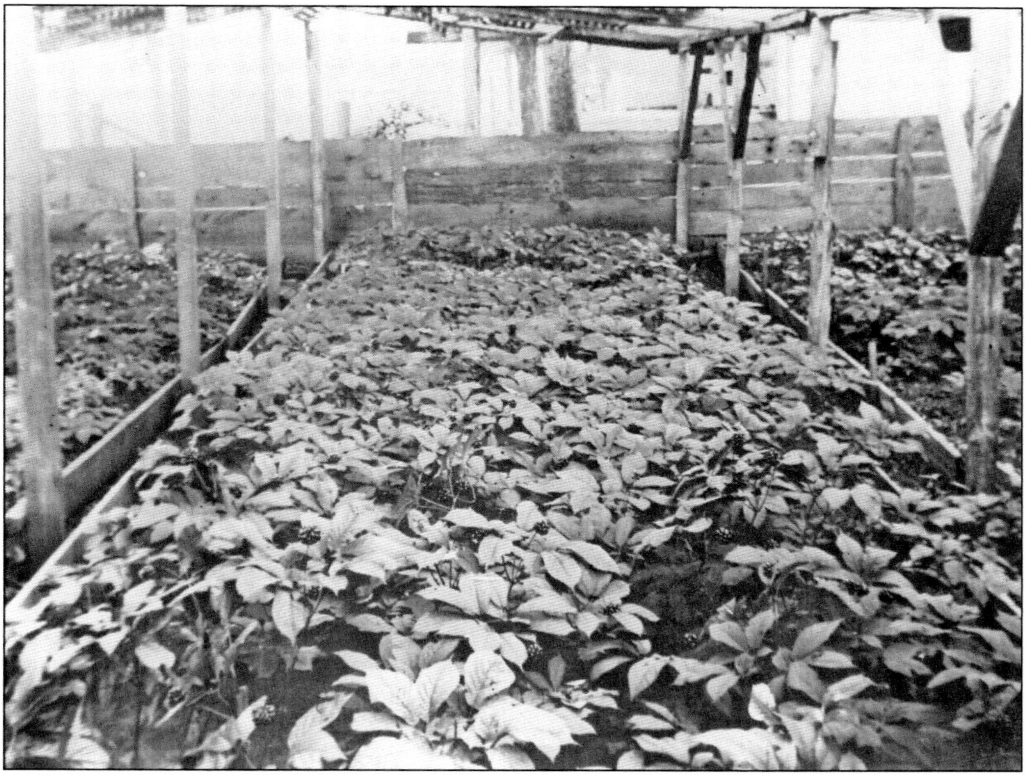

William E. Dyer owned a home and store on Main Street in Maine Village. He also grew ginseng on his property on McGregor Avenue, pictured here in the early 1900s. Ginseng is native to the Nanticoke Valley area and is widely used in making patent medicines. Dyer sold the ginseng to Chinese merchants in New York City for $10 a pound.

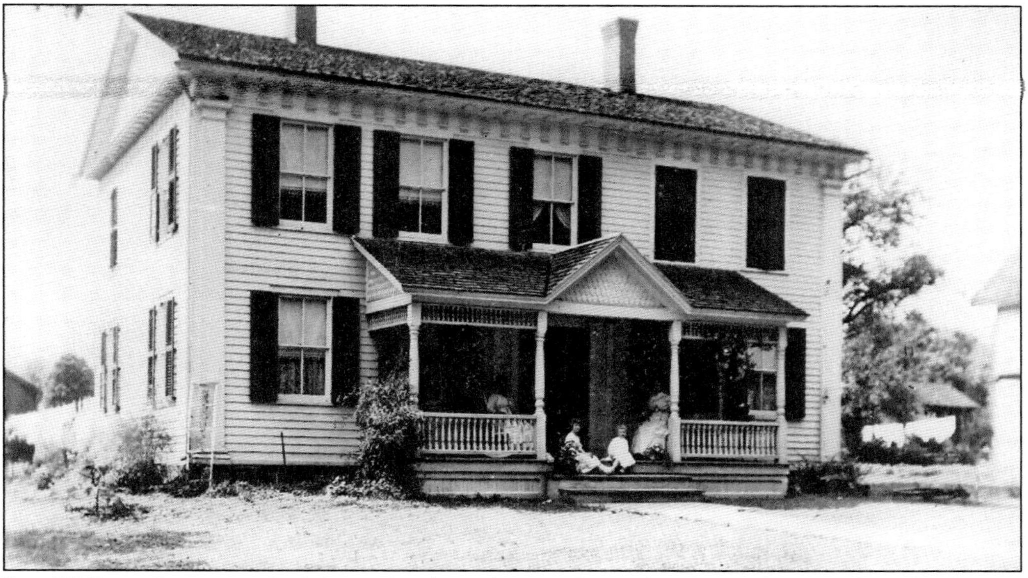

Rev. William Gates ran the Maine Academy from 1837 until 1852. Students at the school came from as far away as Owego. The Baptist minister was pro-slavery and used scripture to support his point of view, and it was also said that Reverend Gates spoke eight languages.

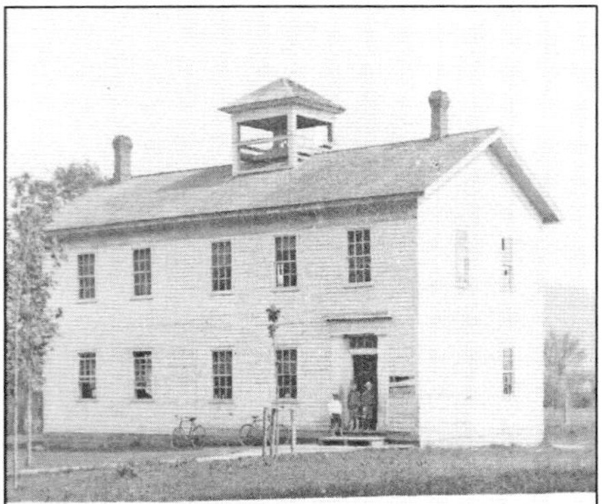

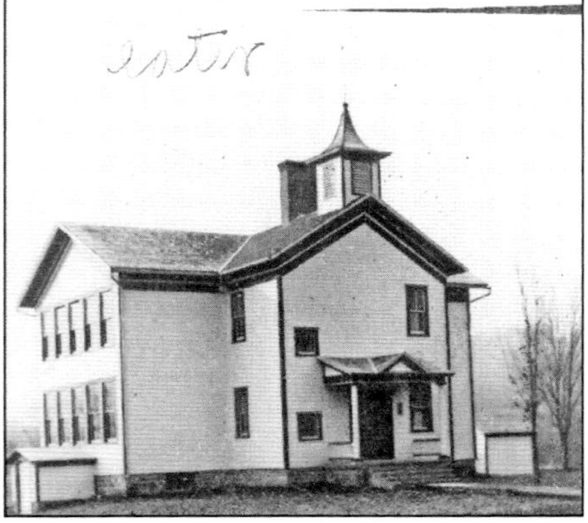

The top photograph at left, of the Maine Village School, shows the school as it looked as early as 1833. The first floor had two classrooms, and the second floor had another classroom for grades six through nine and a large community room with a stage. The photograph below it was taken after a major renovation added two more classrooms to the second floor. This school was in use until 1940, when it was auctioned off and dismantled to make room for a new school.

Bill Berry (left), Ralph Walter (center), and Dale Berry appear to be having a great time in a boat at the school assembly in Maine Village in May 1938. Other children in the chorus included, in no particular order, Warren Ames, Beverly Russell, Norman Rude, Louis Kotasek, Lloyd Ludington, Arlene Haines, Rowena Pitcher, Gerald Padbury, and James Fox. (Courtesy of Nancy Berry.)

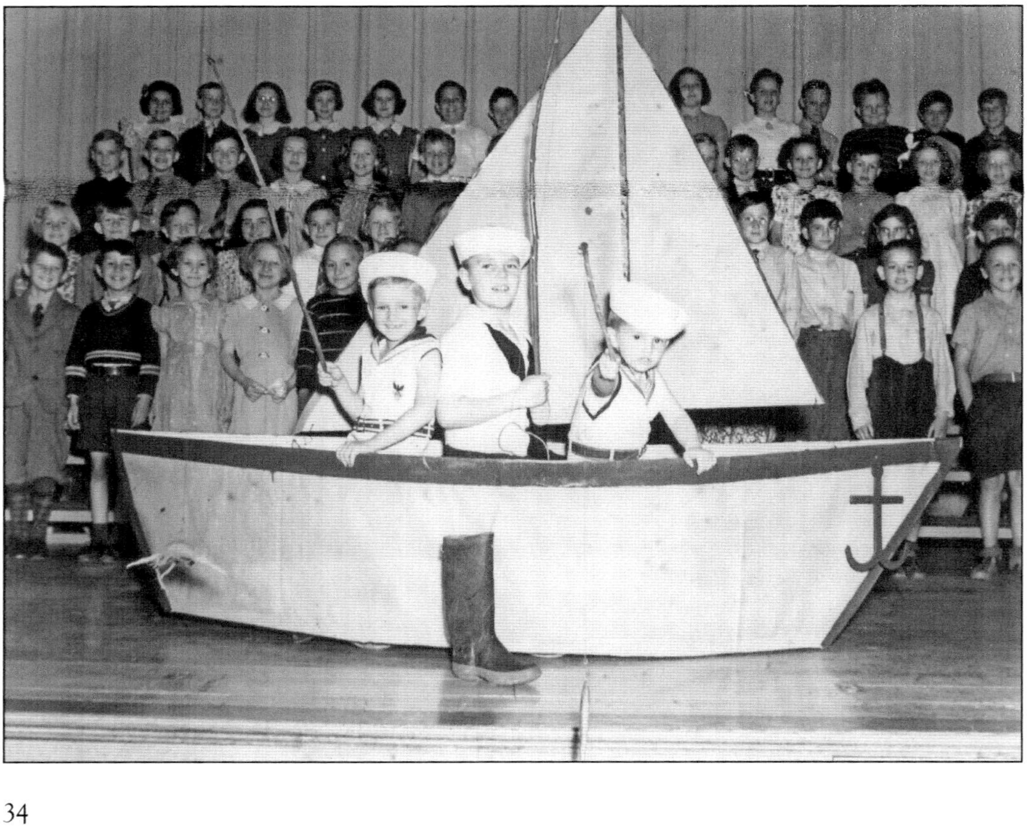

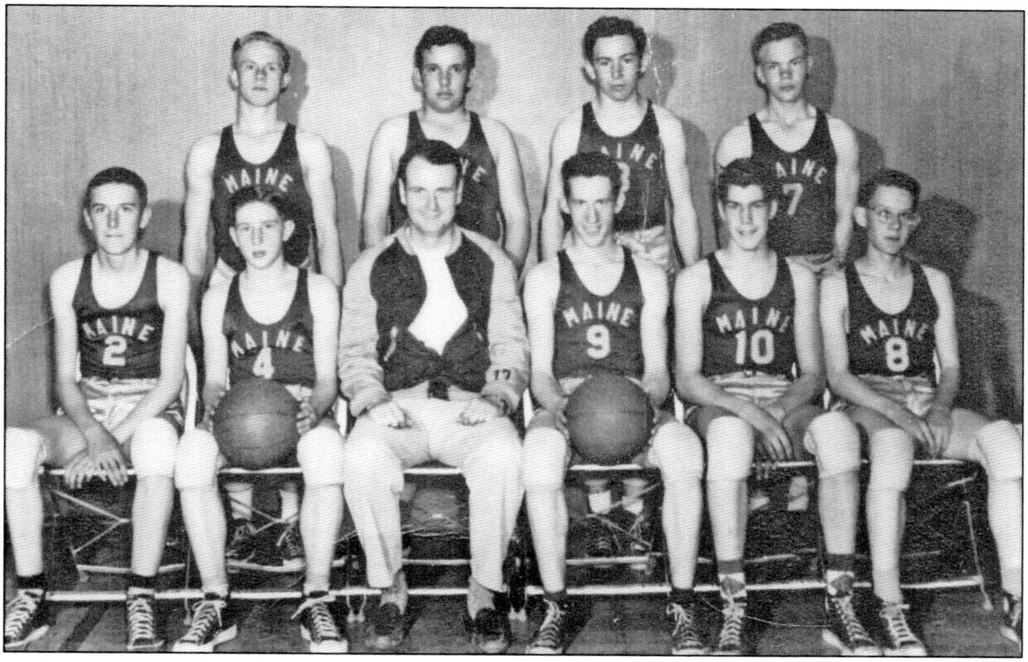

A 1950s Maine basketball team poses for a photograph at Maine Central School on Church Street. A few team members in the first row have been identified, including Gary McManus (second from left), coach Bob Bradley (third from left), Jack Lawton (second from right), and Dean Masland (far right). (Courtesy of Betty Welch.)

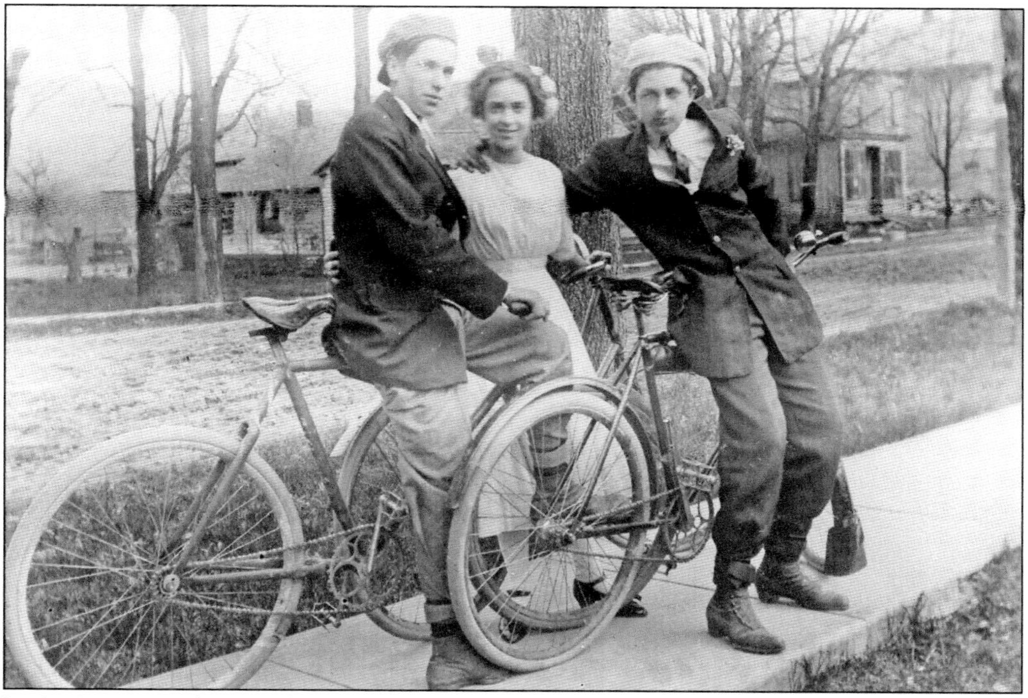
In this May 1912 photograph, 15-year-old Ralph Gray (left), 13-year-old Ethelyn Riley, and 15-year-old Lee Loomis (right) pose with their bicycles on Main Street. In the background behind Loomis's left shoulder is the Nanticoke Grange Hall, with the Hollenbeck store to the right.

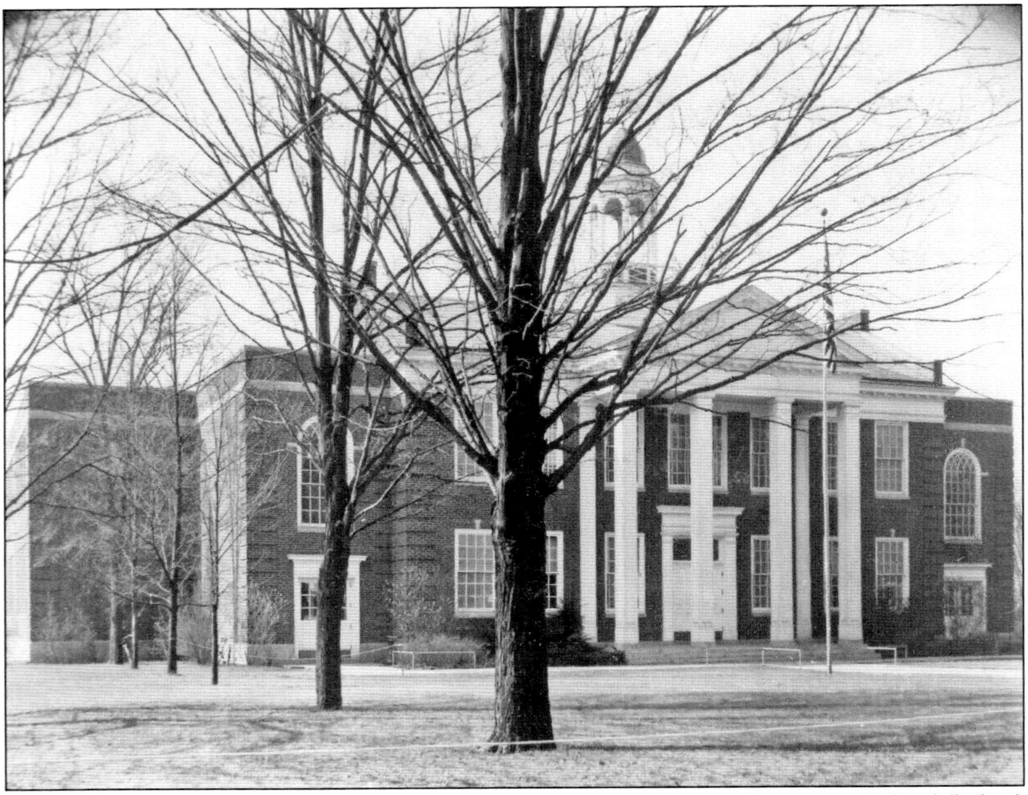

Maine Central School (above) was built in 1939—and Union Center Elementary School (below) was built one year later—to meet the educational needs of students in grades one through nine in Maine, Union Center, Bowers' Corners, Tiona, the Gates Neighborhood, Allentown, Mount Ettrick, East Maine, Brocket Hollow, Pollard Hill, and Broughamtown. Students in 10th, 11th, and 12th grades attended school at Union-Endicott and Johnson City High Schools. In 1969, Maine Central School was renamed J. Ralph Ingalls School in honor of Ingalls, a school board member. The architecturally significant building is now listed in the New York State and National Registers of Historic Places.

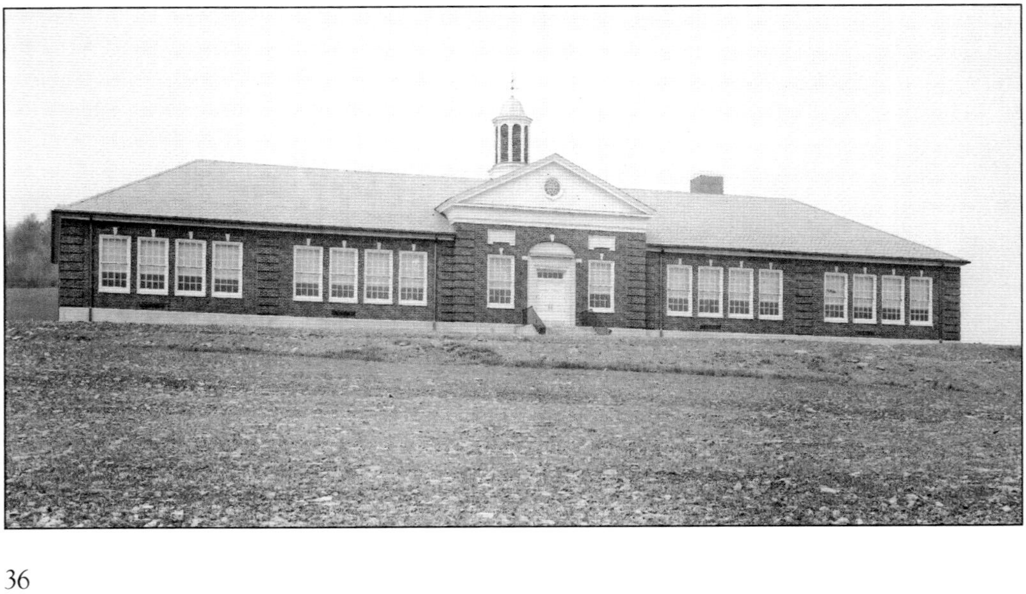

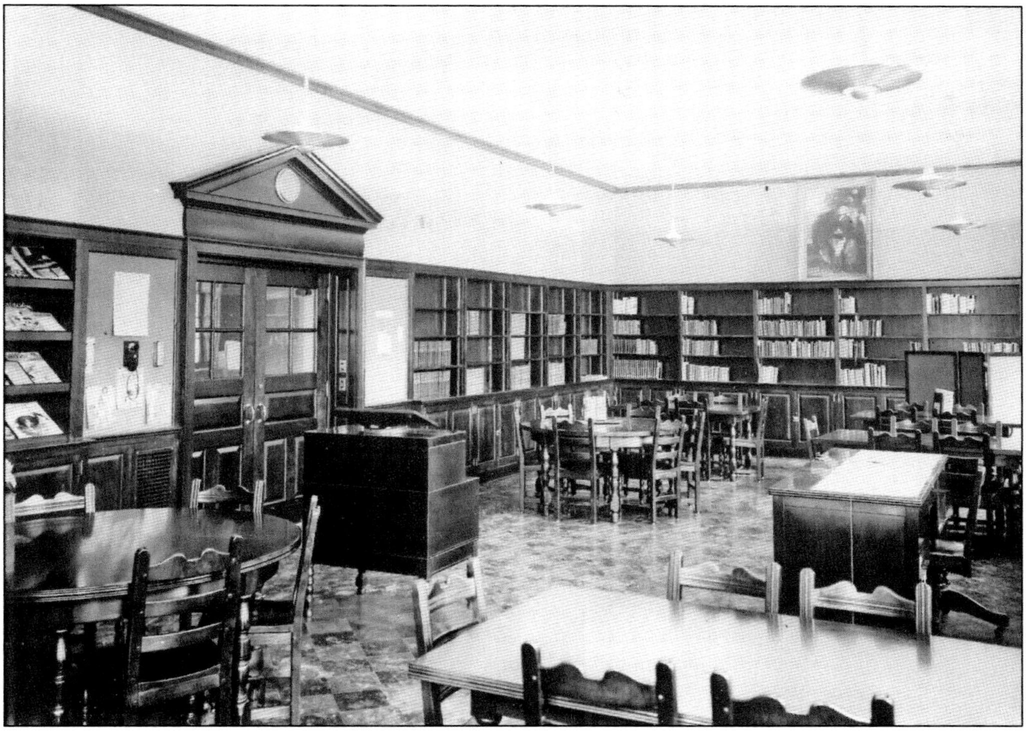

The library at the new Maine Central School is seen above. The whole school followed a colonial design based on Williamsburg, Virginia. The furniture for the school was purchased from Stickley Furniture Company in Fayetteville, New York, and is stained to simulate mahogany. Special oil-painting reproductions were commissioned by the Federal Art Project specifically for this building. The facilities were considered state-of-the-art, as one can tell by looking at the homemaking room pictured below.

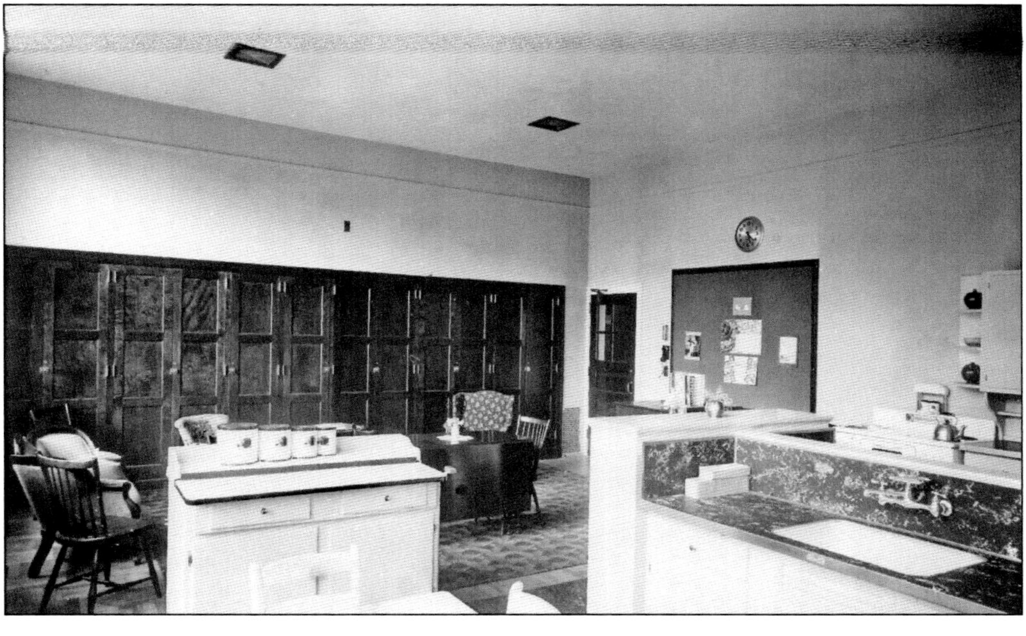

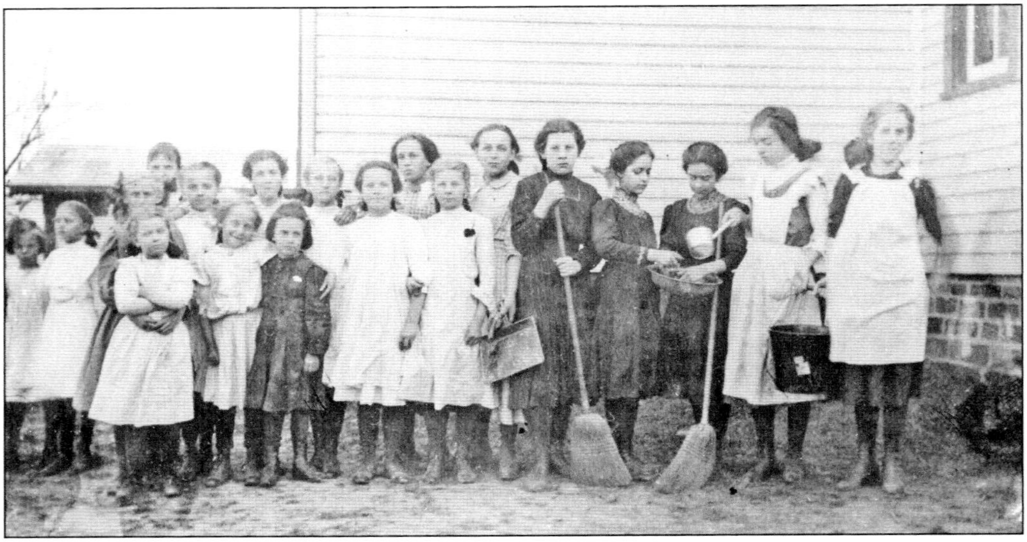

These images from between 1905 and 1910, part of the "Seasons of Childhood" exhibit at the Nanticoke Valley Historical Society museum, show spring-cleaning at the Maine Village School. The children are divided into groups, with girls cleaning up the inside with brooms, mops, dustpans, buckets, and basins and boys doing outside work with rakes in hand. Signs of spring include the spring dresses some of the girls are wearing, but note that most of them are still wearing black winter stockings and boots. The boys are dressed more casually, but half of them are wearing jackets, shirts with celluloid collars, and ties. All are wearing boots, except for one barefoot boy. The boys also display a wide variety of the hats and caps of that time.

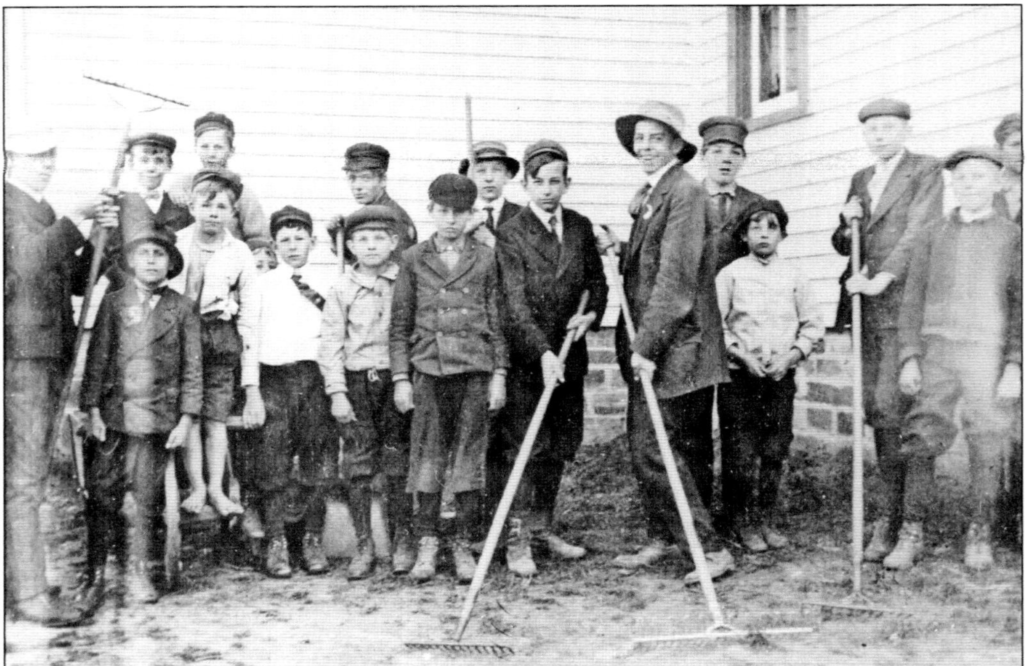

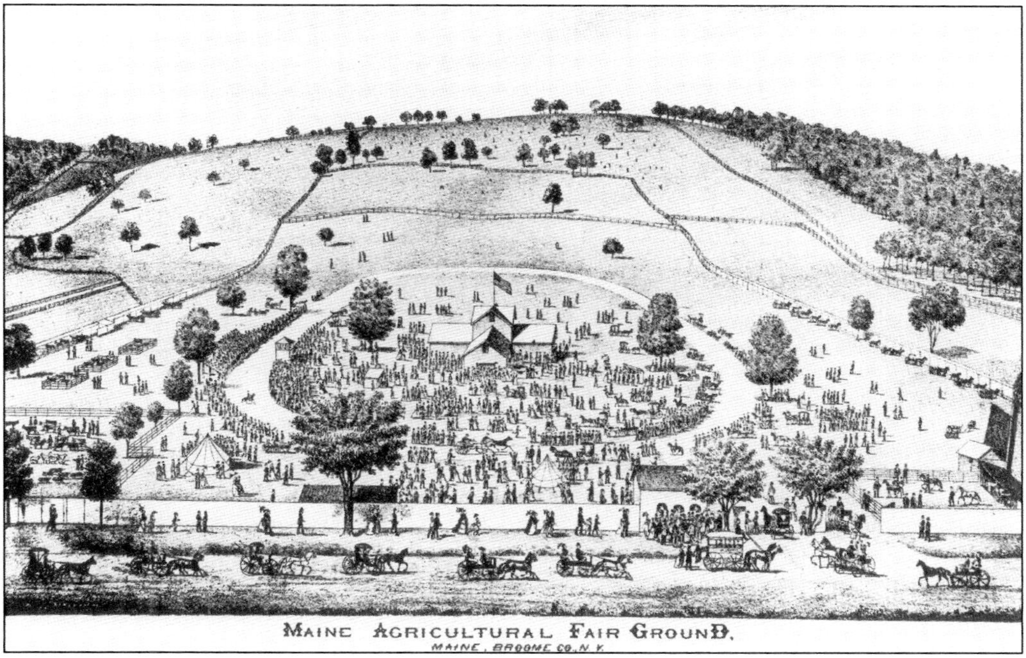

The Maine Agricultural Fairgrounds was built on the property of Ephraim Ketchum. The first fair was held in the autumn of 1876 and was repeated every year for eight years. At the first fair, there were 900 entries in various categories such as livestock, vegetables, cooking, and handiwork. The above print is from the 1876 Broome County atlas. The image below shows a prize bull being entered in a contest for a blue ribbon. There was also a half-mile track for harness racing and footraces. The current Maine Memorial Elementary School was built on the site of the fairgrounds.

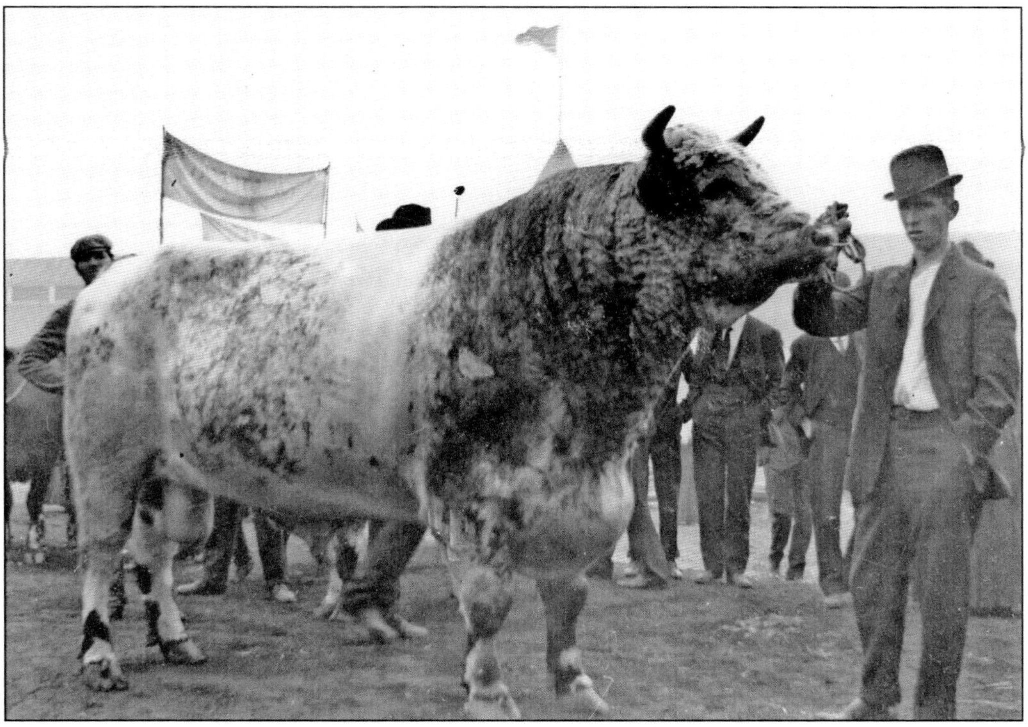

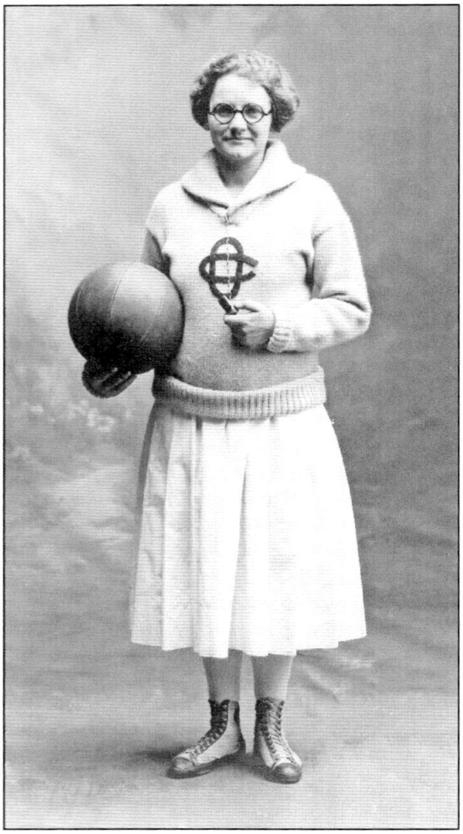

Mary Crocket was a graduate of Oberlin College in Ohio. She and her husband, David, moved to Maine around 1939 and opened a variety store. Mary was hired as a physical education teacher in Maine in the early 1940s. She was also very active in the Girl Scouts, serving as a scout leader and as the Maine troop camp director for many years.

The Lamb twins, daughters of Charles and Nina (Dyer) Lamb, pose outside. One of the girls has a watch in her hand, and the other has her dolly. Charles Lamb ran the Dyer store, which was owned by his father-in-law, W. Emmett Dyer, in 1903. One of the buildings in the background once housed the Bostwick drugstore. This image must have been taken before 1905, as the building far down the street is Asa Curtis's store, which burned down in December 1905. The Niles Creamery is in front of the Curtis store.

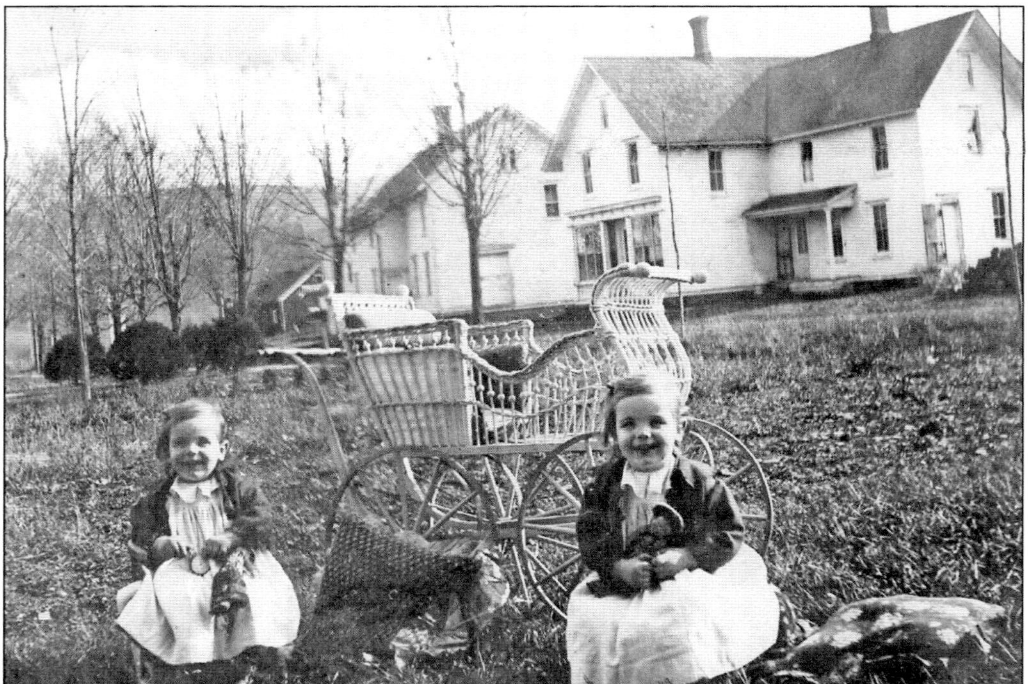

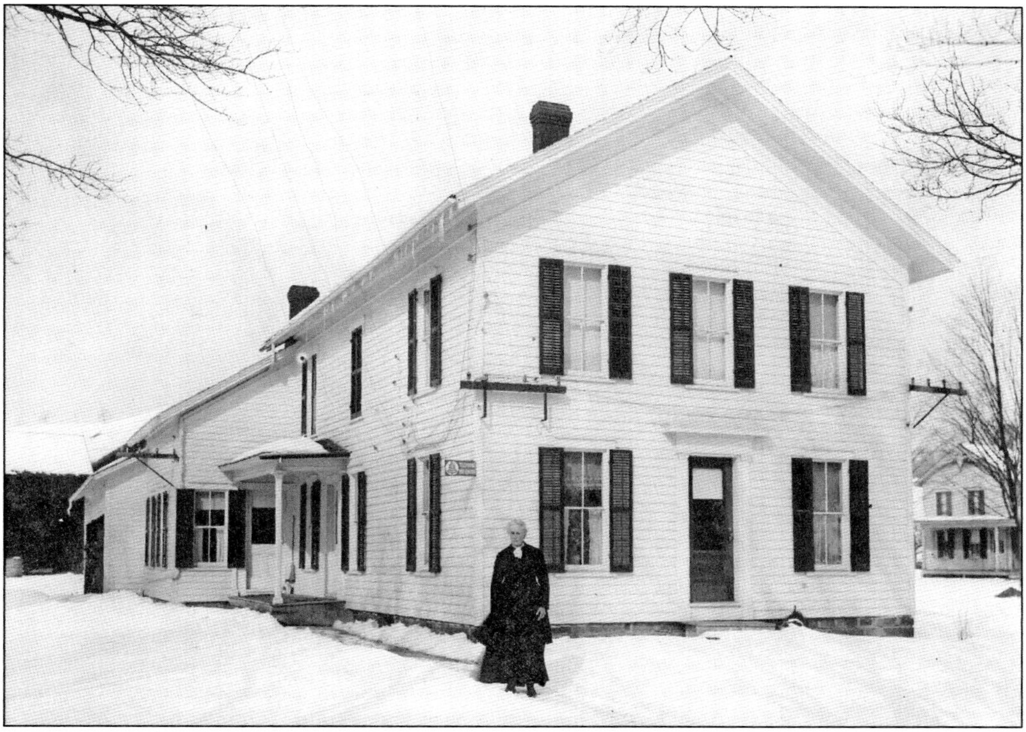

Asa U. Curtis lived in this house with his wife, Mary, and ran a store next to it from 1876 to 1905. It was a general store that also sold feed and housed the post office for a time. This building also contained the town's Bell and York State Telephone exchanges. When the store burned down in 1905, the exchanges moved into the house for a short time.

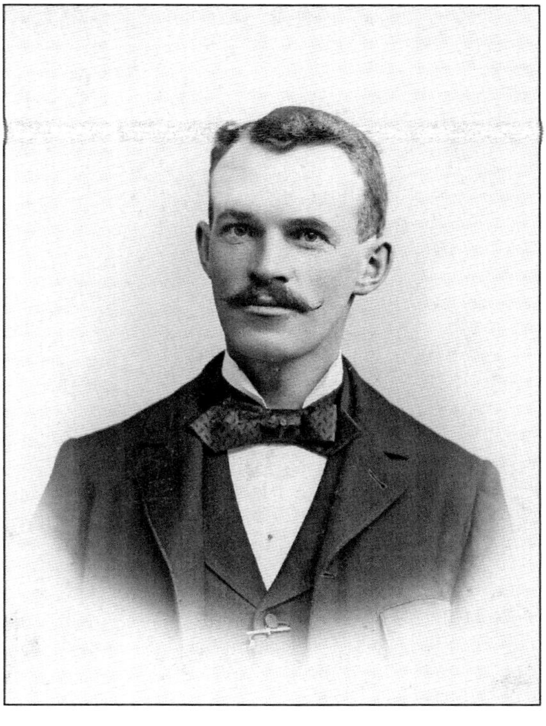

Ollie Ketchum (1869–1960) was born in Union Center and owned a farm there. He was a member of the Union Center Congregational Church for all of his 91 years. Ketchum married Mary Louise Curtis, Asa Curtis's daughter, in 1907 and moved to Maine Village in 1914. He was the town justice in 1916, the town clerk in 1918 and 1920, and the town historian. In 1920, Ketchum also worked as a lineman for the phone company.

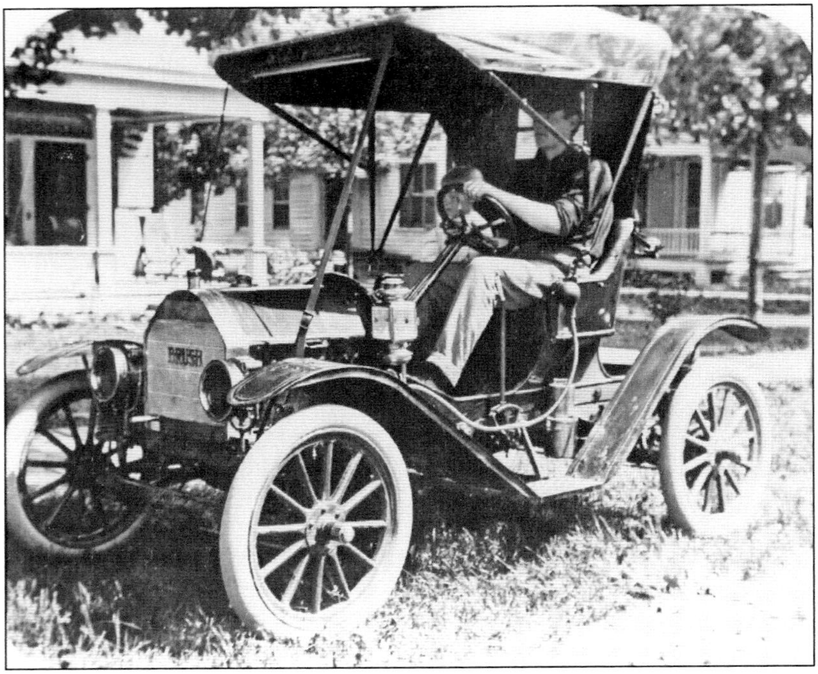

The first automobile in Maine Village was purchased for $500 by J.R. Allen in 1907. It was a Brush Runabout from Detroit and had a six-horsepower engine. The frame, axles, and wheels were all made of oak. The passenger area looked a lot like a buggy and had no protection from the elements.

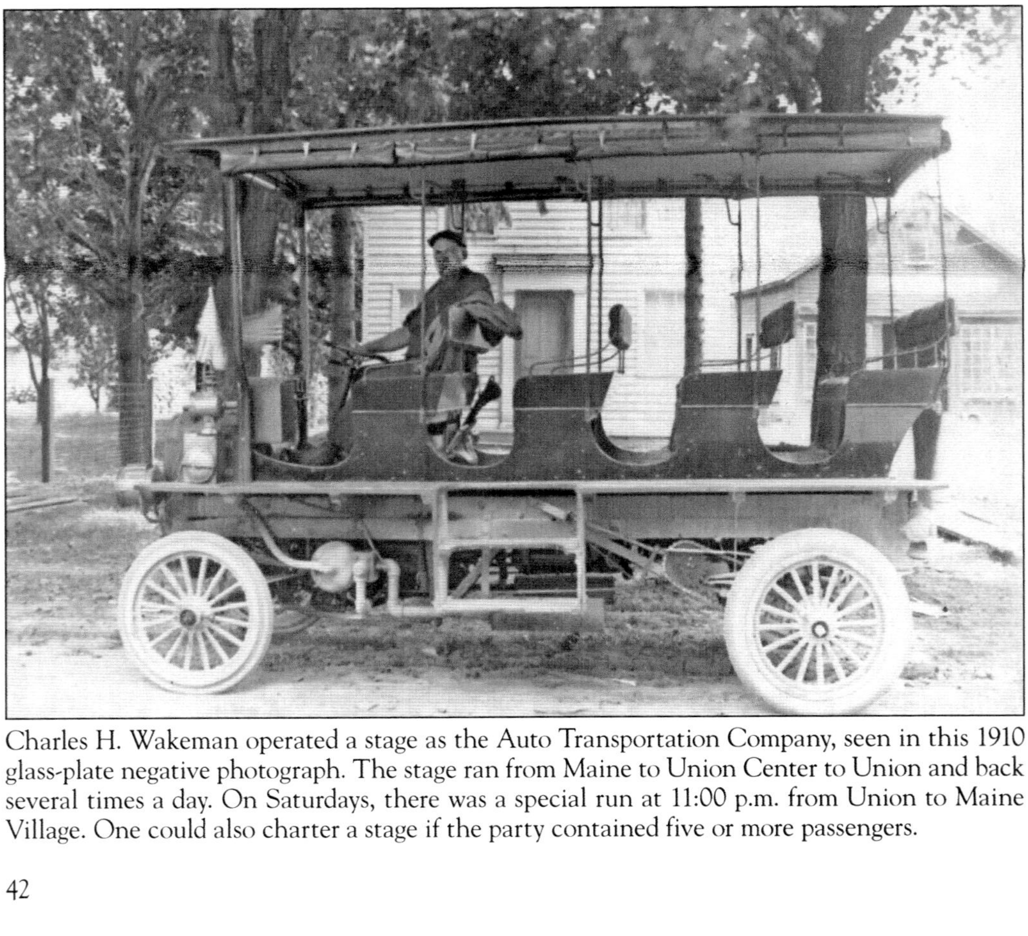

Charles H. Wakeman operated a stage as the Auto Transportation Company, seen in this 1910 glass-plate negative photograph. The stage ran from Maine to Union Center to Union and back several times a day. On Saturdays, there was a special run at 11:00 p.m. from Union to Maine Village. One could also charter a stage if the party contained five or more passengers.

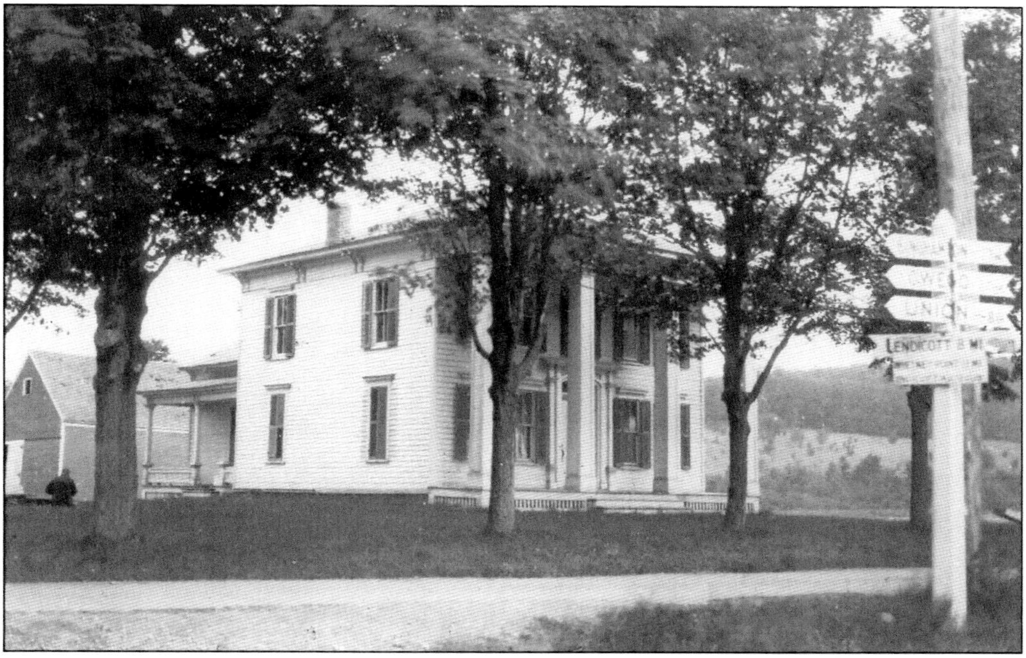

The above photograph of the Bowers homestead appeared on the 1927 Christmas card sent out by LaMont M. Bowers and his wife, Fannie Grey. This house was built in 1871, after the original structure (which was built in 1837) burned down. The area around the home is called Bowers' Corners after LaMont's father, Gardner Bowers, who settled there in 1822.

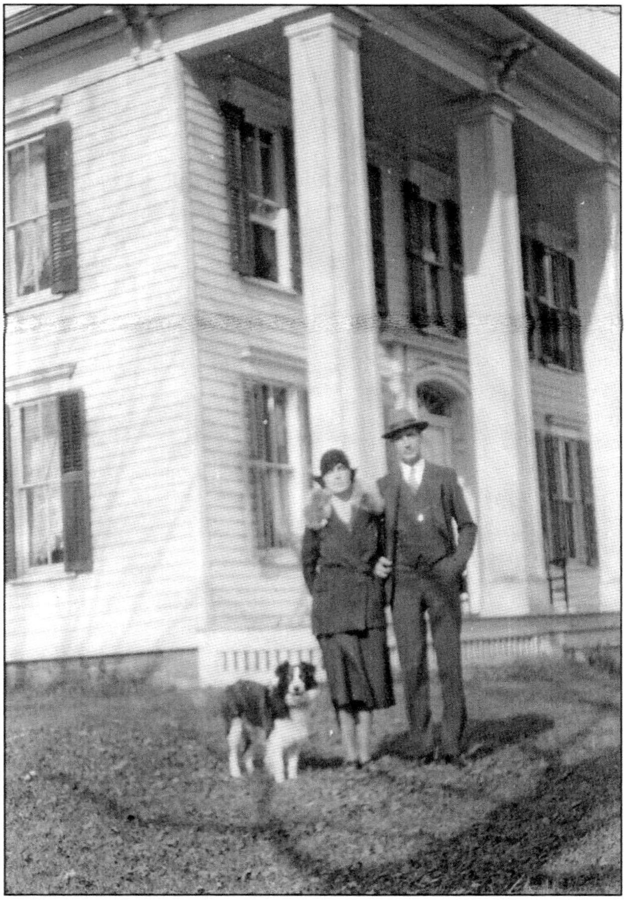

In this 1931 image, Janet W. and Clement G. Bowers and their dog, Buddy, stand in front of their home at Bowers' Corners. Clement Bowers was a scientist specializing in botany. Janet, a nutritionist in her early years, was later the president of Federated Garden Clubs of New York State. They both had a deep love for the history of Maine and Broome County.

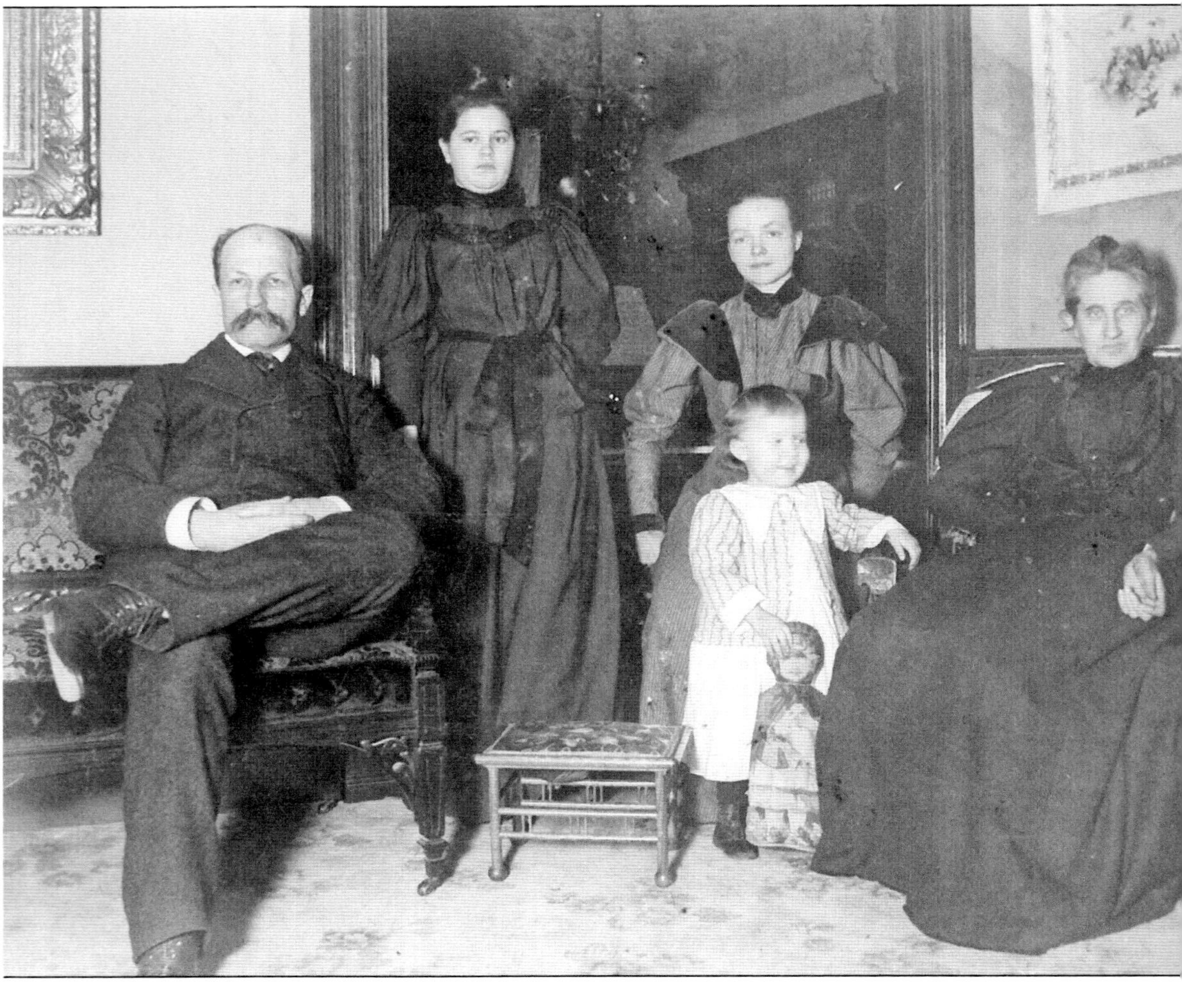

Posing here in 1898 are, from left to right, LaMont M. Bowers, Lori Johnson (Mrs. C.R. Thayer), Katy Shay, Clement Bowers (with doll), and Fannie Grey Bowers. LaMont Bowers was born at Bowers' Corners in 1847 and worked for John D. Rockefeller Jr. for 30 years, organizing shipping on the Great Lakes and serving as chairman of the board of directors for the Colorado Fuel & Iron Company (CF&I).

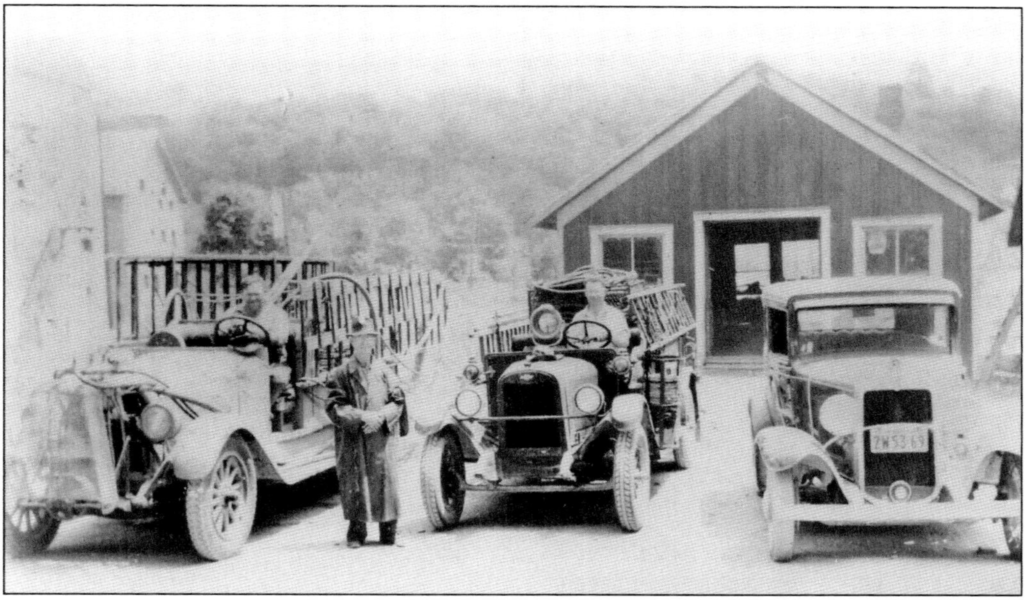

The Nanticoke Valley Fire Company was formed in 1923, and under chief Ray W. Payne, the 22-member group began fighting fires in the area. This 1935 photograph shows Bennett Eckert sitting in the truck at left; Payne, who remained fire chief until 1942, standing between the trucks; and Herman Wheaton at the wheel of the truck in the center. The truck driven by Wheaton, which was once a Meteor hearse, was donated to the company by J.R. Allen. The first Nanticoke Valley fire station was located in the converted Columbian block.

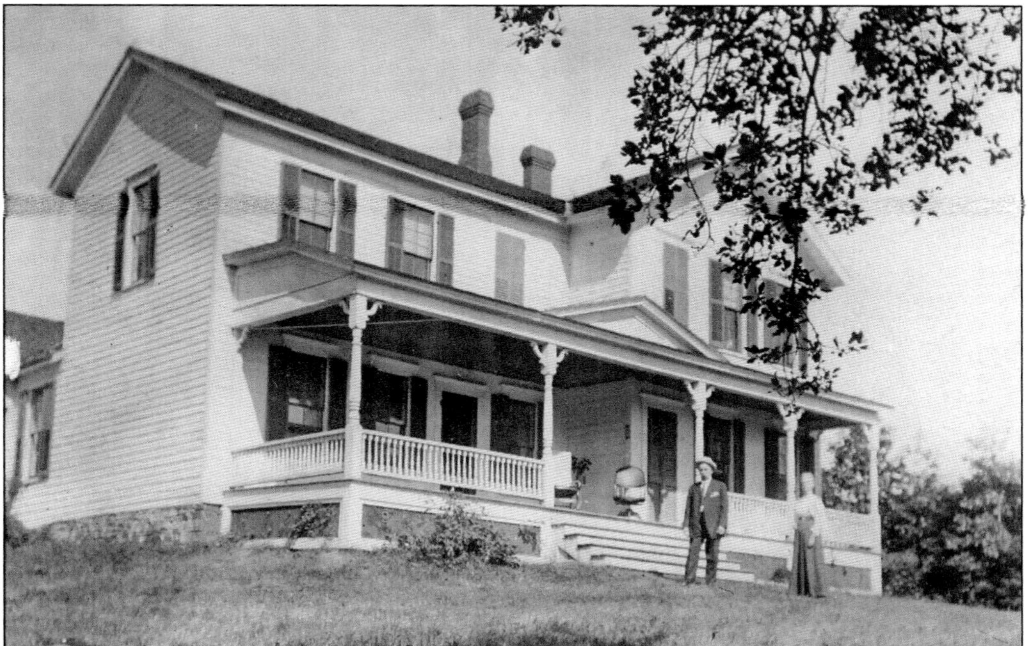

Marietta and Orin Holden lived in this home at the bottom of King Hill. Orin was a Civil War Navy veteran who served on the ironclad *Dictator*. He also served as the town highway supervisor and the town supervisor, and he worked at the custom house in New York City for a time.

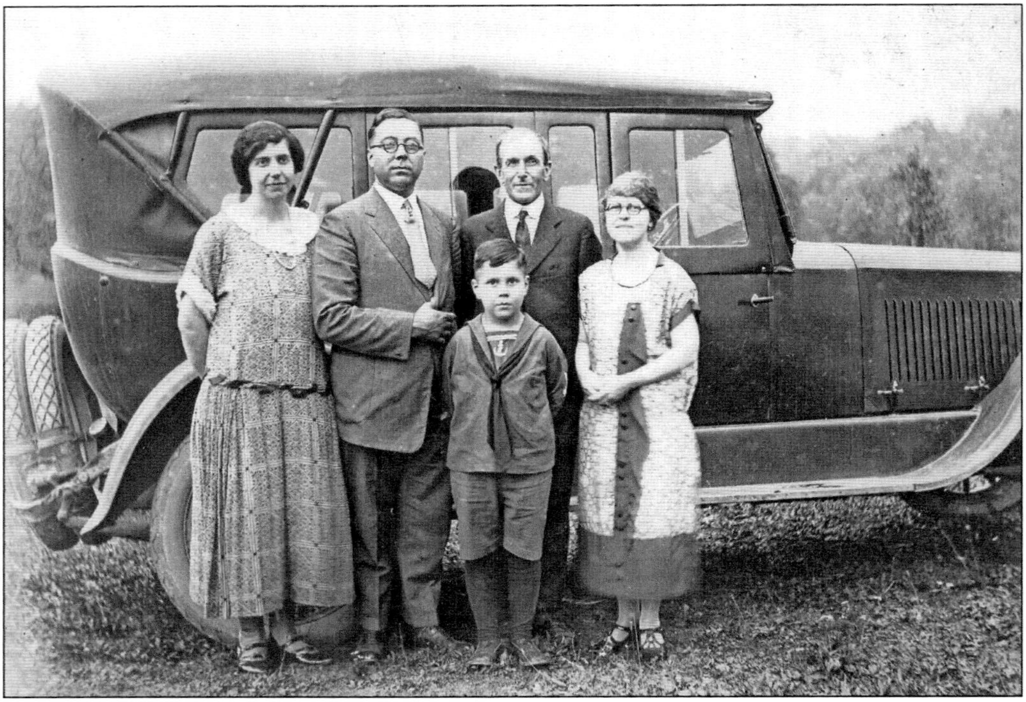

Posing in front of an automobile in the 1920s are, from left to right, Ina Tymeson, Wellington Tymeson, Rob Taylor, Lena Taylor, and young Glen Tymeson (in front). Ina and Wellington owned the Tymeson Brothers store, where Ina worked as the postmistress at the post office in the store. Their son Glen grew up to be a doctor in Whitney Point. Rob and Lena Taylor donated the land for the Masonic lodge that was built on Main Street in 1955 and lived just south of the lodge.

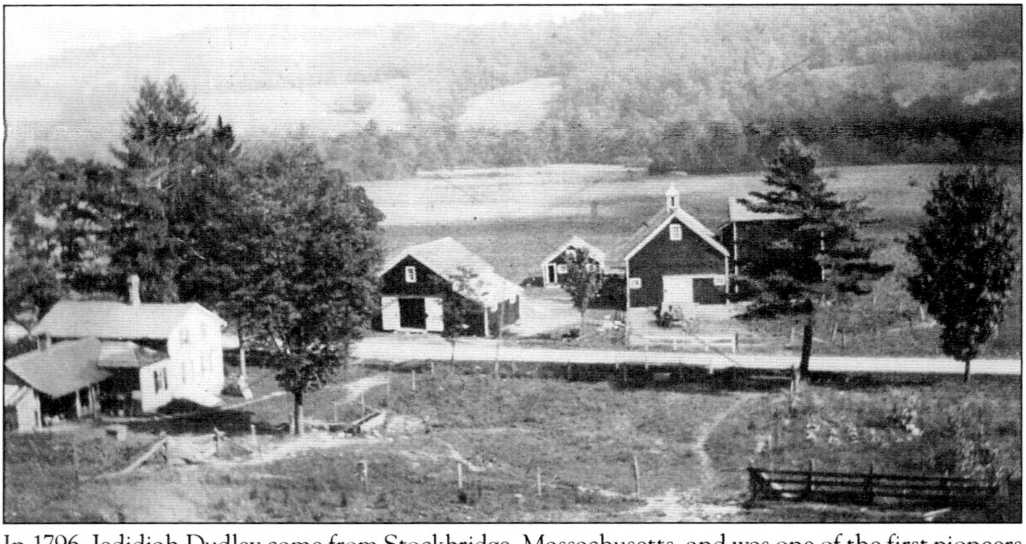

In 1796, Jedidiah Dudley came from Stockbridge, Massachusetts, and was one of the first pioneers to settle in the Nanticoke Valley. This house, pictured in August 1915, was built between the late 1820s and the early 1830s by Dudley's son, Jedidiah Jr., who was born here and farmed this land with his wife, Emeline. Dr. Dwight Dudley (son of Jedidiah Jr.) later inherited the family homestead. Eventually, after his brother and mother died, Dr. Guilford Dudley (son of Dwight) subdivided the farm to create Shadowbrook.

Dr. Dwight Dudley was born in Maine in 1841, graduated from the College of Physicians and Surgeons at Columbia University, and enlisted in the Union army during the Civil War. After the war, he returned to Maine in 1870 and set up his practice, which he kept for 50 years. He married Alice Haskins Turner in 1884 and retired in 1920, moving to Endicott in 1921.

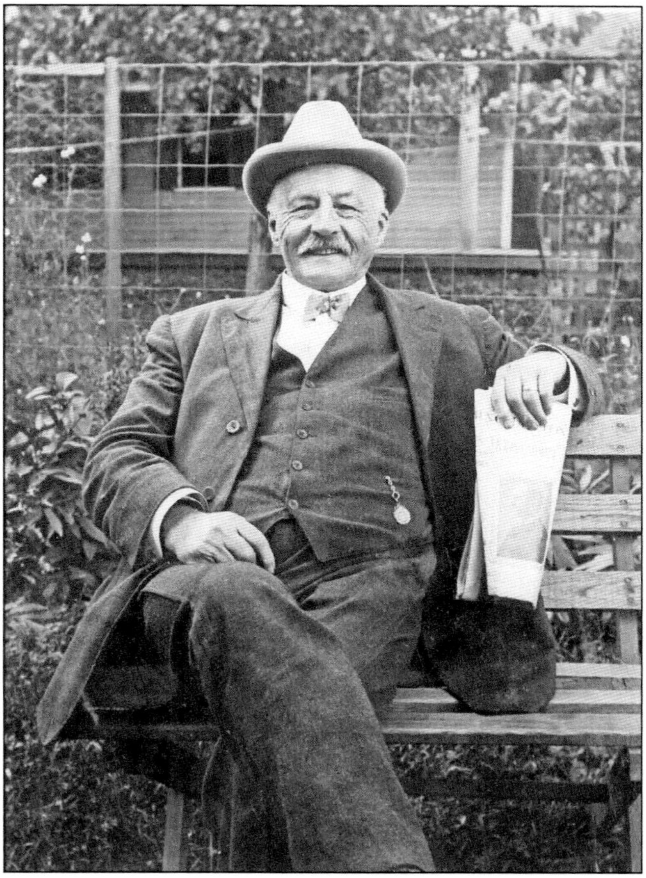

When the Civil War broke out, Dr. Dwight Dudley convinced secretary of war Edwin M. Stanton to appoint him as one of the first 140 medical cadets. At age 23, he became the youngest commanding officer when he was put in charge of Barracks A at the Elmira Prison. The photograph below, taken in Frederick City, Maryland, in 1862 or 1863, shows Dudley (center) with two fellow cadets.

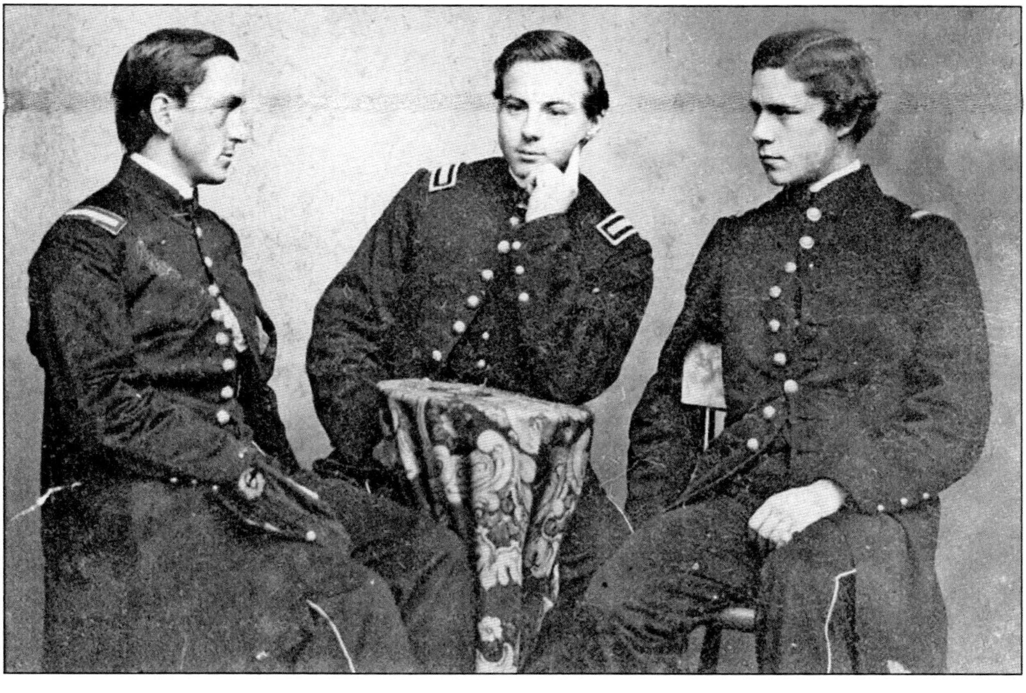

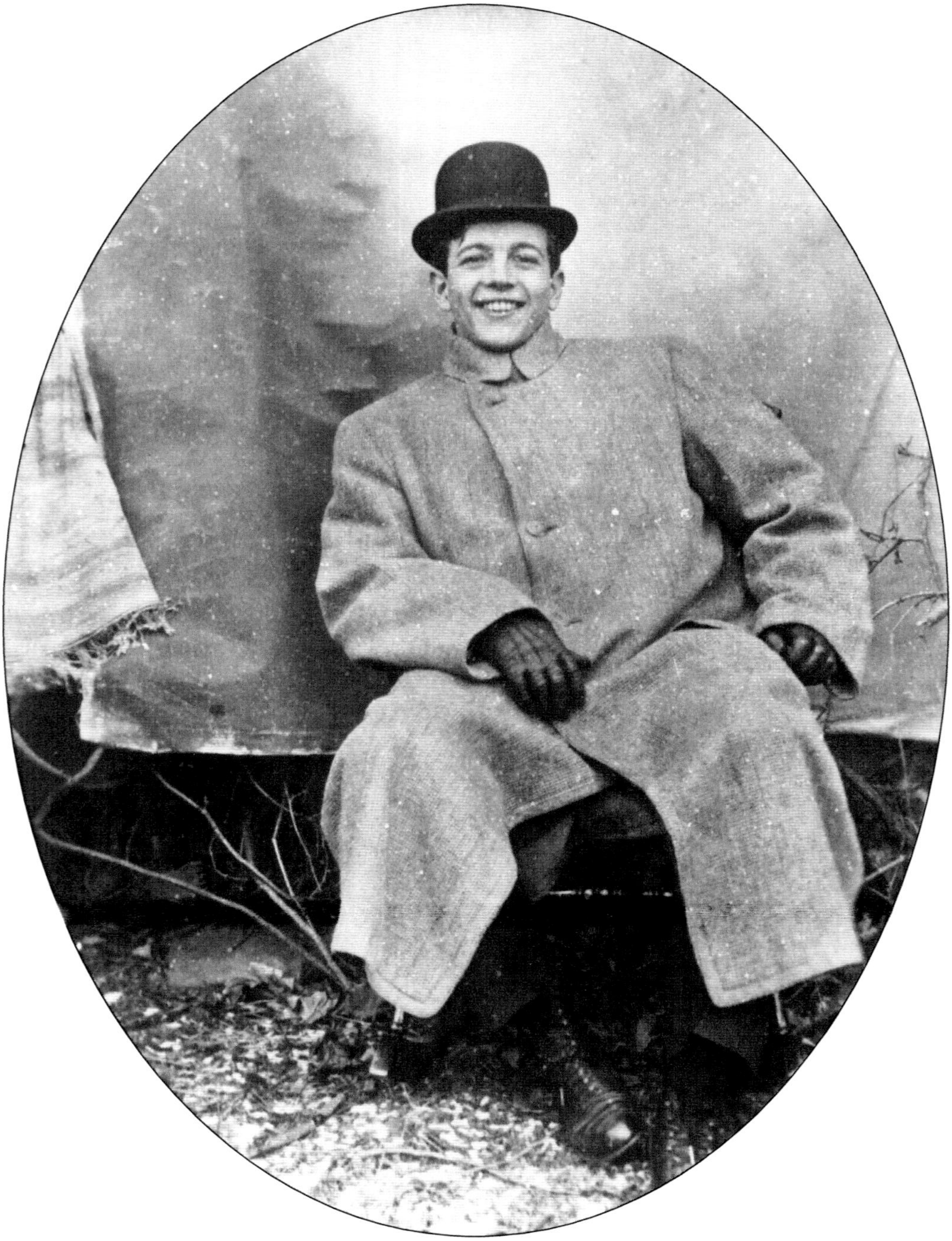

Dr. Dwight Dudley's son, Dr. D. Guilford Dudley, was born in 1890 in Maine. In 1913, he graduated from Albany Medical College and opened a practice in Maine for two years before moving to Endicott. In World War I, Guilford served as a first lieutenant in France from 1917 through 1919. He helped develop an anti-anthrax serum that was much needed, as many soldiers were dying after contracting the disease from shaving brushes. Dr. Guilford Dudley went on to become president of Ideal Hospital and died in 1972.

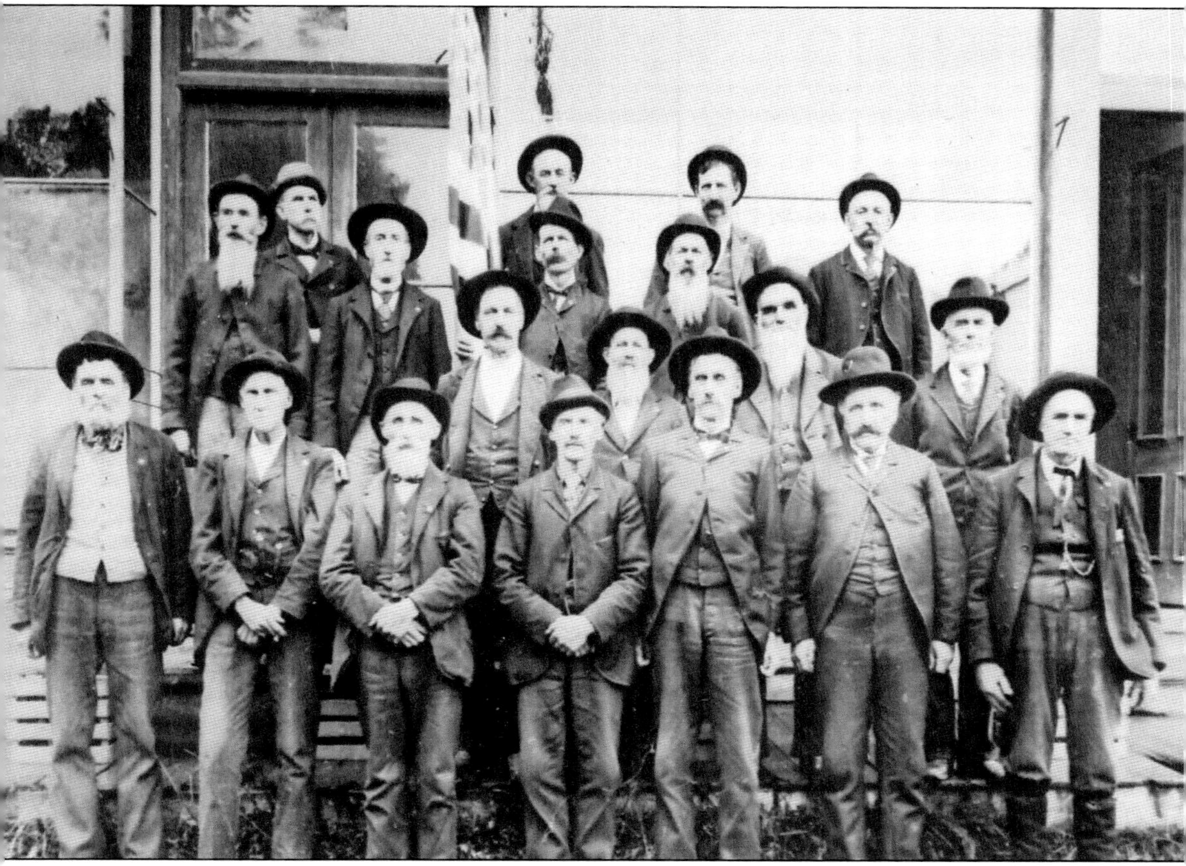

Veterans of the Civil War from the Maine area formed the Howard Post No. 474 Grand Army of the Republic (GAR). It was named in honor of Asa L. Howard, who was wounded in the first battle of Bull Run, reenlisted, and then died in December 1862. Of the 190 men from the area who went to defend the Union, 15 died in battle, from disease, or after suffering wounds. Of the 190 men, 100 of them served in the 50th New York Engineers under Capt. O.E. Hine. On October 8, 1898, the GAR posed for this photograph in front of the Mareans' store. They are, from left to right, (first row) Aaron Travis, Orin D. Gray, John Riordon, Fernando Chancey, William Bronk, Marsden Durfee, and William Holbrook; (second row) Horace Butts, Garrett Rozelle, James M. Emerson, and Judson T. Brown; (third row) James Riddle, LeRoy Bostwick, Norman Brown, Joshua Murch, Nelson Baird, and Rufus W. Porter; (fourth row) Morgan Yarnes and F.F. Corwir. The last Civil War veteran from the Maine area was George Norton, who died in 1931.

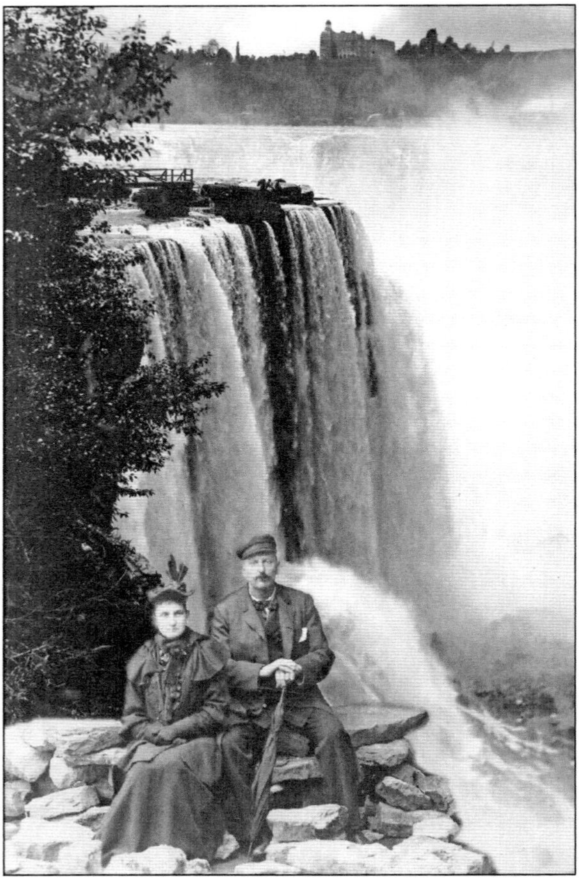

Niagara Falls has always been a popular vacation destination, including in the 1890s, when Baker Taylor and his wife, Eva Hathaway Taylor, posed for the photograph at left. The Taylors' love of nature was reflected in their parlor, which was full of collections from the natural world, such as seashells, pressed and dried flowers, and other items.

Many small towns across the country swelled with excitement when the one-ring circus came to town to entertain enthusiastic crowds with horseback riding, acrobatic acts, and tightrope walking. The clowns and animal acts also thrilled the audience. When the circus came to Maine Village, the group set up their tents at the fairgrounds.

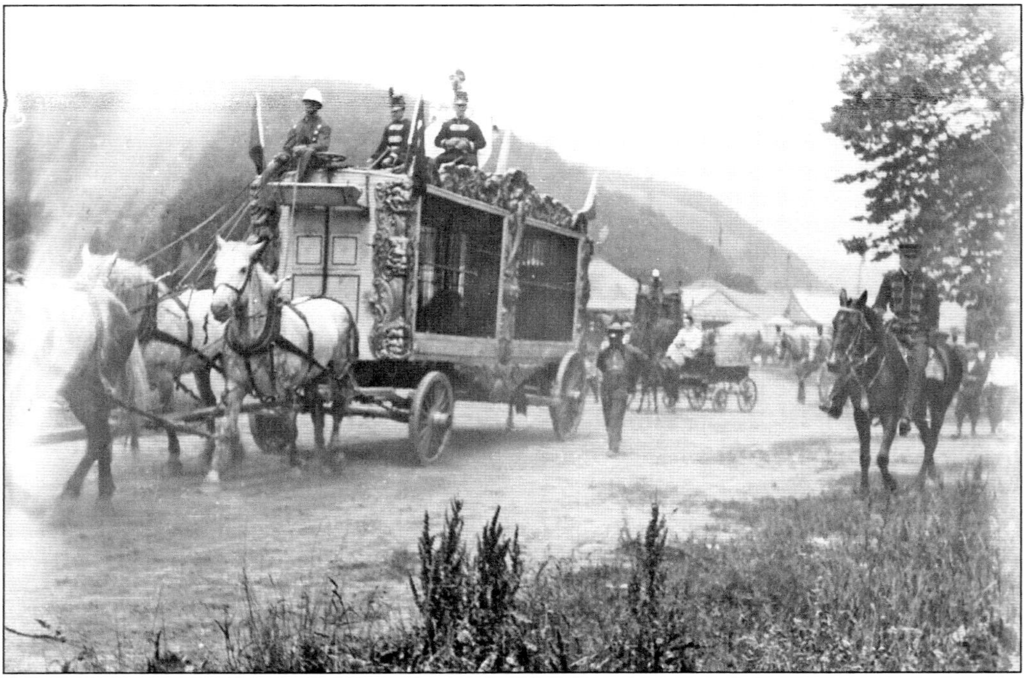

This young man poses in a World War I uniform with an authentic rifle. He was likely dressed up for Decoration Day or a Fourth of July celebration. The Tymeson Brothers store, on the corner of Main and Church Streets, is in the background. The horse block in the background is still on the site today.

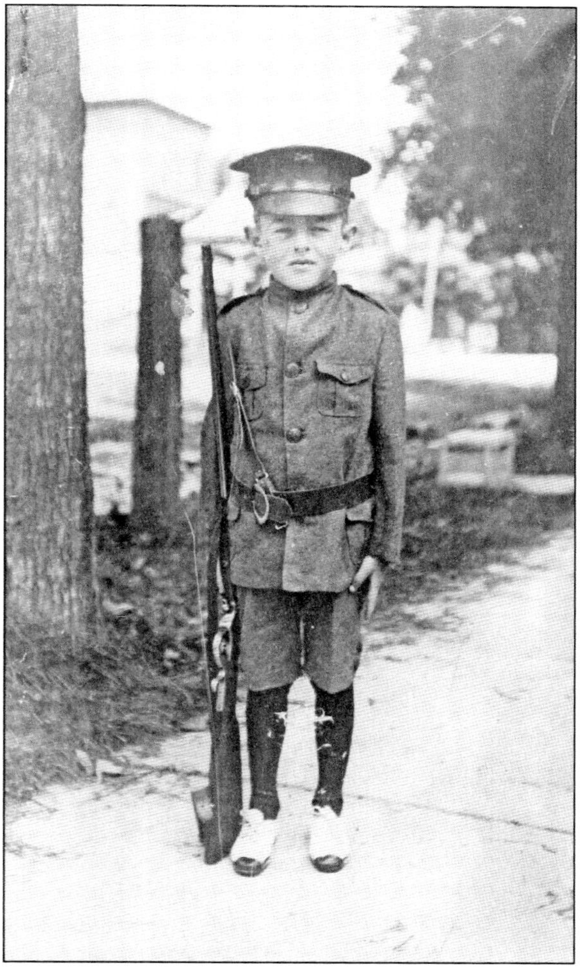

Below, Padbury and Loomis family members and neighbor Donald Lawton pose in front of a car around 1922. From left to right are Doris Padbury, Lawton, Lee Loomis, Mary Loomis, Leslie Padbury, and Geraldine Padbury. Lee Loomis took the photograph with the aid of a tripod and a timing device.

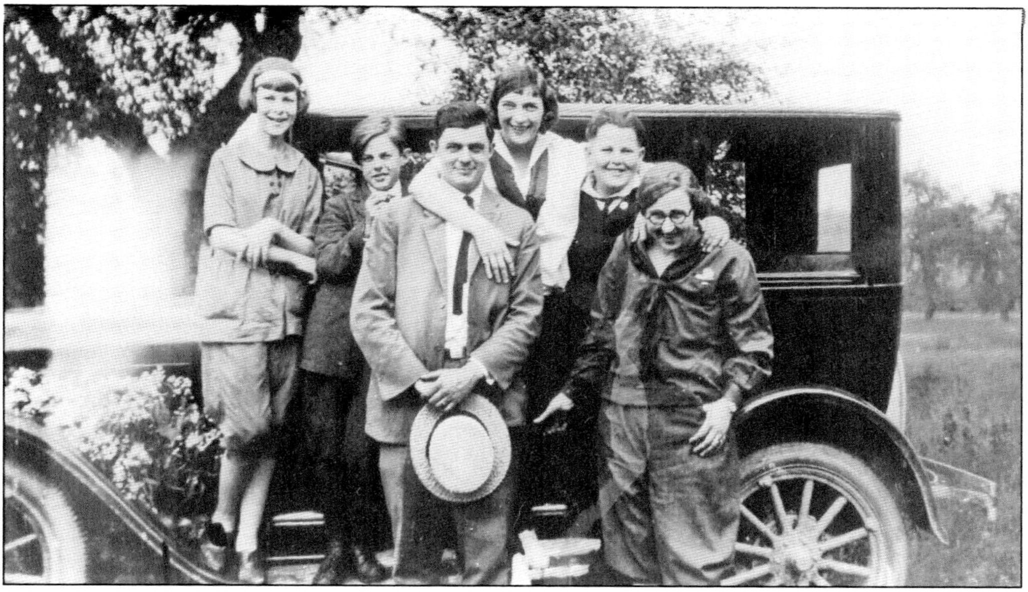

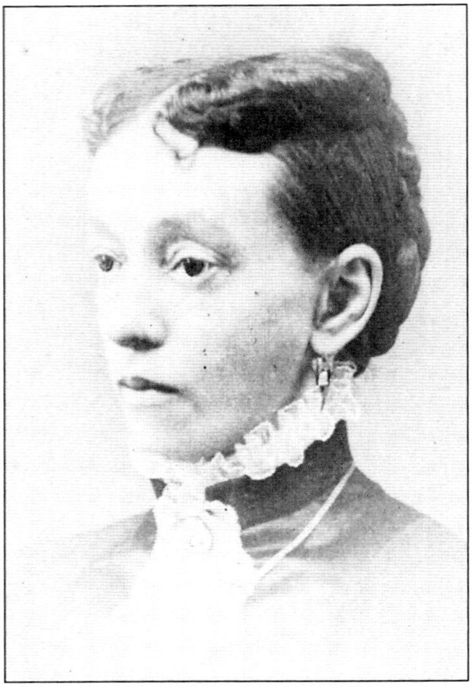

Mary Delano Emerson, who sold policies for the Home Insurance Company around 1900, was quite an unusual woman for her time. Emerson was one of the first women in the area to own a bicycle, which she called "the wheel." She rode it all over the area, up and down the hills, all without brakes. She was also an accomplished organist at the Congregational Church.

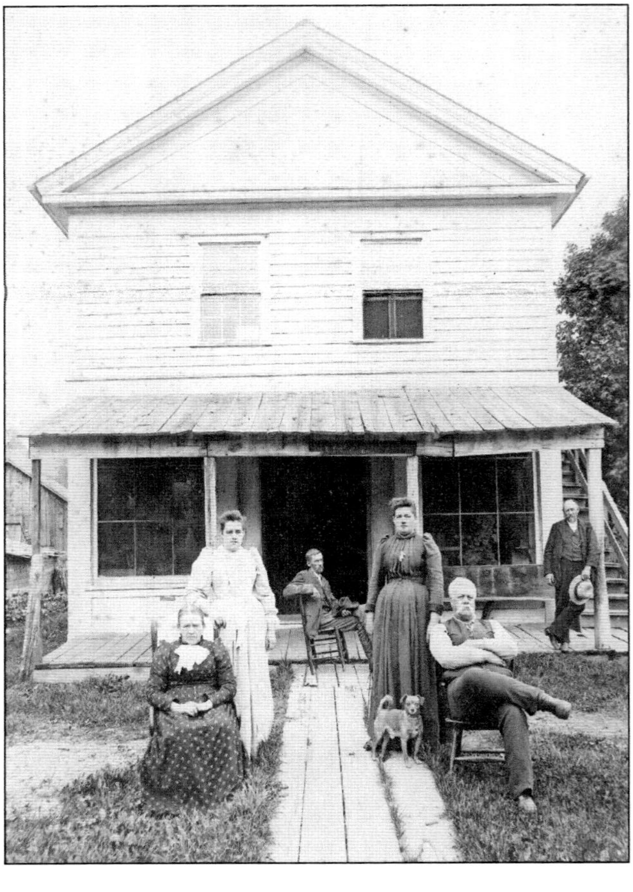

This house, the former home of Lee Loomis and his family, still stands on Main Street. Loomis took many of the photographs in this collection, including this one from 1895. Pictured here are, from left to right, (seated) Eliza Whiting Ellis Johnson and her husband, shoemaker George Johnson; (standing) their daughters, Laura Irena Johnson and Alice Johnson Loomis; William Bronk (seated in background) and Eliza's brother, John Ellis (leaning on the post at right).

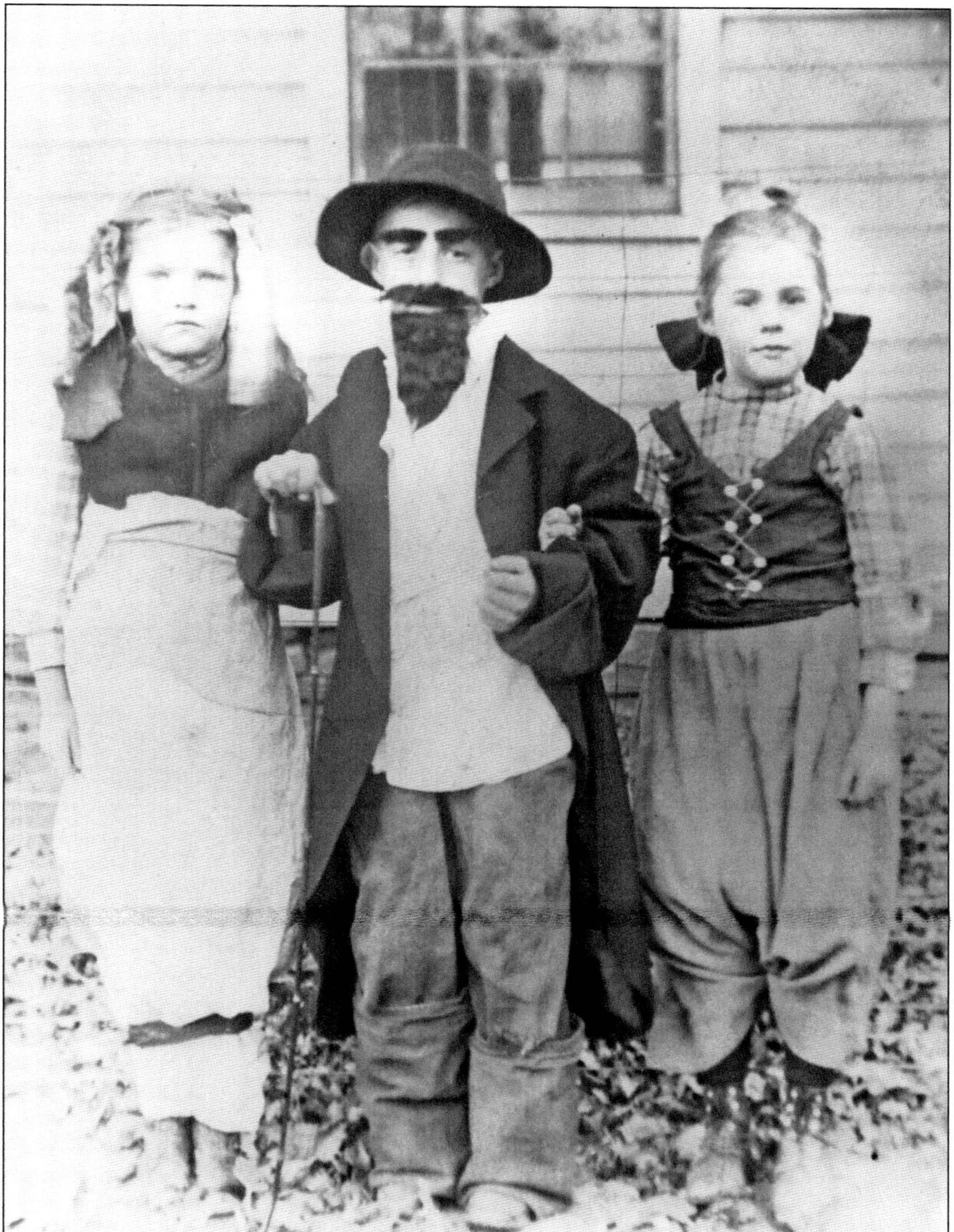

The Lawton children—Adelia (left), Kenneth (center), and Dorothy—are dressed up for Halloween in 1912. In those days, purchasing a costume was unheard of, so children (or their parents) had to make costumes at home. Halloween was an exciting time for young folks, and some of the older children made trouble by pulling pranks like putting a wagon on top of the schoolhouse or tipping over the outhouses.

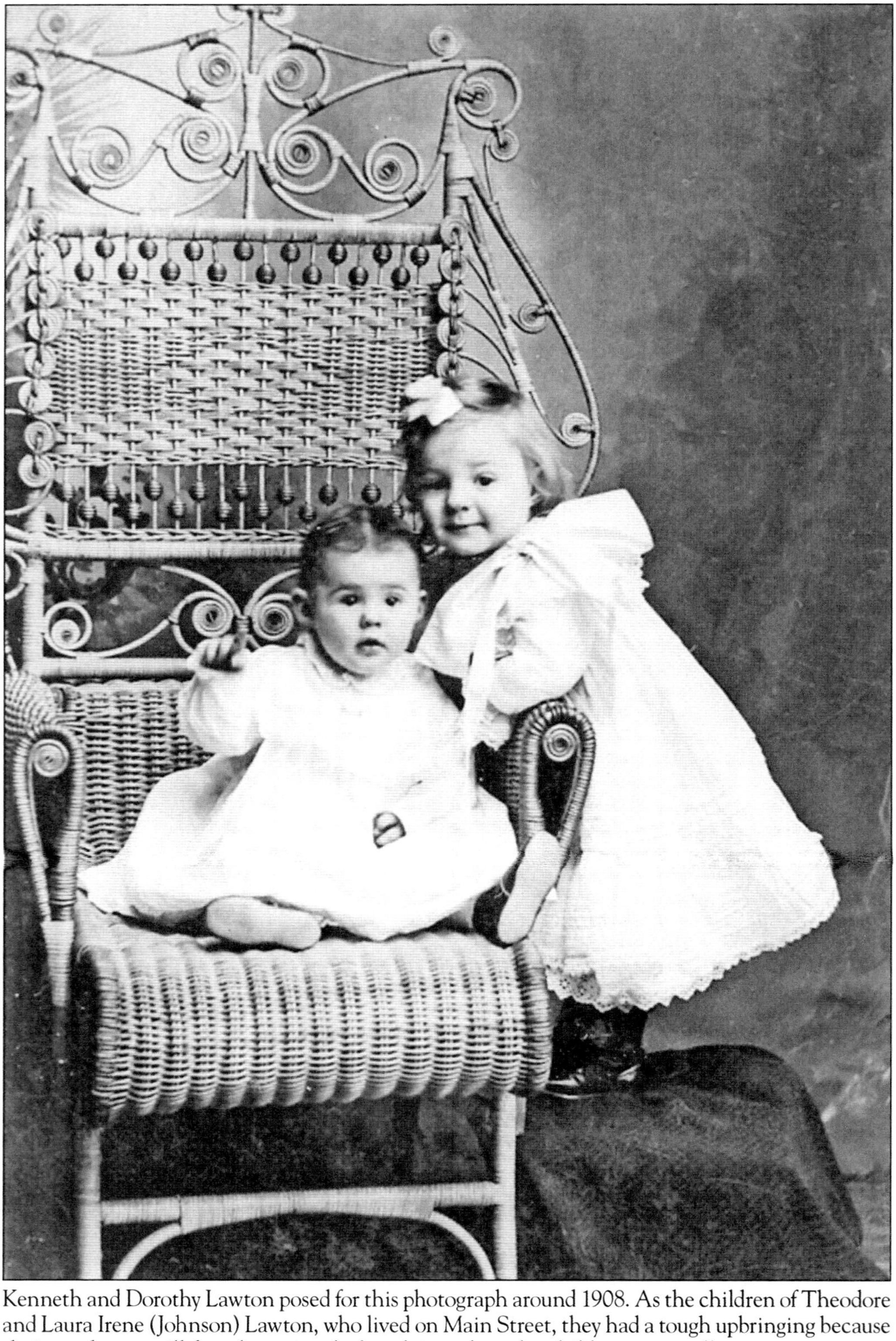

Kenneth and Dorothy Lawton posed for this photograph around 1908. As the children of Theodore and Laura Irene (Johnson) Lawton, who lived on Main Street, they had a tough upbringing because their mother was ill for a long time before dying when the children were still very young.

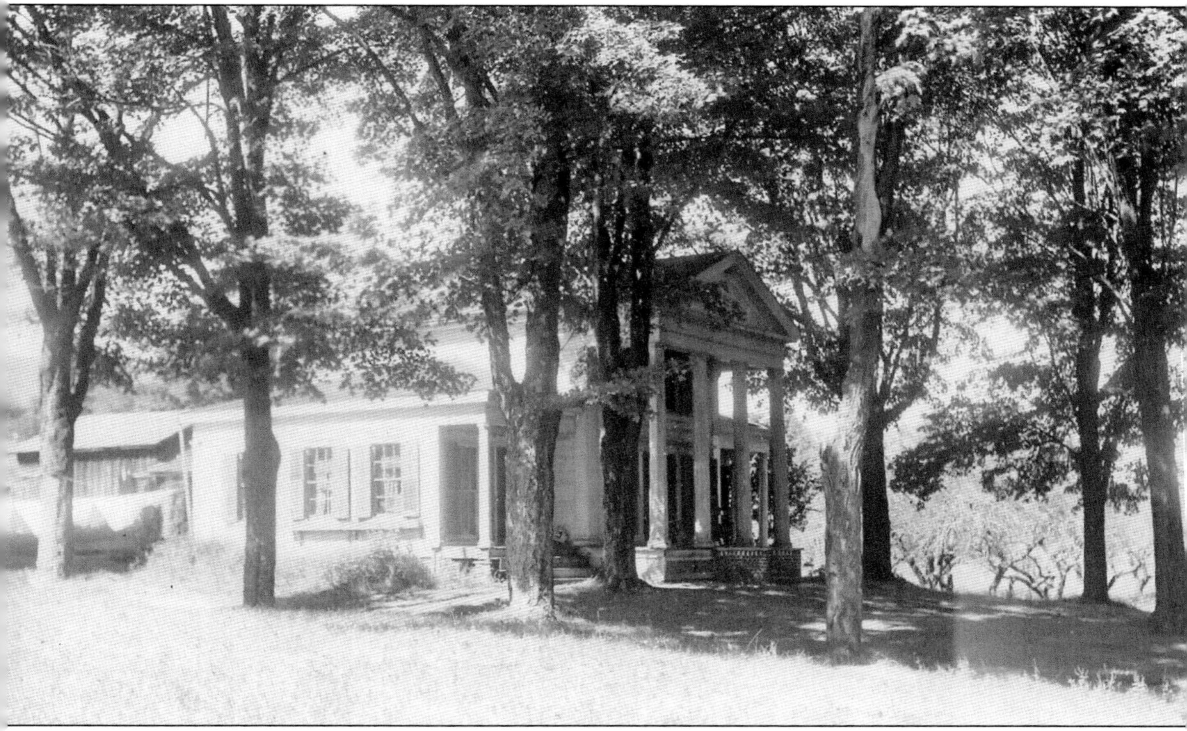

The home of Cyrus and Arabella Gates was built in 1848 on Old Nanticoke Road in Maine. Cyrus was a surveyor and cartographer. This home was once a station on the Underground Railroad, and the Cyrus Gates Farmstead is now listed in the New York State and National Registers of Historic Places.

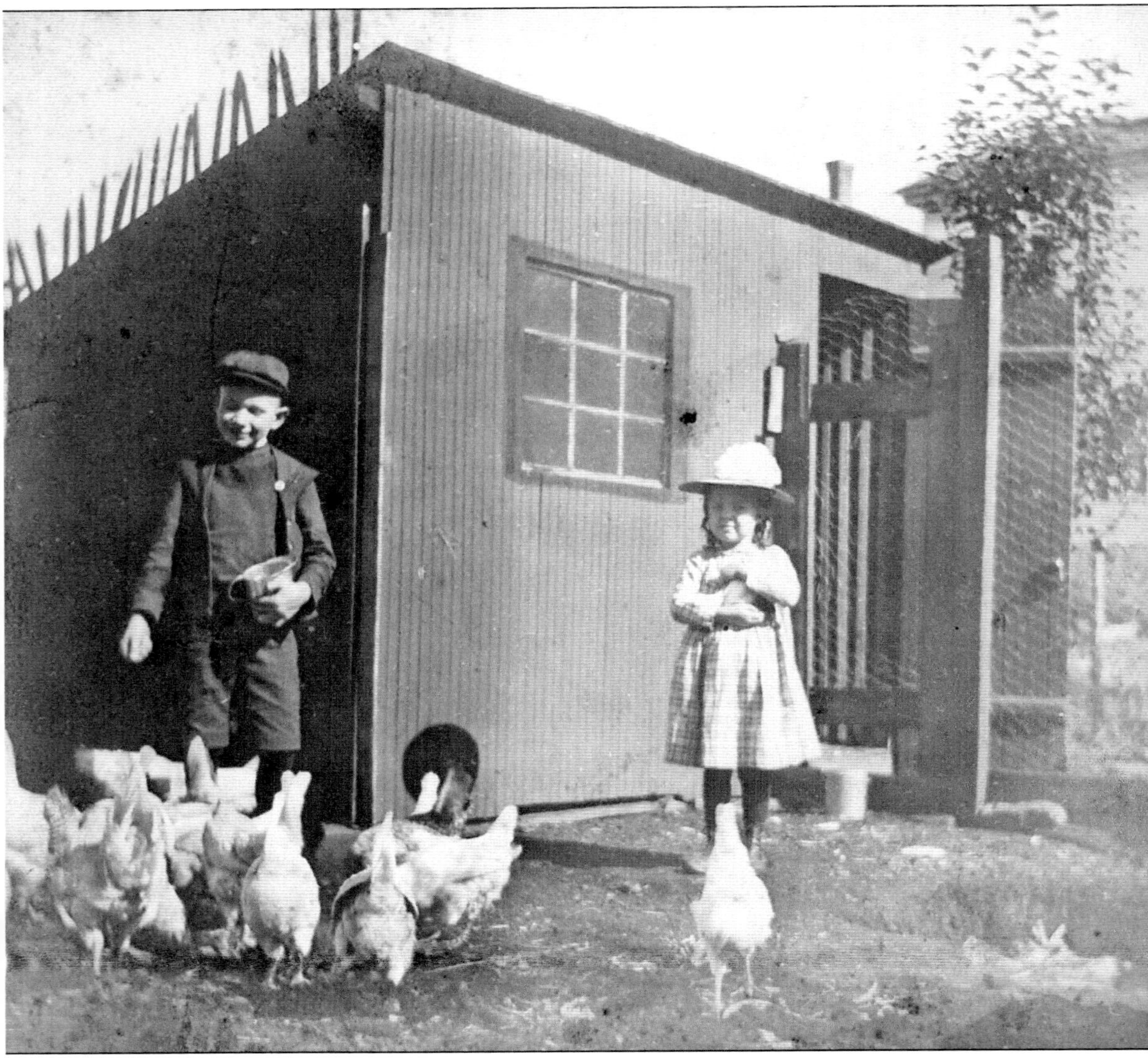

A lot of farm families in the Nanticoke Valley kept chickens for their own needs and to bring in cash or trade from stores in Binghamton or New York City. Farm wives would kill and dress chickens and gather eggs for sale. Here, the Norton children feed the flock at the chicken coop in 1901.

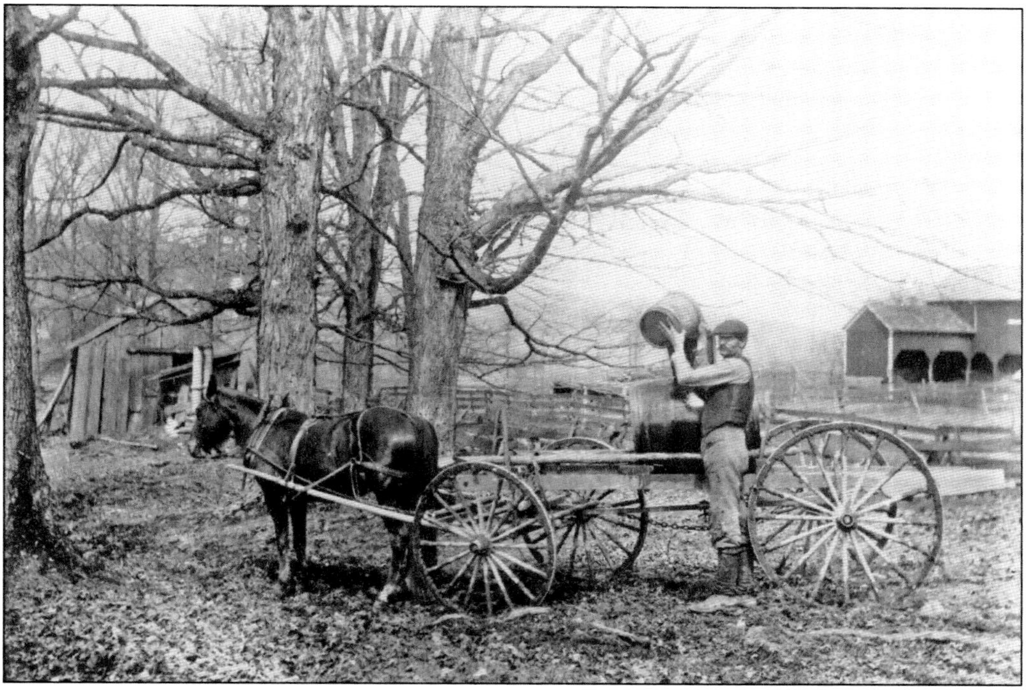

The following newspaper report was found in an 1883 scrapbook: "Eighteen hundred and seventeen for a good many years was referred to as the greatest sap season ever known. A few days before the seventeenth day of April of that year there had been a cold disagreeable storm when it suddenly turned very cold. On the seventeenth when it seemed too cold for sap to flow it commenced to running and freezing to the spouts and continued to run till icicles were formed from the spouts to the tubs as large as a man's arm. Nor did the flow cease when the tubs were full. The boiling apparatus was driven to its full extent and the storages were filled. The sap still run, run til the tubs could hold no more. It is said that the sap, that sap lost upon the ground at that sap run raised the waters of the Nanticoke Creek." In the image above, an unidentified man is collecting sap; in the image below, Charles Bowers is finishing off sap inside the house.

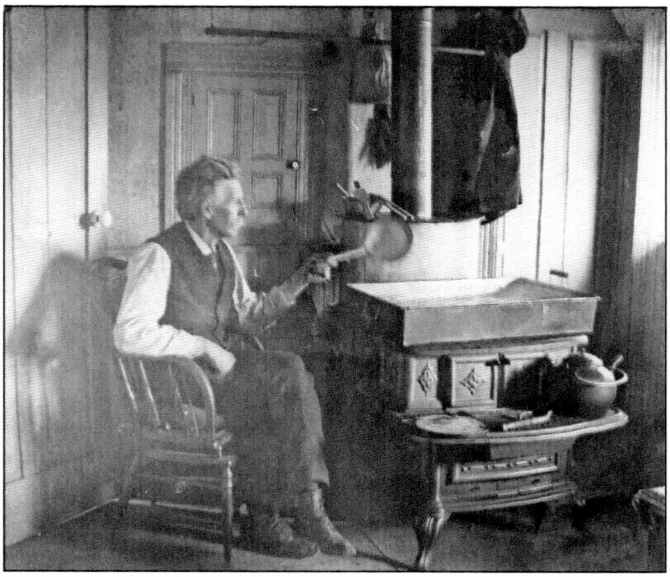

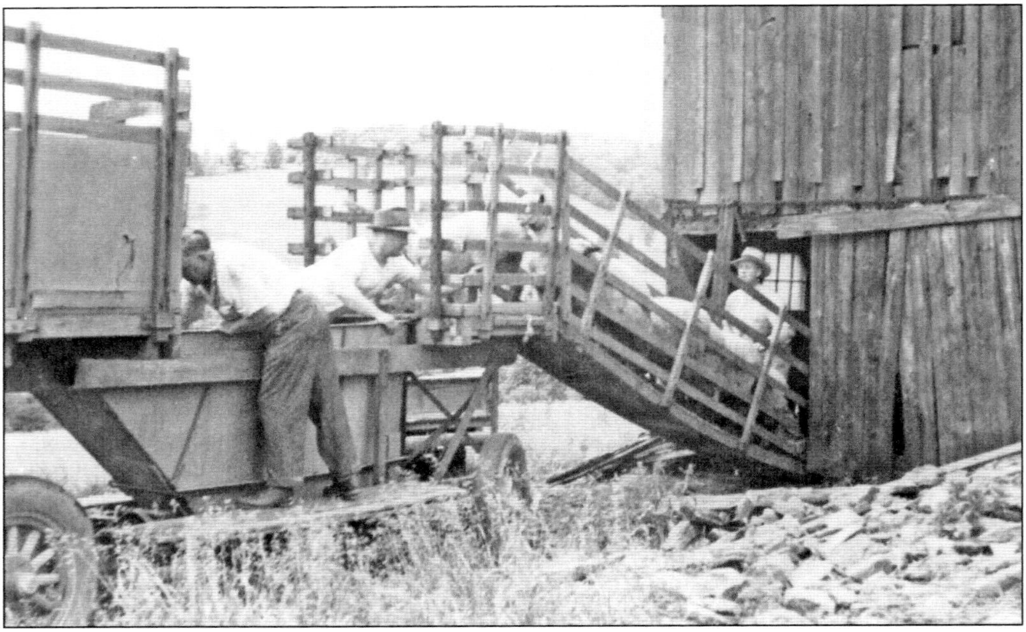

Before the sheep-dipping trough was invented in Scotland in the 1830s, sheep were pushed into a stream and rubbed all over to clean them before they were shorn. Most farms in the Nanticoke Valley had small flocks and used a sheep-dipping trough cooperatively. The Scottish shepherds on Mount Ettrick had large flocks and owned the machines. Their farms were rough uplands that were perfect for sheep but too steep for cattle or gardening.

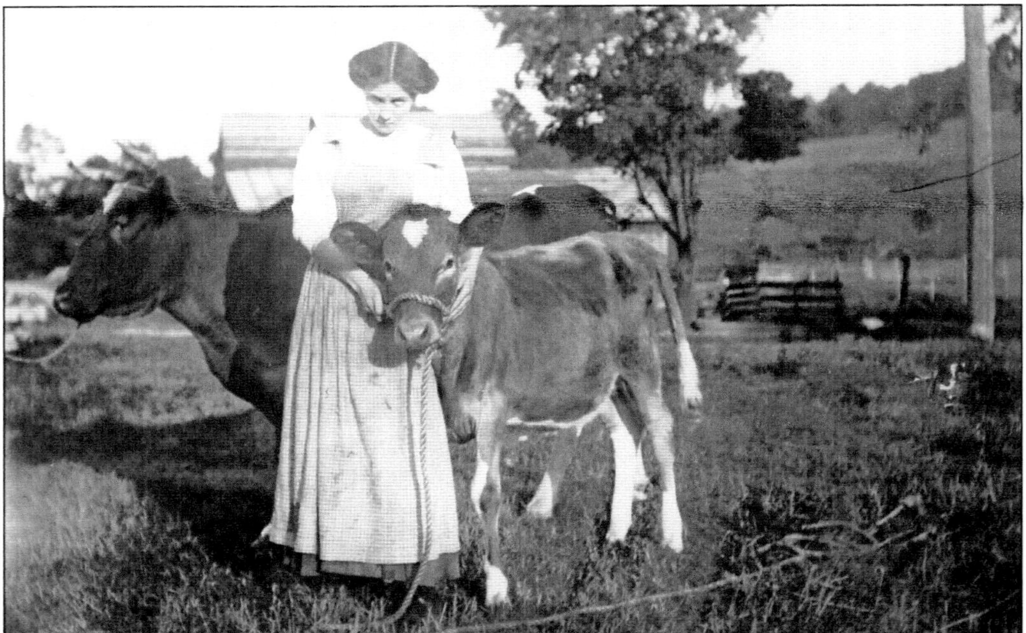

The Nanticoke Valley was a prosperous dairying community in the late 1800s. The work of women was essential to the dairies, because it was women who processed the milk products before they could be sold. Some women also milked cows, but most, like Ina Tymeson (pictured), skimmed cream and churned butter.

A large group of Scottish families settled in East Maine in the 1830s and 1840s. The settlement was initially called Hogg Hill after its first settlers, but the name was later changed to Mount Ettrick after the settlers' birthplace in Scotland. The Scottish settlers were well educated and raised sheep and sheared their own wool, as they had as shepherds in Scotland. Isabelle Hogg (right) was born in 1809 and her husband, William Paisley (below), was born in 1792.

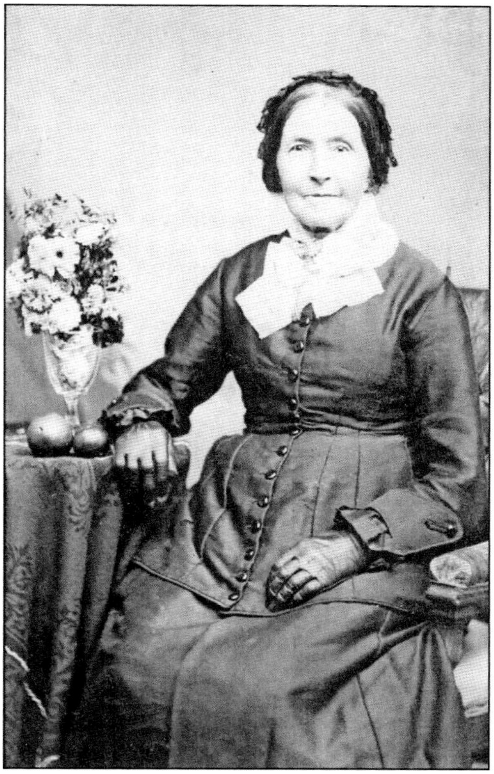

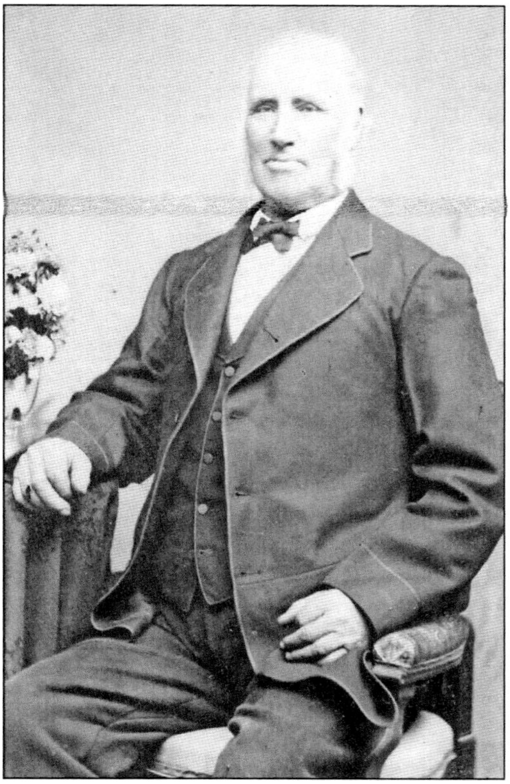

The Paisleys came to Maine from Scotland in the early 1840s and had nine children, four of whom—Mary, Margaret, Jemima, and Olive—died of scarlet fever. Their home, located on Kolb Road near the present-day Broome County airport, still stands.

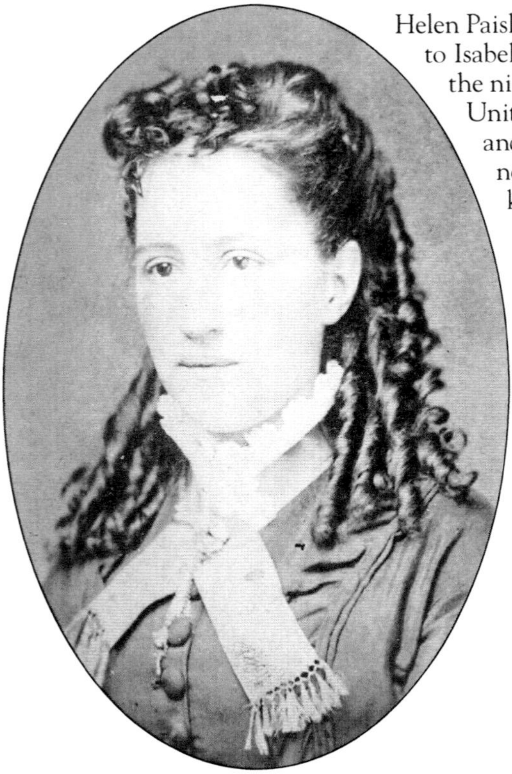

Helen Paisley (left), also known as Nellie, was born in 1848 to Isabelle and William Paisley. She was the seventh of the nine Paisley children and the first one born in the United States, followed by her brother John (below) and sister Olive. Nellie taught school for 10 years, never marrying but coming back to the farm to keep house for her parents and brother.

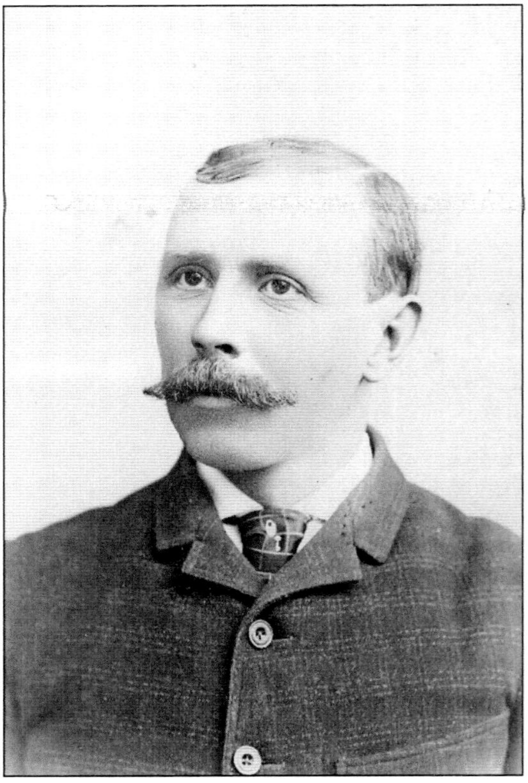

John Paisley, born in 1856, stayed and worked on the family farm. In 1891, John married Grace Howard, who was 12 years younger and lived on a neighboring farm a half-mile away. Howard had studied dressmaking and was a skilled seamstress. When she joined the family, she took over the housework, giving Nellie the opportunity to work outside on chores such as tending chickens, making butter, boiling down sap in the spring, beekeeping, and gardening. John and Grace had two daughters, Mary and Mildred, but Grace died when her children were very young, leaving Nellie to help her brother raise the girls.

Sledding was a fun wintertime activity in Maine. According to George Dudley's diary, on Sunday, February 22, 1920, "In the P.M. after cleaning the stables Audley [Allen, pictured] got out my old sled and started riding downhill up back of the house in the orchard. I went out and then we both went over on the steepest part of the pastures and had a great time."

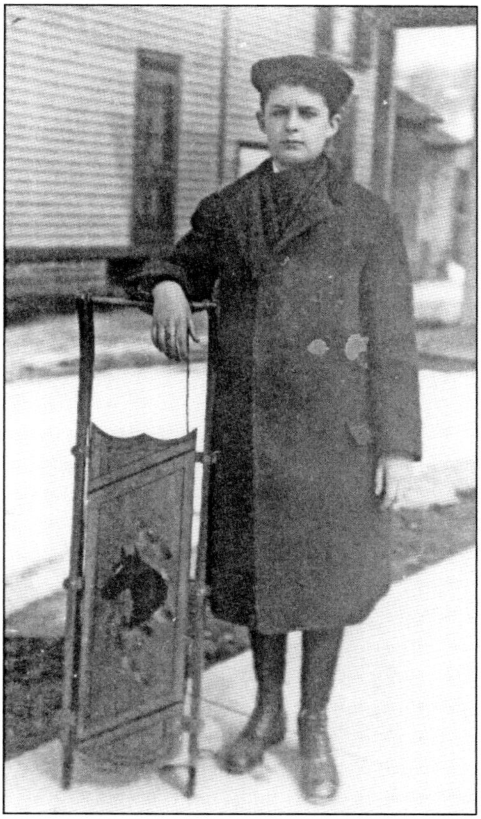

The c. 1910 image below shows the unidentified son of the pastor of the Maine Baptist Church as photographed by neighbor Lee Loomis. Loomis, who bought a camera when he was a teenager, was one of the first people in Maine to record local life during that time period.

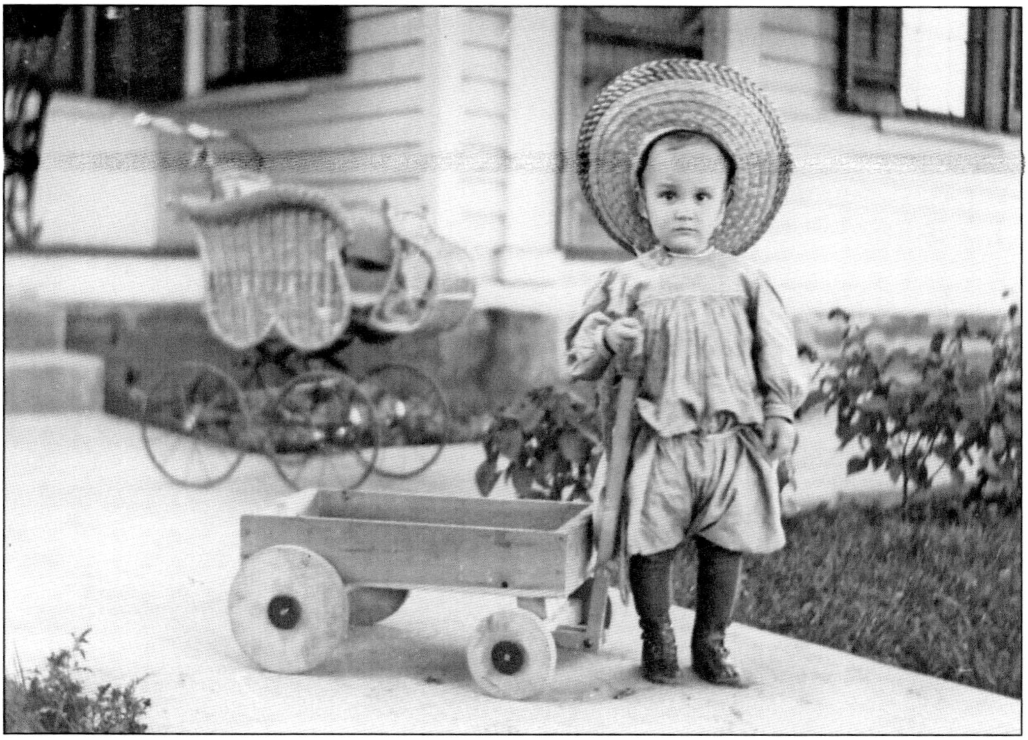

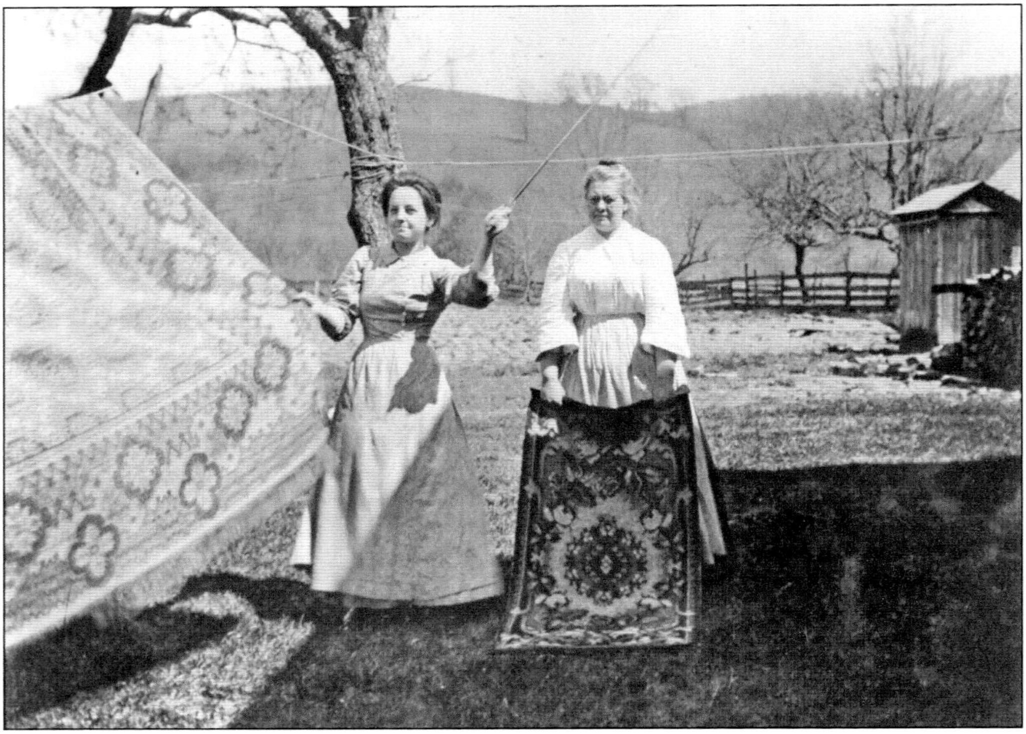

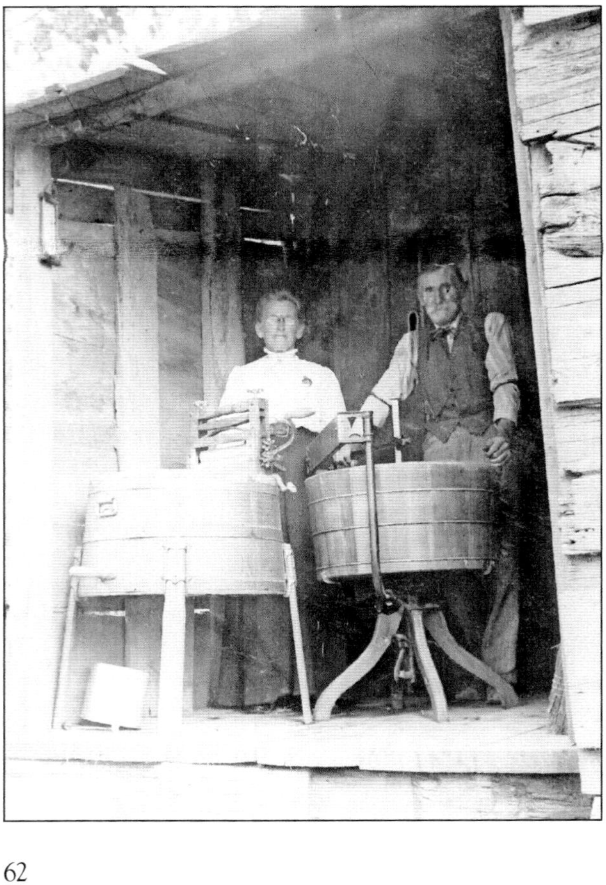

The arrival of spring each year meant a thorough housecleaning that included beating and shaking the dirt and dust out of rugs. Above, Jessie Dudley Allen (left) and her mother, Alice Dudley, clean the family homestead, just south of Maine Village; Jessie is beating the rug with a horsewhip.

Doing the weekly laundry was one of the biggest hardships women had to endure in the Nanticoke Valley. They would start the night before, soaking clothes to remove stains. On Monday morning, they would get an early start in order to fetch the water and heat it on the stove before washing the clothes and hanging them on the line. This 1900 dual-tub washer, which could be purchased for around $10 in 1905, made the job much easier.

These two images are very unusual, as there were not many photographs taken of women doing housework in 1912. Alice Johnson Loomis, pictured on this page doing the dishes and washing the laundry, was photographed by her son, Lee Loomis, who likely took them to practice his skills or try out a new camera.

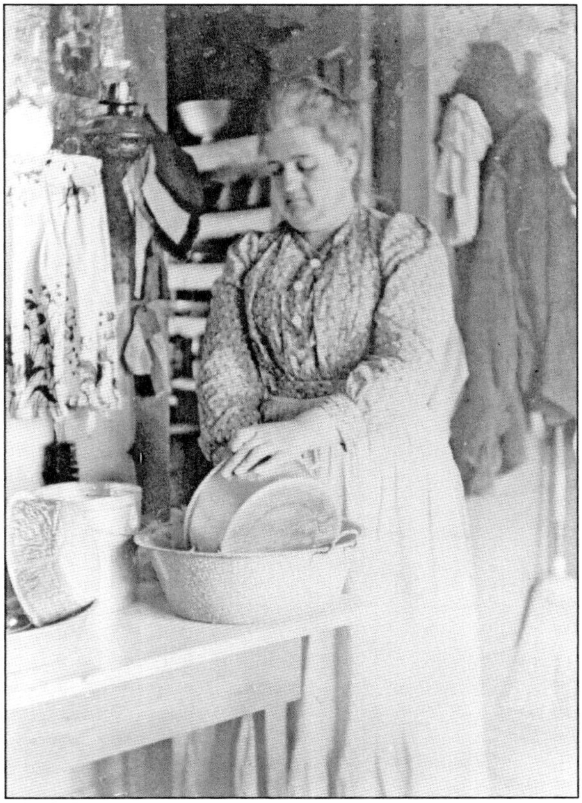

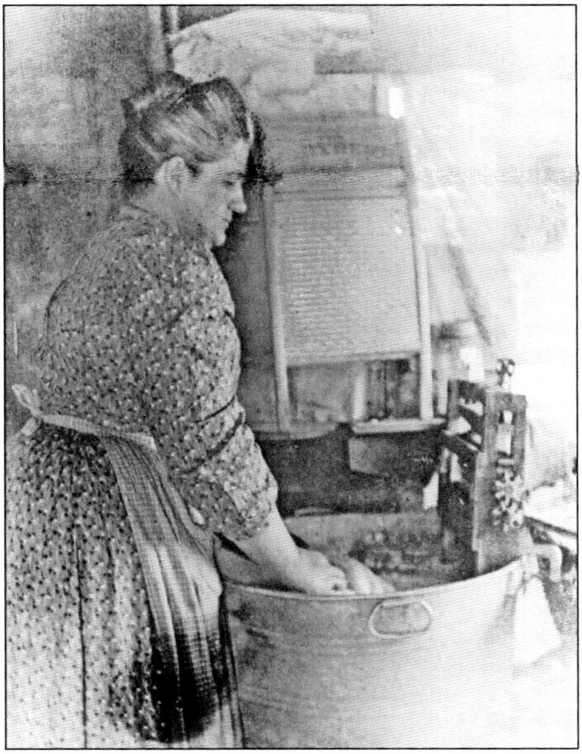

For these chores, Alice Loomis had to heat up the water and haul it to the basin. She used Fels-Naptha soap or soft soap she made at home. The washboard in the background is at the ready to remove any stains on the clothing.

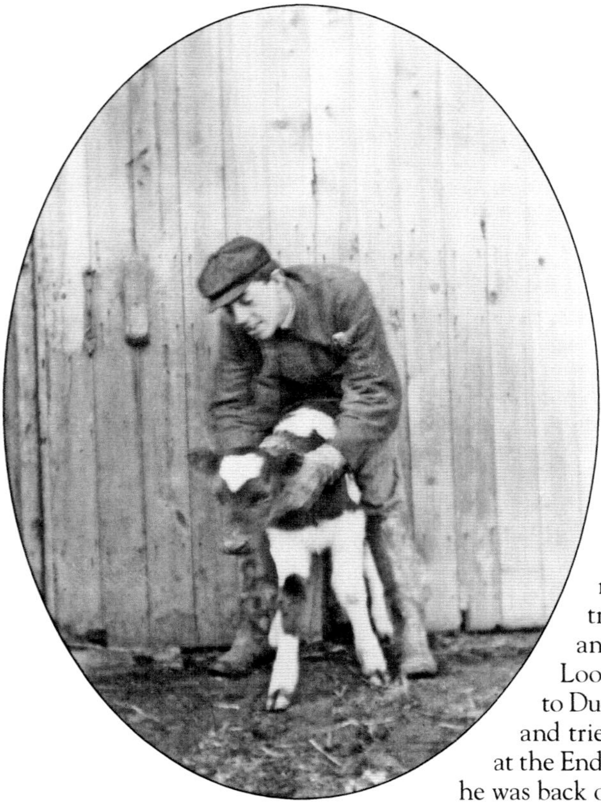

George Dudley started farming the family homestead in 1914, when he was 18. He attended classes and lectures in modern agriculture, taking winter courses at Cornell University in Ithaca. He also attended Farmers Week each year. Dudley used his horses, Simpson and Harry, to haul wood, manure, and milk; to plant crops; and to provide transportation. He also raised veal calves and sold them for $20 each. His friend Lee Loomis took these photographs. According to Dudley's diaries, he gave up farming in 1916 and tried to go back to high school or to work at the Endicott Johnson Corporation, but by 1919, he was back on the farm.

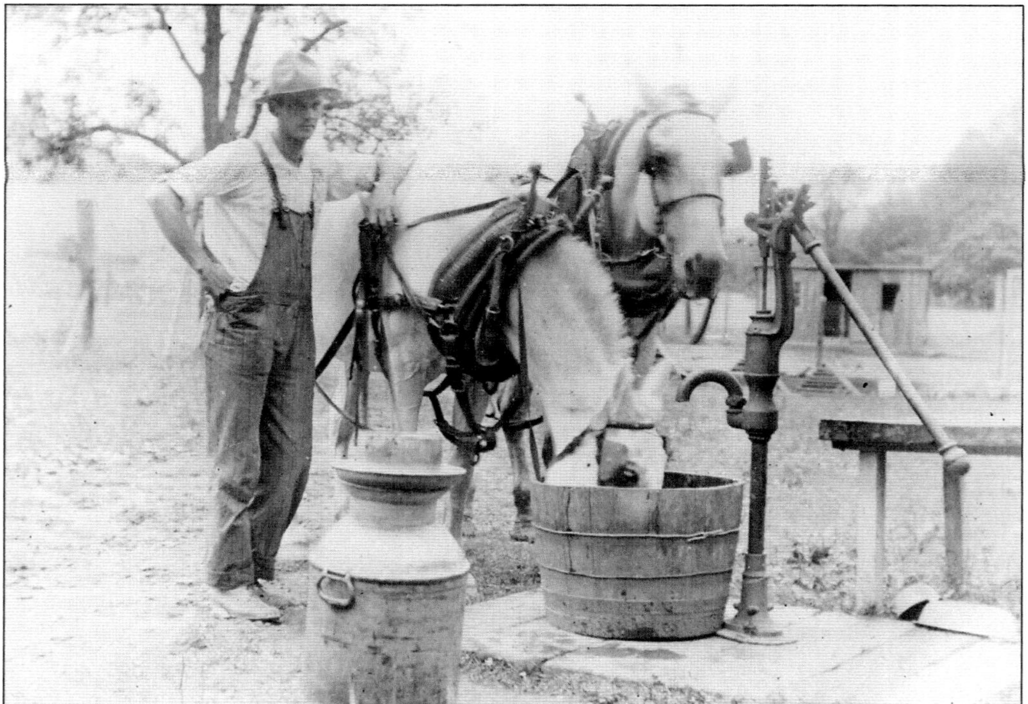

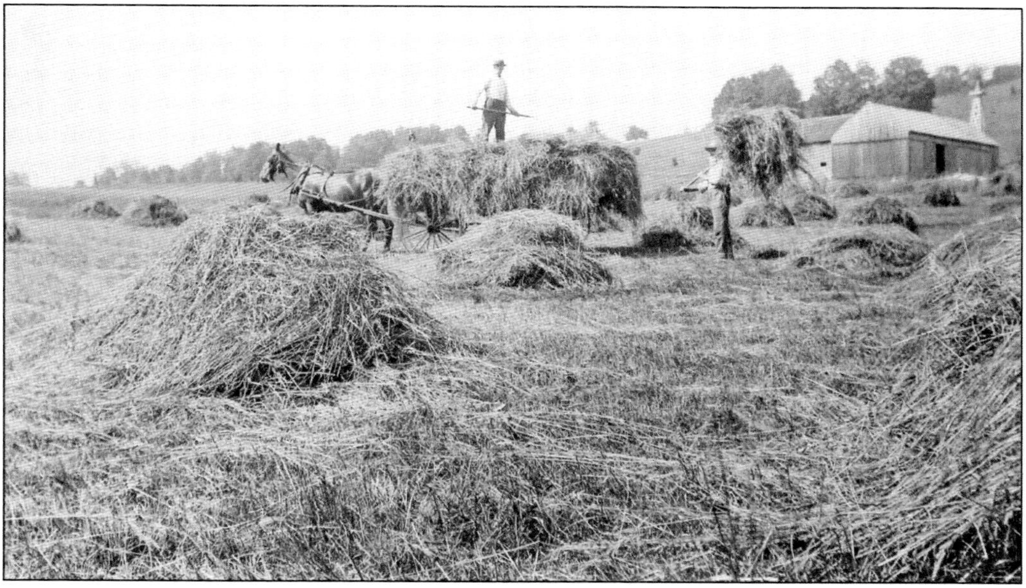

Hay is an important food source for farm animals in the Nanticoke Valley, so it must be harvested and stored for winter consumption. The process starts with mowing the hayfield and leaving the hay on the ground for a number of days to dry. After the hay has dried, a dump rake is used to make small piles; a worker then comes behind the dump rake with a hand-held hayfork to make the piles larger before they are loaded onto the hay wagon. The hay is then carried to the barn, where loose hay is put in the hayloft. During haying operations, women and children may have operated the dump rake or loaded hay into the wagon. The woman below wears a large sun hat to protect her face and neck from the sun; women wore older, shorter dresses to perform these activities in order to avoid getting their clothing caught in the machinery.

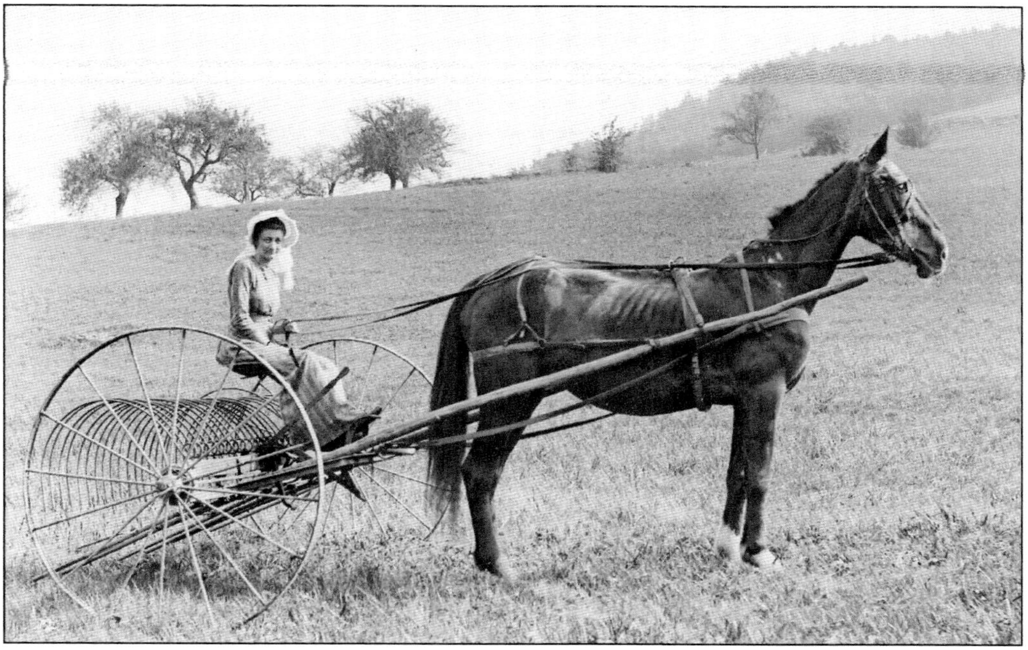

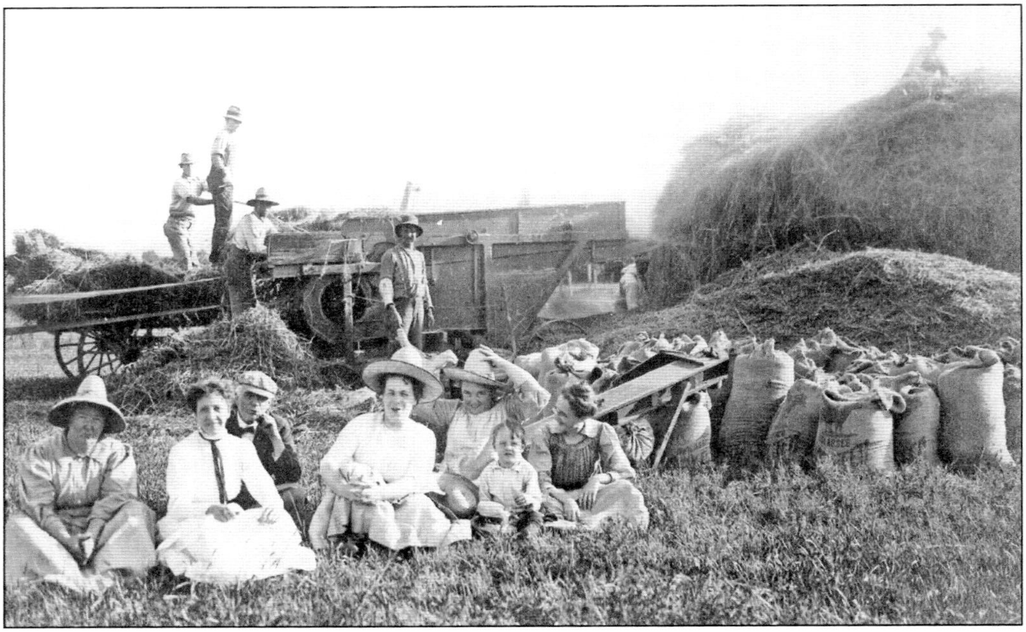

Oats were an important element for feeding the farm animals and were the major grain crop grown by Nanticoke Valley farmers. Once the oat crop was cut, it was raked and put in shocks in order for the grain to dry. After the were dried, it was time for the threshing machine. Most threshers at that time were powered by steam, and sometimes the straw was used for fuel to run the machine. The whole shock was put on the conveyer belt and pulled into the machine, where the grain heads were pulled off and the straw was pushed out of the back. The grain was then loaded into bags, which were taken to the mill to be processed when needed. The straw became animal bedding or was applied to other uses in the house and around the farm.

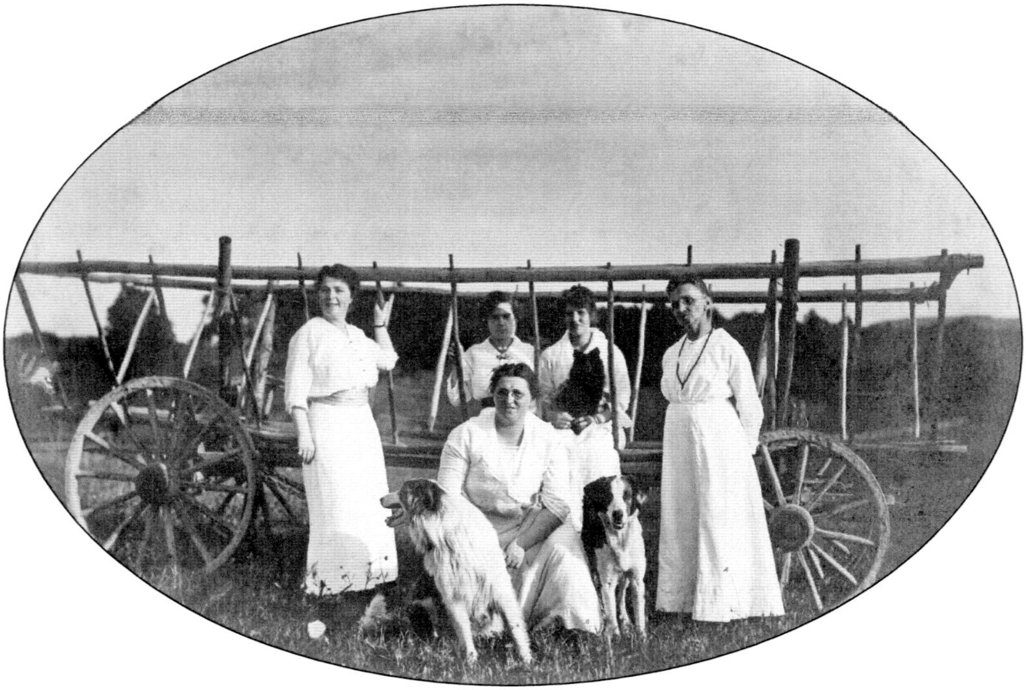

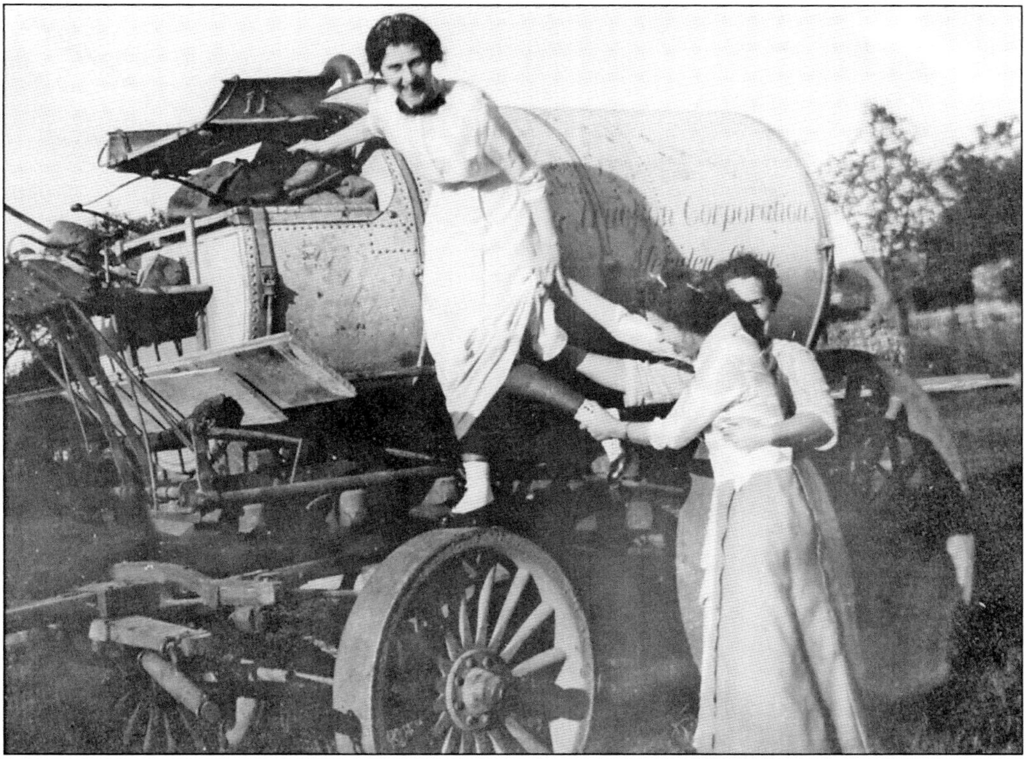

This photograph is from an album owned by the Oliver family of Union Center. The women are climbing onto an unusual piece of farm equipment that has an older wooden base combined with a more modern metal tank-like part. This may have been used to distribute the part of the milk that was left after making butter or to distribute liquid cow manure on the fields.

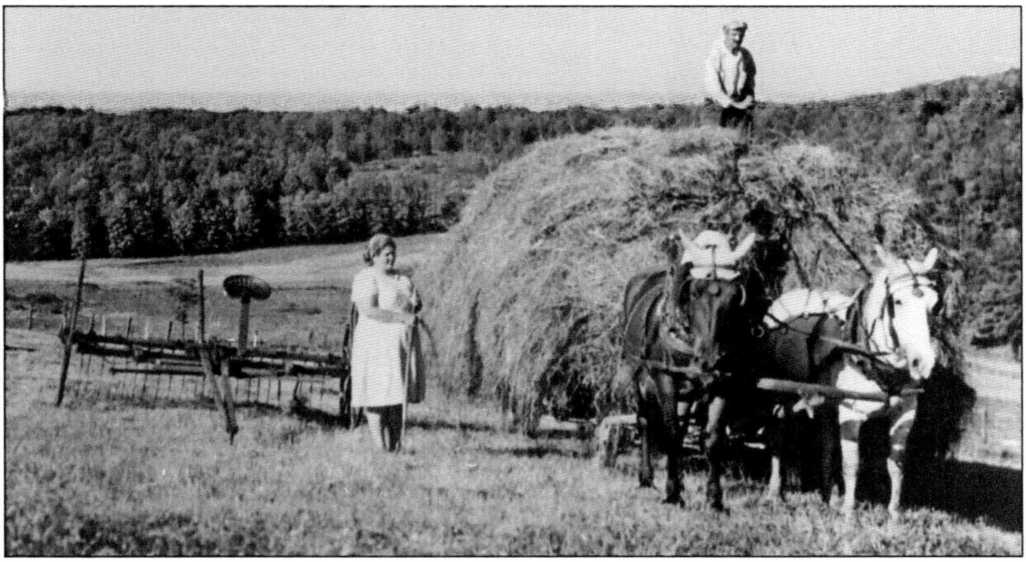

In 1875, George Riley wrote in his diary, "Lucy Ann helped me hay it as good as a man," indicating that his wife, Lucy Ann Riley, did her share of the raking and turning the hay even in July 1866, when she was six months pregnant. In this photograph, Mary Tartanian is helping her husband, John, with the haying on their farm.

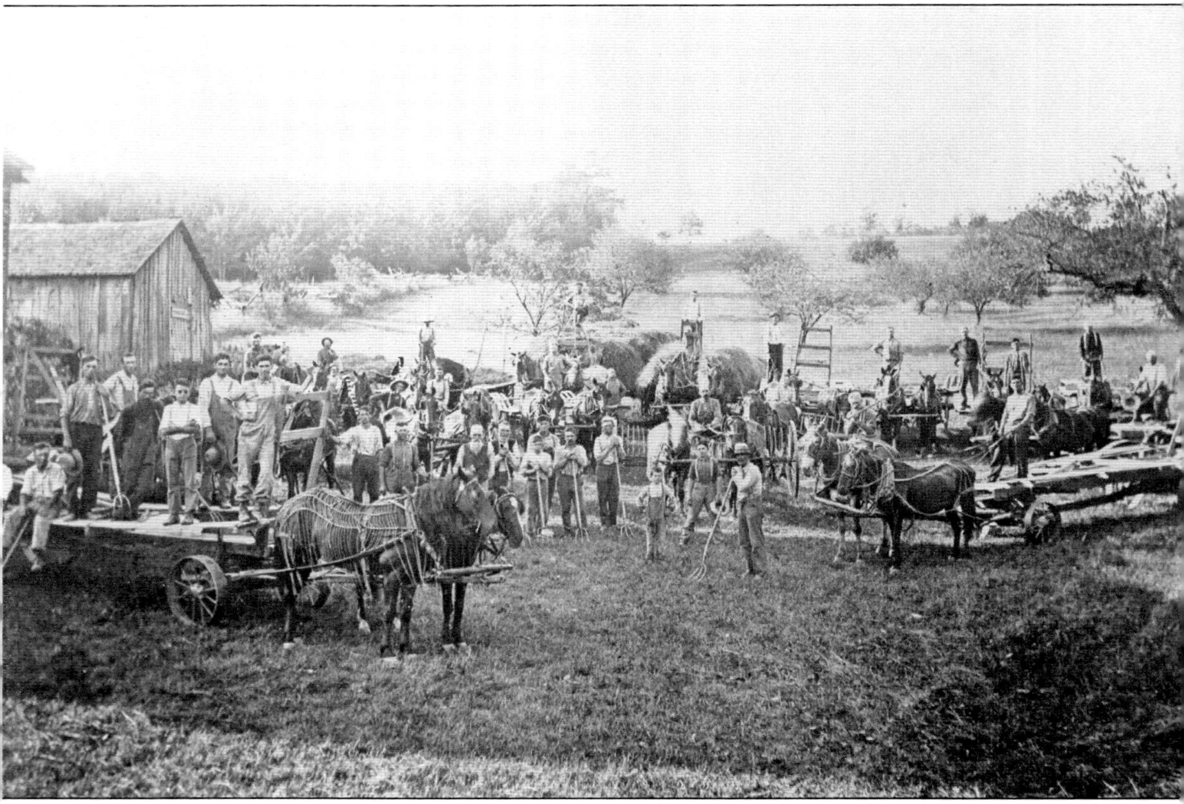

This 1905 photograph shows Frank Brigham's farm in Maine. Local farmers would travel from farm to farm in a group, hauling horse-drawn mowers, wagons, and raking machines, then working until everyone's hay was in. The women were not expected to help, as they were busy preparing the large meals for all who participated.

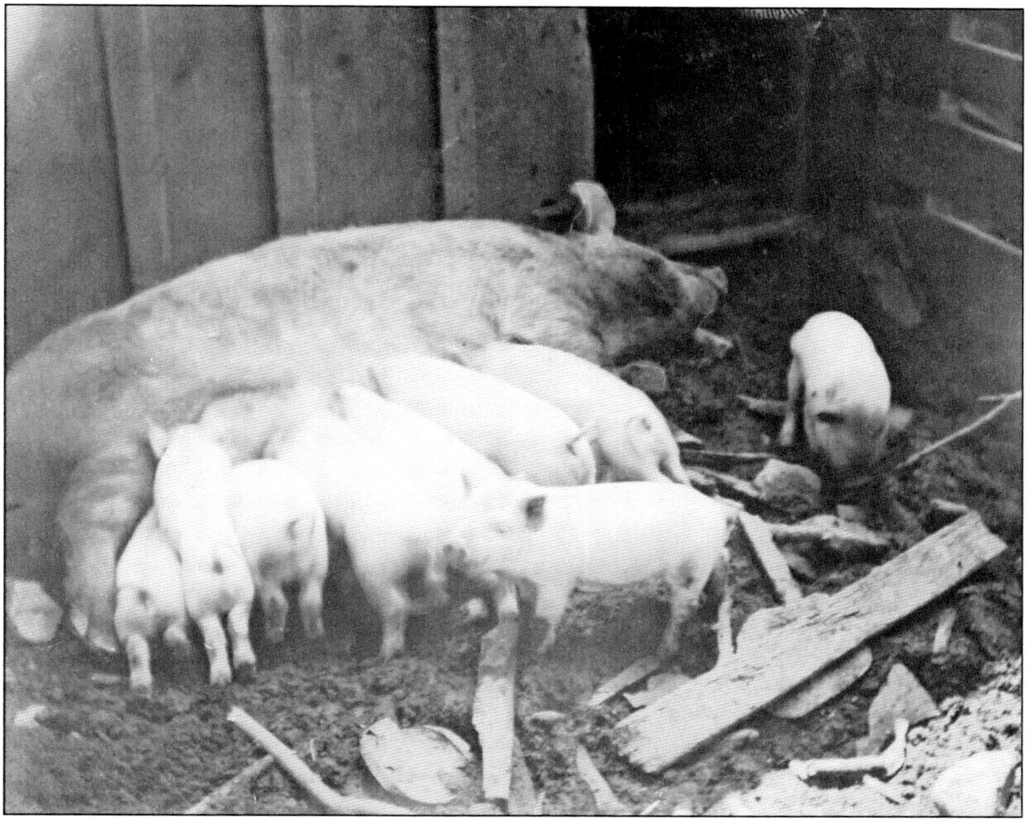

On April 24, 1920, George Dudley recorded in his diary, "It was rainy and warm. Charles Payne and I drove up to Konstantine Kaczynski's farm to get some pigs but he had sold them." Most farms had a pig or two that they could butcher in the fall to provide meat for the winter.

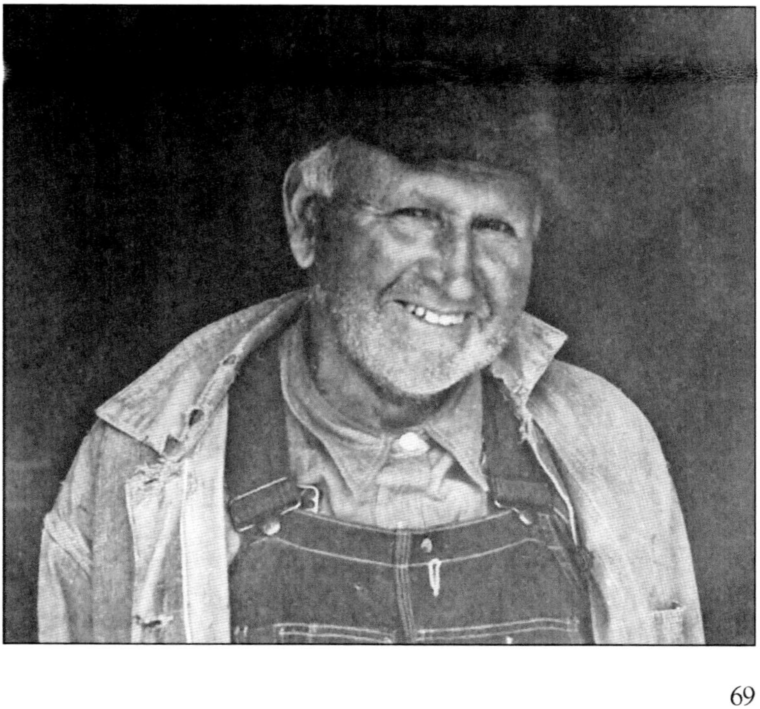

George Durfee was a farmer just north of Maine Village. He and his wife, Gurtha Mooers Durfee, had a house on the present-day location of the NBT Bank; the house was demolished in the 1970s. George's sisters were Myrtie Durfee McIntyre and Clara Durfee McGregor. (Courtesy of Owen Loomis.)

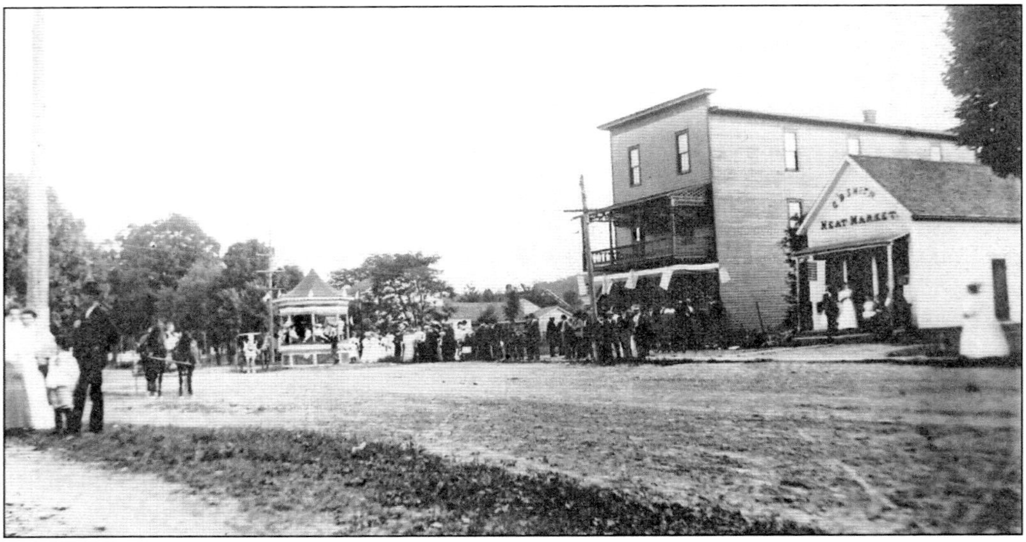

In 1907, when the American flag still only had 45 stars, the Fourth of July was celebrated in Maine with a parade, speeches, a band concert, picnics, and fireworks. Many participants were veterans and members of the GAR. The bandstand in the middle of Main Street was filled with townspeople enjoying the day. Clement Bowers wrote in his history of Maine that local boys would break into the churches and ring the bells on the eve of the Fourth of July.

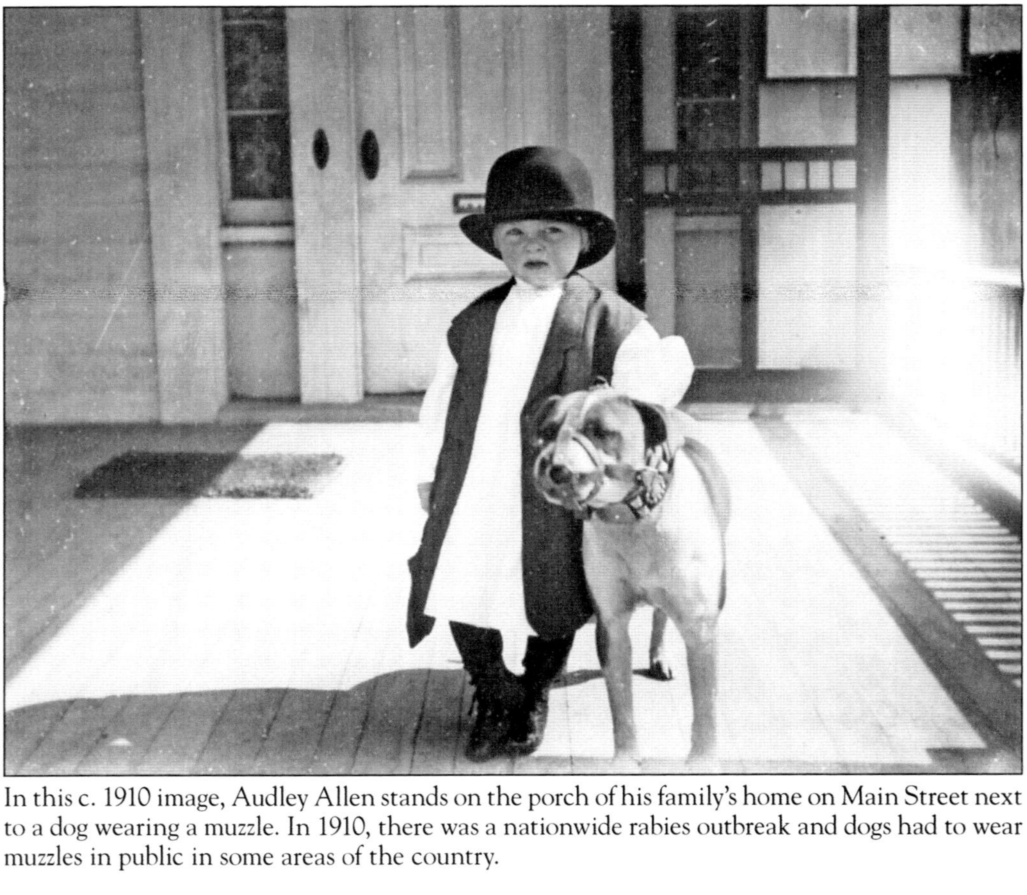

In this c. 1910 image, Audley Allen stands on the porch of his family's home on Main Street next to a dog wearing a muzzle. In 1910, there was a nationwide rabies outbreak and dogs had to wear muzzles in public in some areas of the country.

In old-fashioned houses, the parlor was used for entertaining visitors and for special occasions such as Christmas. Most Christmas decorations and gifts were handmade, as the Victorians were avid crafters. The doll in this photograph was probably purchased, printed on a piece of fabric, and then cut out, sewn, and stuffed; the mother may have made a new outfit for a doll the daughter already had. Fathers often carved wooden farm animals or locomotives for their sons.

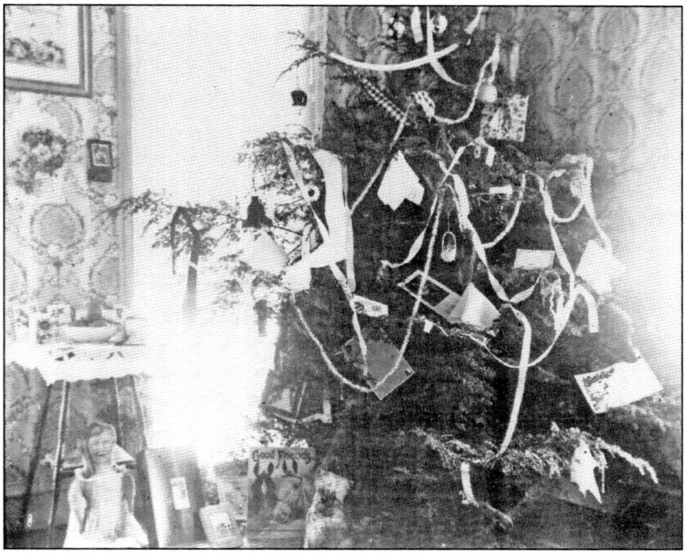

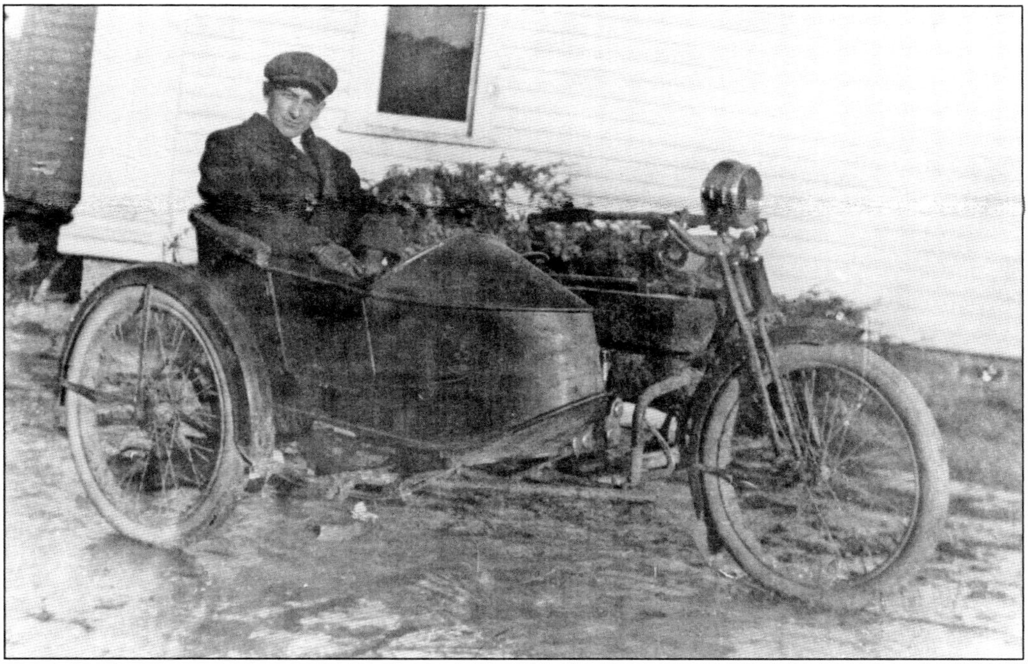

On May 2, 1915, George Dudley wrote in his diary, "I have converted my bike into a racer. Rode up to Bingo propelled by a Smith Motor Wheel." In that same time period, one of his friends, Ralph Grey, was riding in this early motorcycle with a sidecar. It was an exciting time, since the first car had arrived in Maine only eight years earlier.

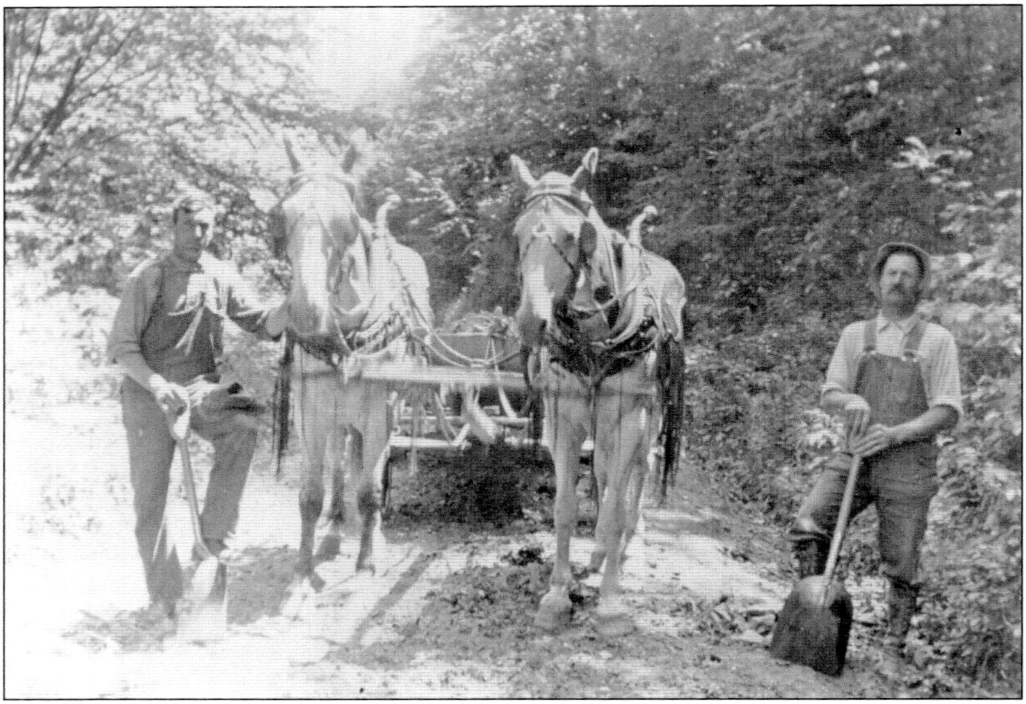

Elijah Butts (right) and an unidentified man work on the roads with shovels. It took three teams of horses to work the roller and another three teams to pull the scraper. Many farmers used their teams to assist in construction of the roads; it was a helpful way to pay one's taxes.

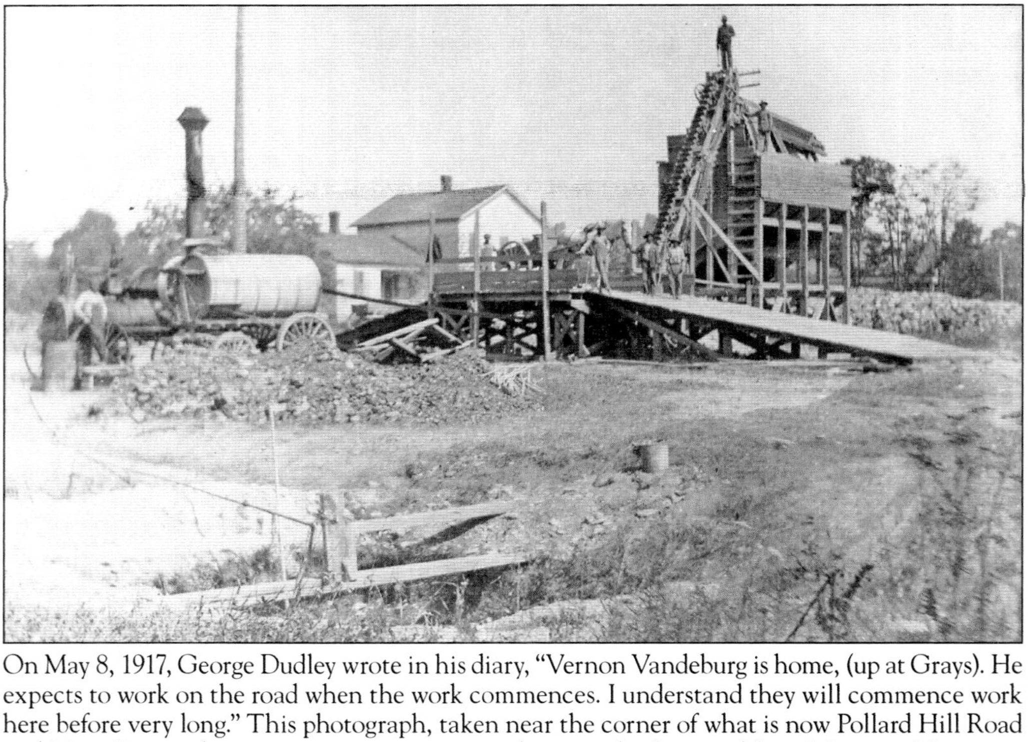

On May 8, 1917, George Dudley wrote in his diary, "Vernon Vandeburg is home, (up at Grays). He expects to work on the road when the work commences. I understand they will commence work here before very long." This photograph, taken near the corner of what is now Pollard Hill Road and Main Street, shows a construction crew working on the first road from Maine to Union.

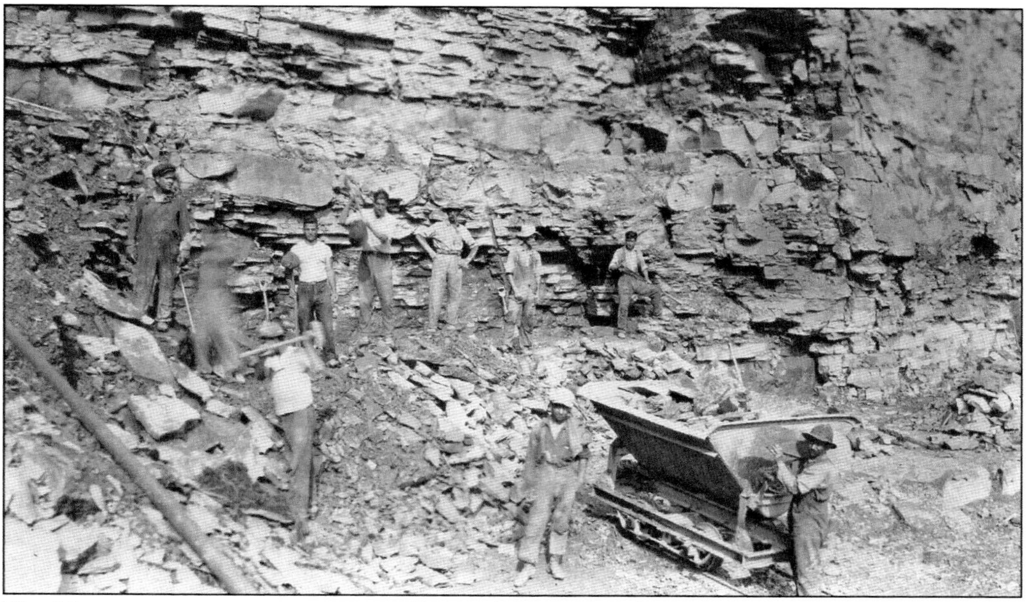

The Maine stone quarries were located behind the present-day Maine highway barn. These men are filling a wagon with gravel, likely for road building or maintenance.

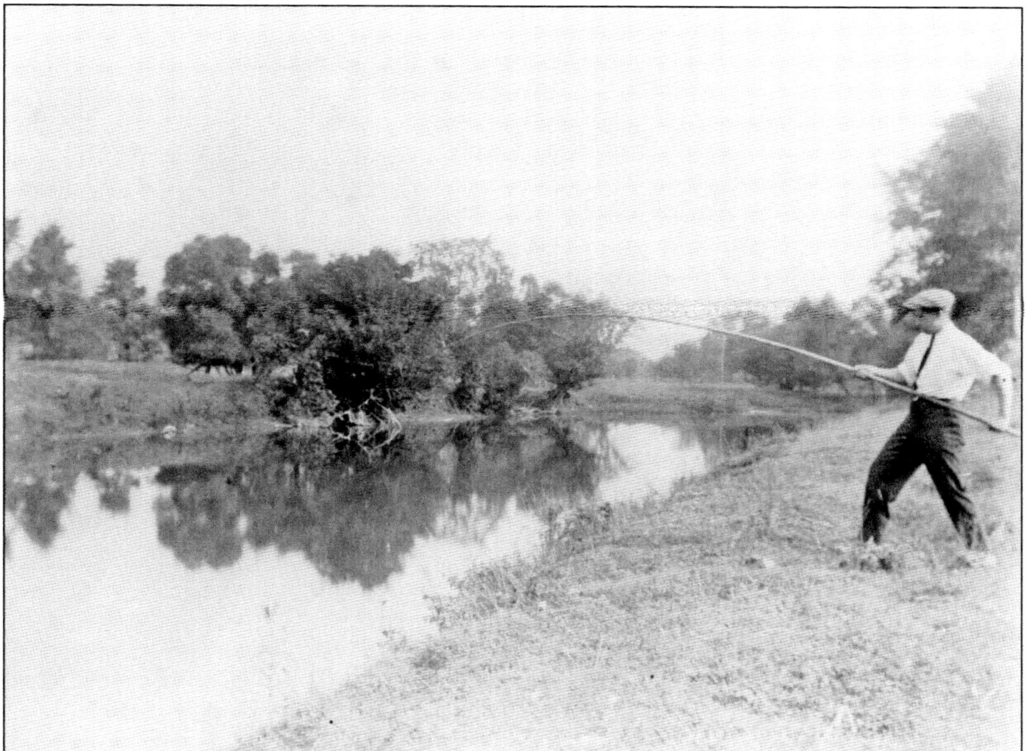

This early-1900s image captures a leisurely afternoon spent by Nanticoke Creek. The unidentified man's white shirt and tie indicate that it is probably Sunday, as people usually fished in more casual attire. The bamboo pole was used to catch large bass that people told stories about; just like today, many tried but few actually caught them. Women also enjoyed fishing.

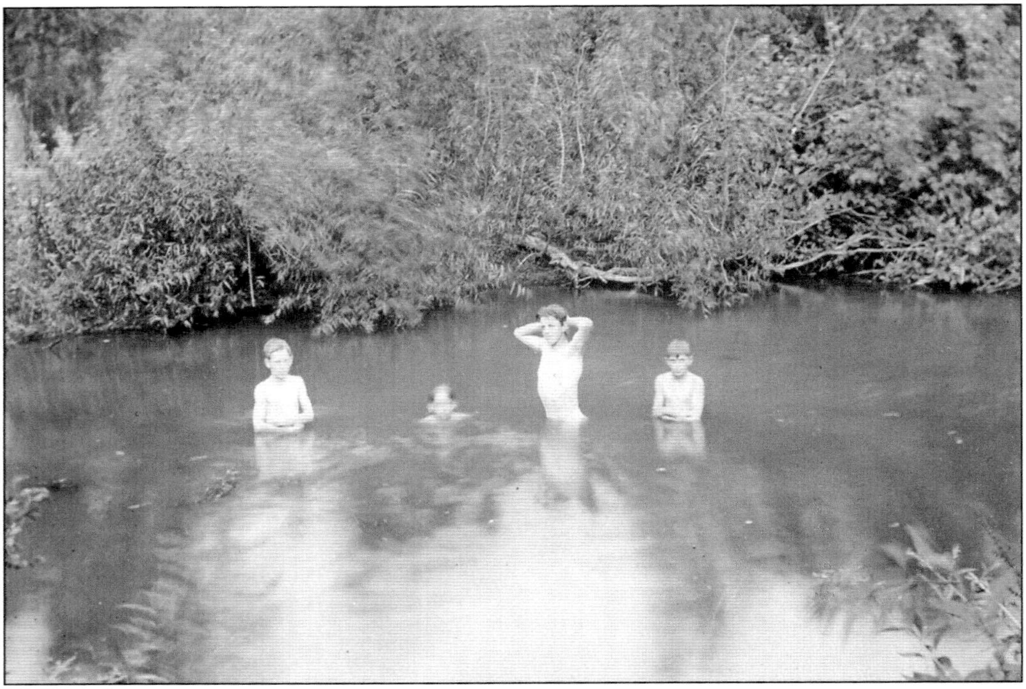

Children did lots of chores every day, especially in the summertime. Afterward, most local kids looked forward to a refreshing dip at the old swimming hole in Nanticoke Creek. This photograph was taken in the early 1900s, when bathing suits were not necessary for these country boys. When girls went swimming, they usually wore wool swimming dresses. When it was really hot, some girls swam in their regular dresses and were dry by the time they arrived home.

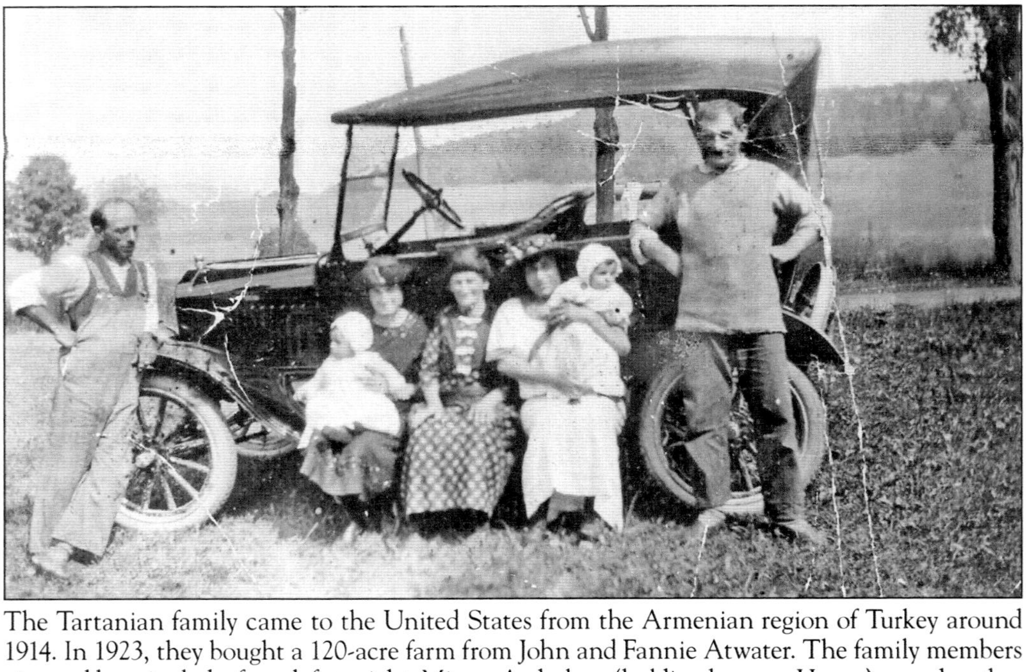

The Tartanian family came to the United States from the Armenian region of Turkey around 1914. In 1923, they bought a 120-acre farm from John and Fannie Atwater. The family members pictured here include, from left to right, Minas, Arshaloos (holding her son, Hagop), grandmother Eskouhi, Paris Mesrobian (with baby Julia), and John. (Courtesy of Alice Hopkins.)

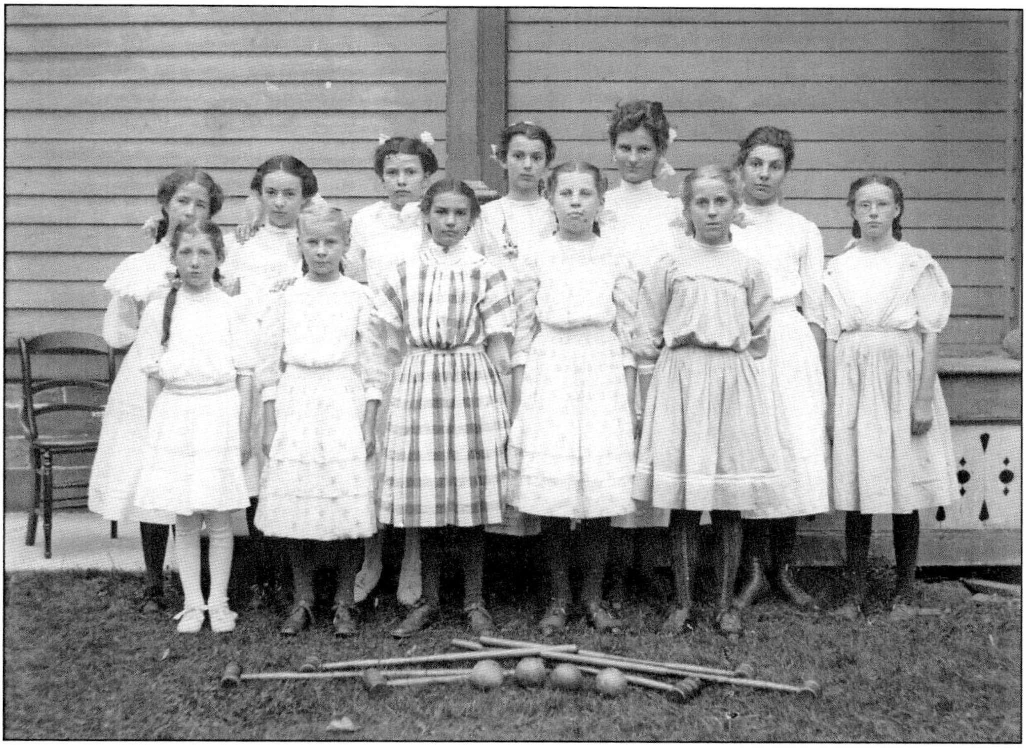

These 12 unidentified young ladies attended Elma Pearce's 12th birthday in Maine Village. In the early 1900s, croquet was very popular in the Nanticoke Valley. Part of the reason for its popularity with young people was because men and women could play the game together. In her 1899 diary, Mary Delano (Emerson) frequently mentions mowing her croquet lawn.

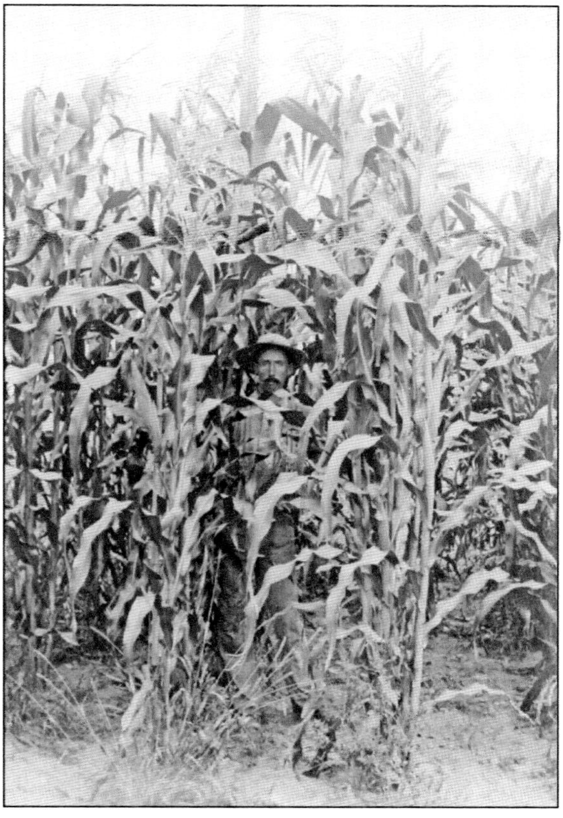

Judging from the height of this corn, Maine had a great growing season around 1909. Warm weather and just the right amount of rain is the recipe for corn this high. This unidentified member of the Pitcher family must have been proud of the corn crop that is almost twice as tall as he is.

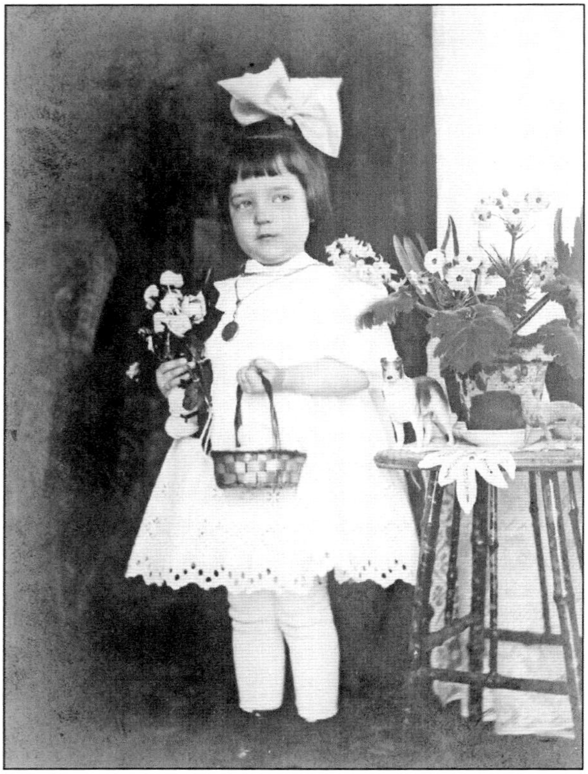

This little girl all dolled up for Easter is Dorothy Lawton. She poses with a basket of eggs and a bouquet in hand. Wearing a beautiful big bow in her hair, she also has a white eyelet dress, which was probably made by her mother, Laura Irene (Johnson) Lawton, who was an excellent seamstress. Dorothy's mother's locket is hanging around her neck.

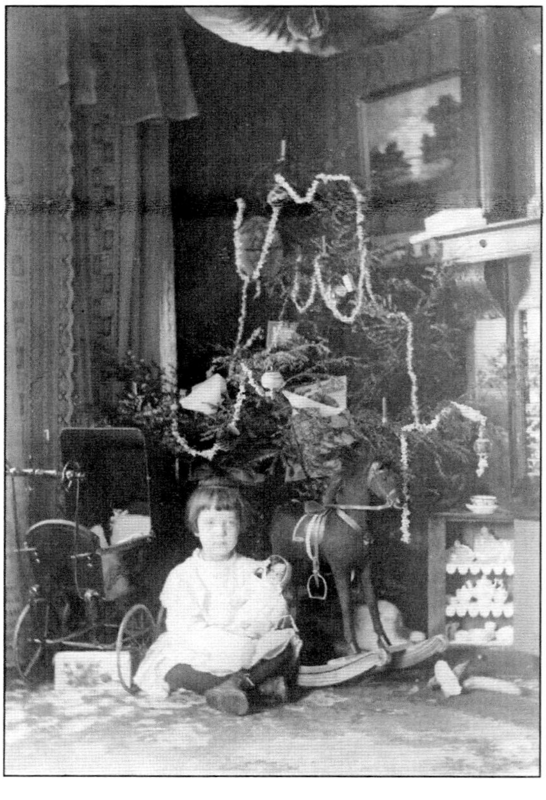

Dorothy Lawton poses for a photograph taken by her cousin Lee Loomis around the start of the 20th century. She is under her Christmas tree holding her new baby doll in front of her elaborate rocking horse. She was enjoying a wonderful Christmas when her mother was alive and in good health.

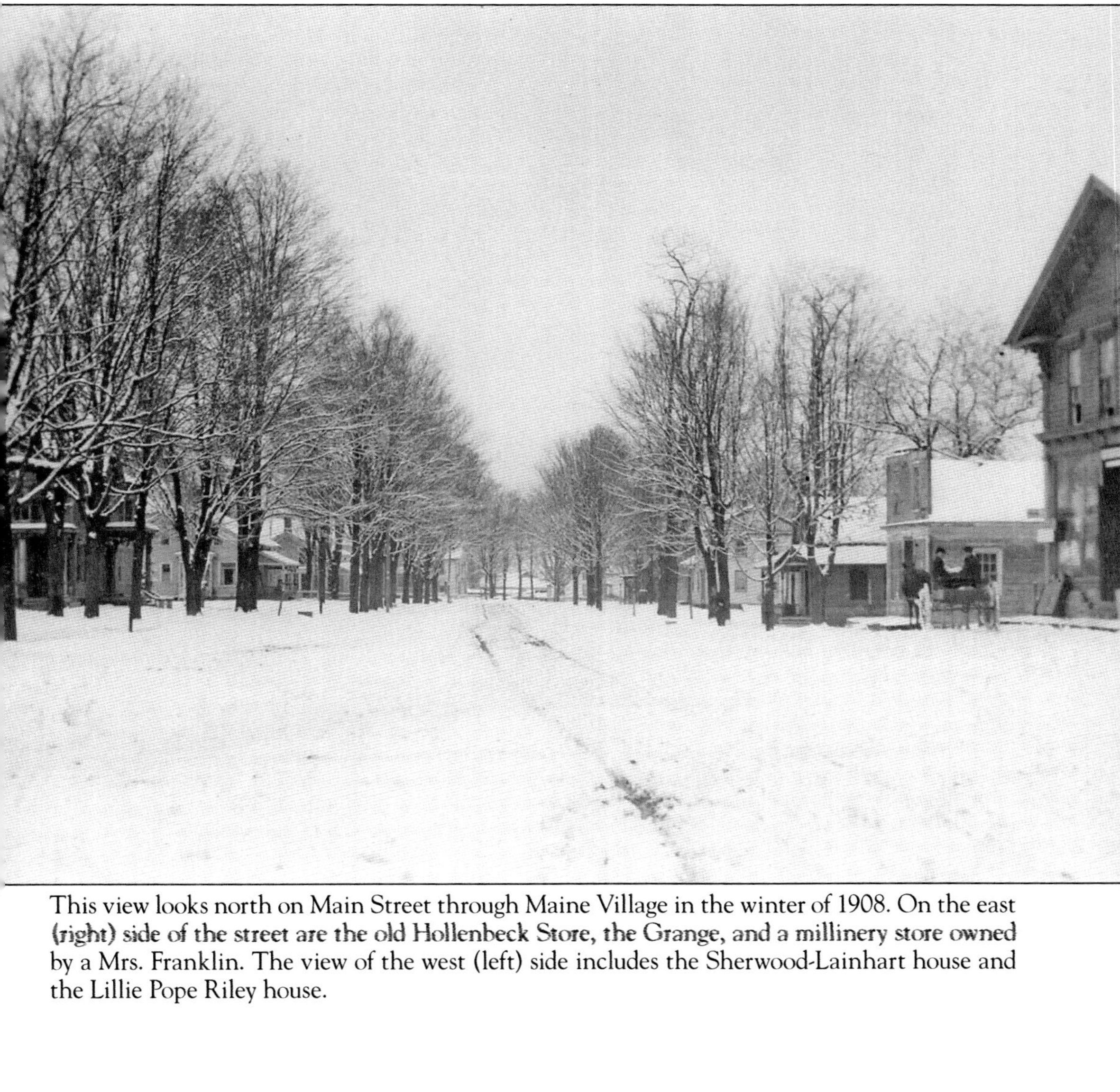

This view looks north on Main Street through Maine Village in the winter of 1908. On the east (right) side of the street are the old Hollenbeck Store, the Grange, and a millinery store owned by a Mrs. Franklin. The view of the west (left) side includes the Sherwood-Lainhart house and the Lillie Pope Riley house.

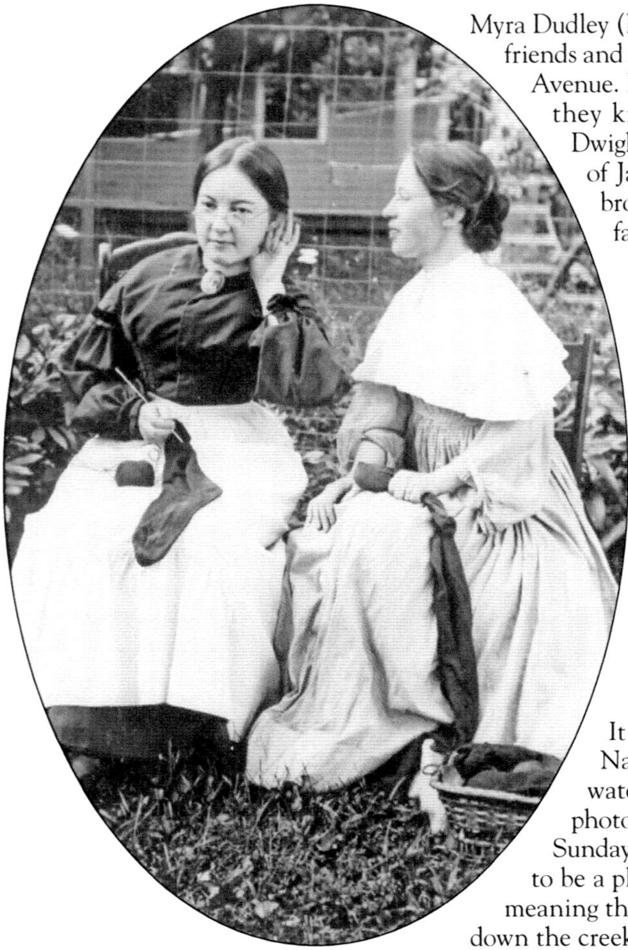

Myra Dudley (left) and Mabel McGregor were good friends and neighbors who grew up on McGregor Avenue. Here, they take time for a visit while they knit. Myra was the daughter of Dr. Dwight Dudley, and Mabel was the daughter of James McGregor, a carpenter, whose brother, Venley McGregor, started the family poultry business.

It is wonderful to ride through the Nanticoke Creek in a buggy when the water is low and still. Perhaps this 1910 photograph, taken by Lee Loomis, shows a Sunday excursion, as there does not appear to be a place to drive into or out of the water, meaning these riders must have come from up or down the creek.

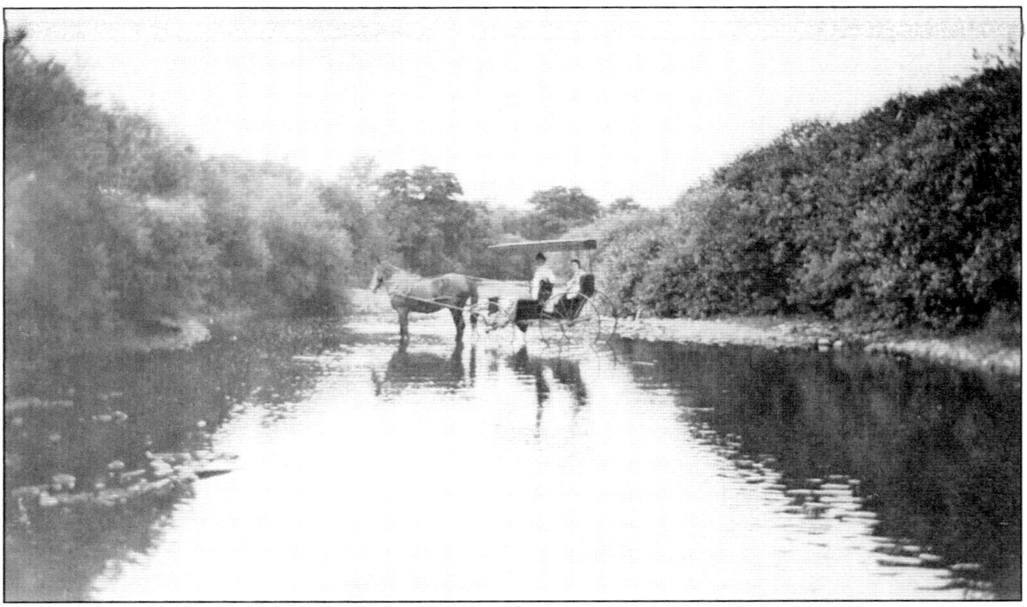

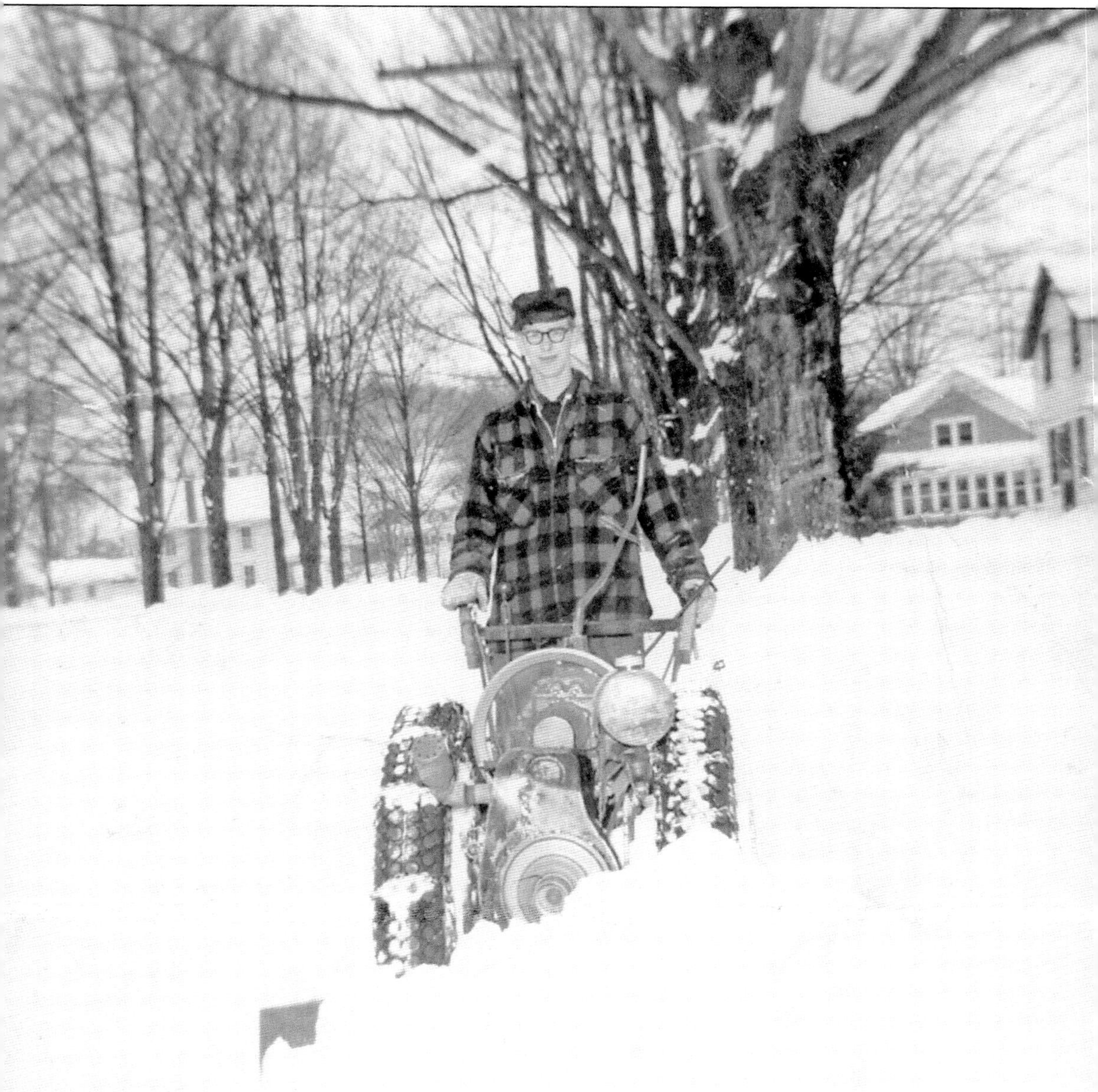

The Loomis family is well established in the Nanticoke Valley. In 1958, Owen Loomis plowed the sidewalks on Church Street, then Main Street, and all the way to the Federated church using a homemade garden tractor he made with a Briggs & Stratton engine and a plow; the snow was quite high. Loomis's father, Ralph, started the Maine Steam Engine Show in 1973. Only four people exhibited that first year, but there were more than 200 in attendance; the show is still held today. Ralph, the grandson of Chauncey F. McIntyre, worked at the sawmill and rake factory. For 10 years, Owen Loomis delivered the *Binghamton Press*, the *Sun-Bulletin*, and the *Binghamton Morning Sun* in the hamlet. (Courtesy of Owen Loomis.)

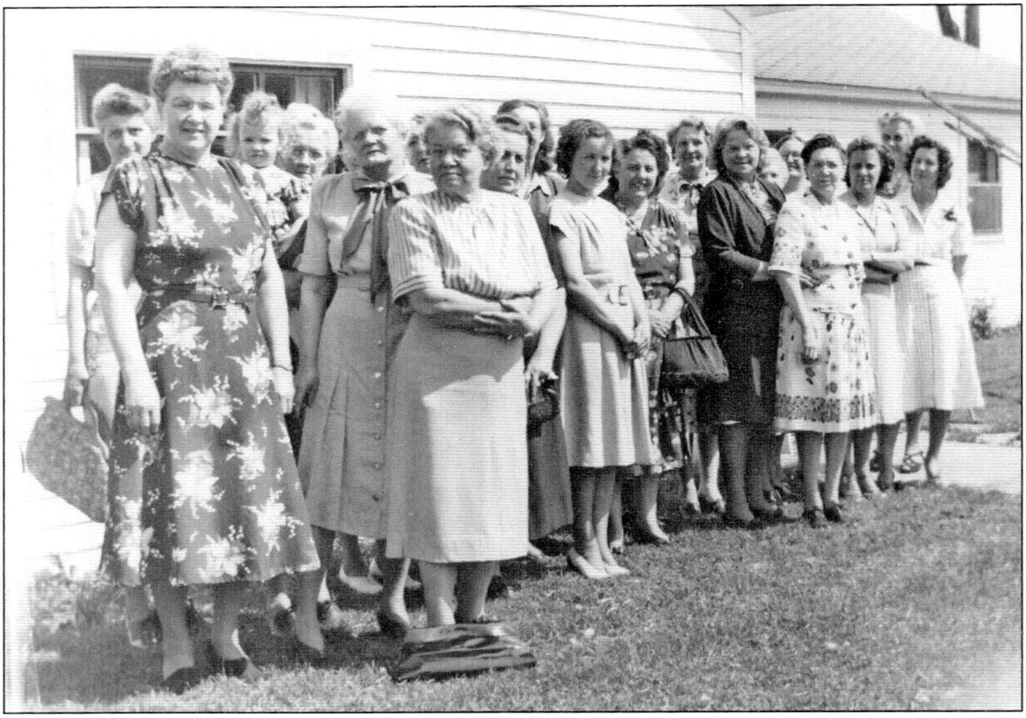

The Home Bureau, pictured here in 1948, came into being during World War I and was active in the Maine area until the mid-1960s. The association was formed to help women deal with wartime rationing, nutrition, home nursing, sewing, economizing, and household efficiency. In 1938, the Home Bureau sponsored the first 4-H Club in Maine. In the 1940s, it was renamed the Broome County Home Extension.

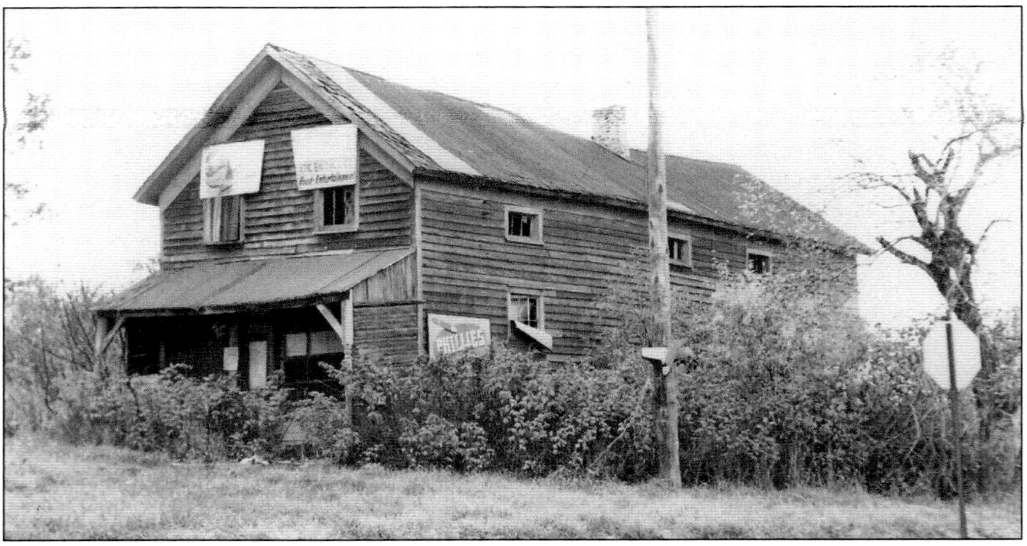

In the 1870s, there was a thriving corner at East Maine and Farm To Market Roads. This general store was run by a Mr. Aker, who was the postmaster from 1892 to 1912. From 1912 until 1928, his daughter, Lizzy, was the postmistress until rural free delivery ended her job. A stage from Binghamton dropped off the mail at the East Maine post office, and local residents came there to pick up their letters and newspapers.

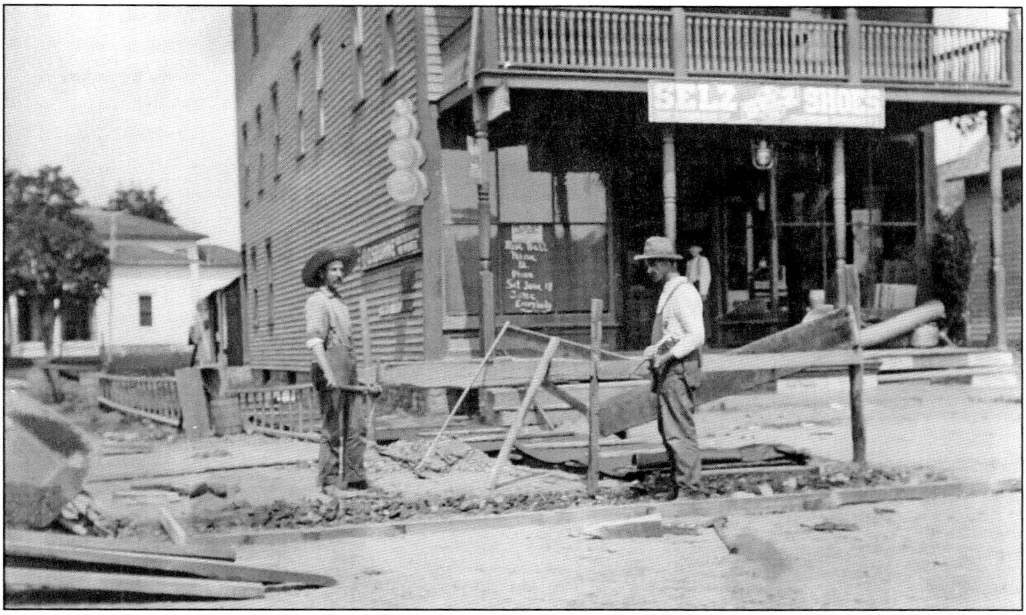

In 1910, on the corner of Main and Church Streets, George Loomis (left) and an unidentified man constructed a sidewalk in front of the store owned by J.W. Coleman, who also owned a lumber company. It later housed the Tymeson Brothers store. The Clarence Earl Lewis home is in the background.

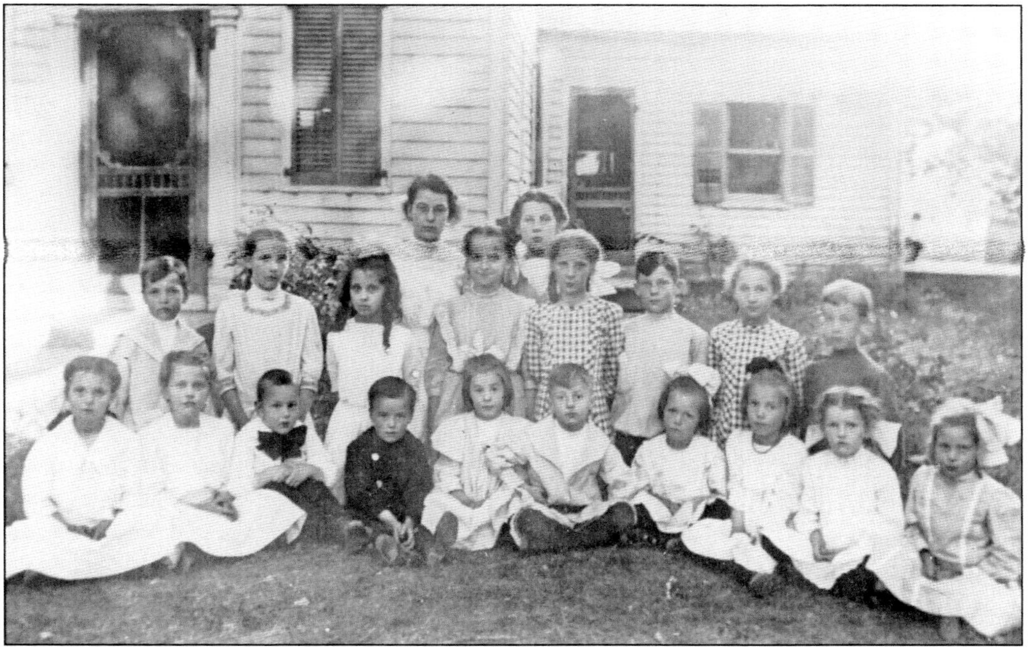

In 1910, Dorothy Lawton celebrated her fifth birthday in front of her home on Main Street. Helping her celebrate are, from left to right, (first row) Ruth Saddlemire, Mary Tibbits, Elton Tibbits, Alton Lewis, Dorothy Lawton, Kenneth Lawton, Marian Saddlemire, Lula Lewis, Adelia Lawton, and Laura Tibbits; (second row) Clyde Saddlemire, Mildred Durfee, Grace Taylor, Marie Merle, Irene Lawton, Leland Lawton, Cecil Monk, and Eugene Vandeventer; (third row) Elizabeth Kattell and Caroline Lawton.

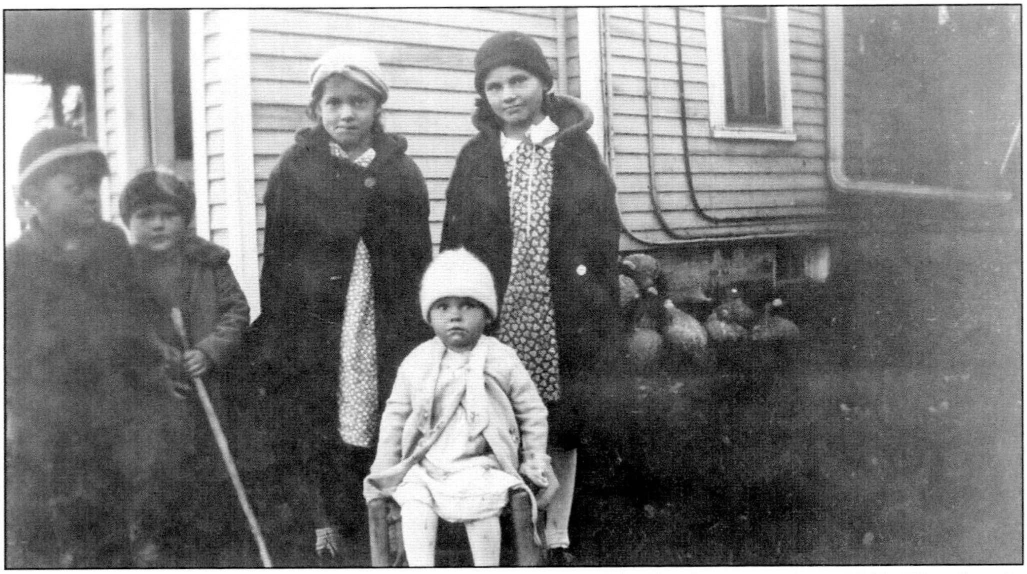

The Chopiack family was originally from Ukraine and had a farm on King Hill. The family members pictured here are, from left to right, Russell, Sam, Martha, Lydia, and Dorothy. (Courtesy of Owen Loomis.)

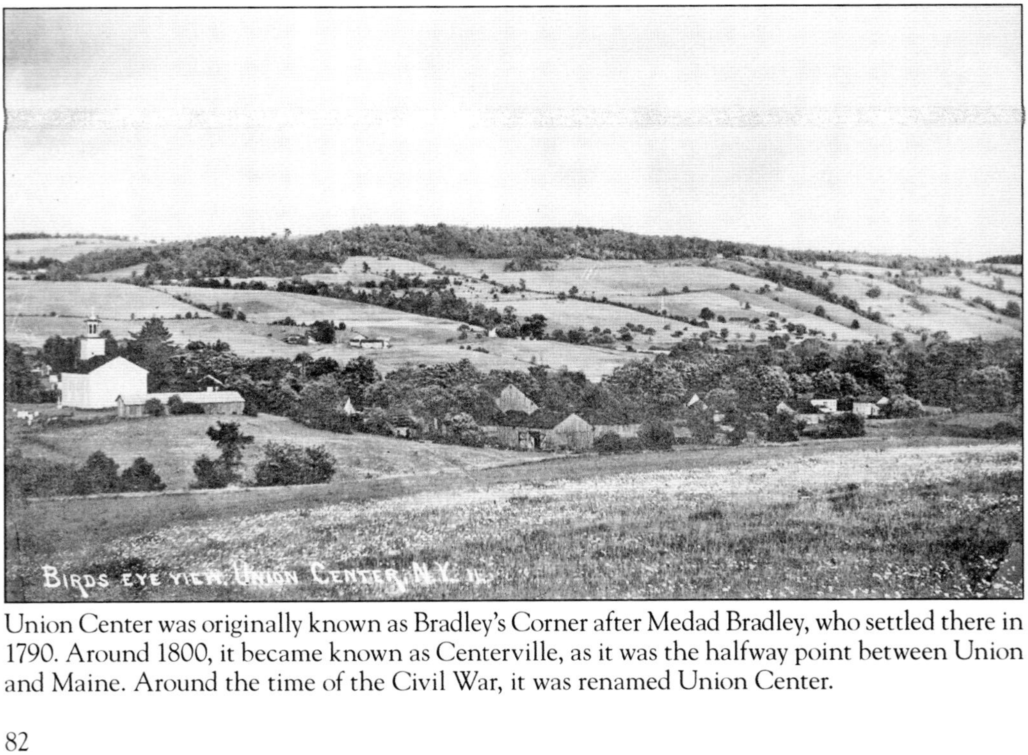

Union Center was originally known as Bradley's Corner after Medad Bradley, who settled there in 1790. Around 1800, it became known as Centerville, as it was the halfway point between Union and Maine. Around the time of the Civil War, it was renamed Union Center.

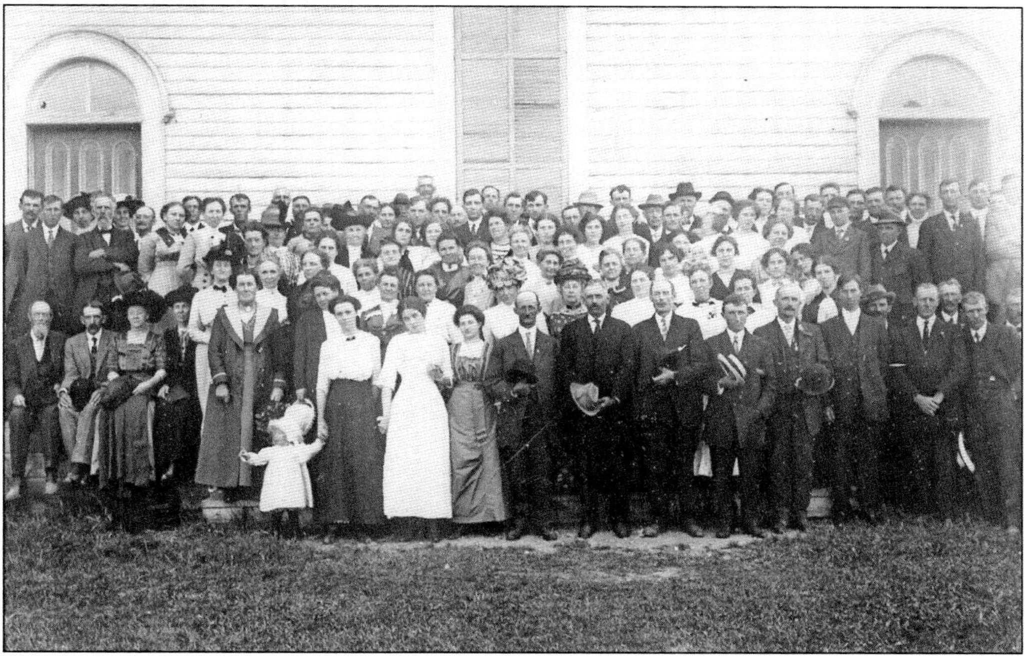

This Broome County Grange meeting was held at the Union Center Congregational Church around 1912. Union Center Grange No. 1153 was organized on December 26, 1908. In 1940, the Grange was moved to Maine and the name was changed to Nanticoke Valley Grange.

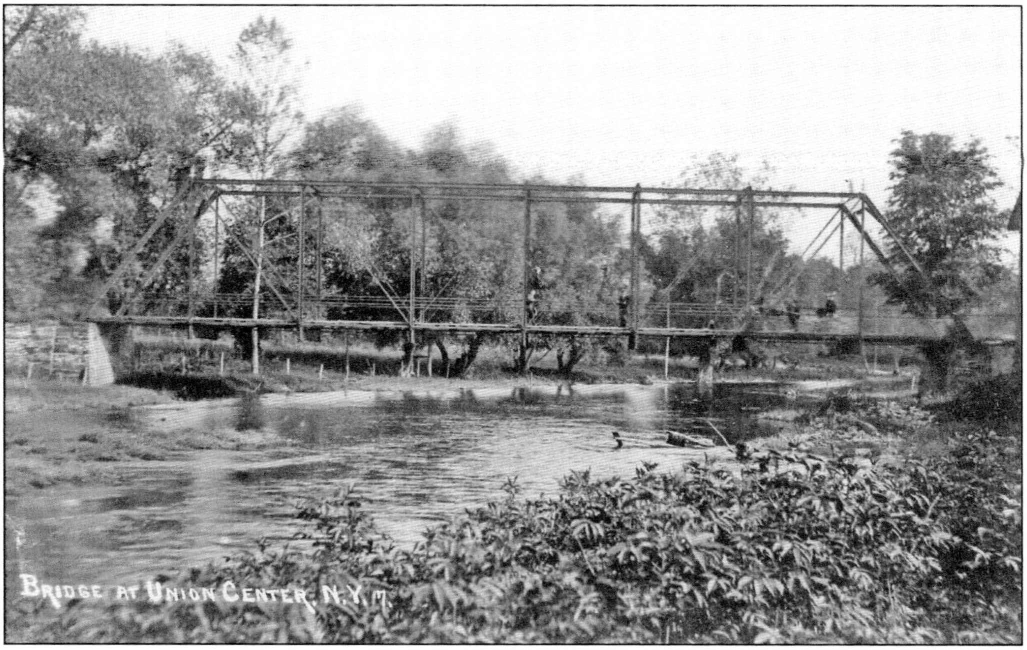

In 1907, the Union Center Bridge was built over Nanticoke Creek. The 150-foot iron bridge was built by the Groton Bridge Company for $2,200. Until it was washed away in an 1880 flood, a wooden bridge spanned the river at this location.

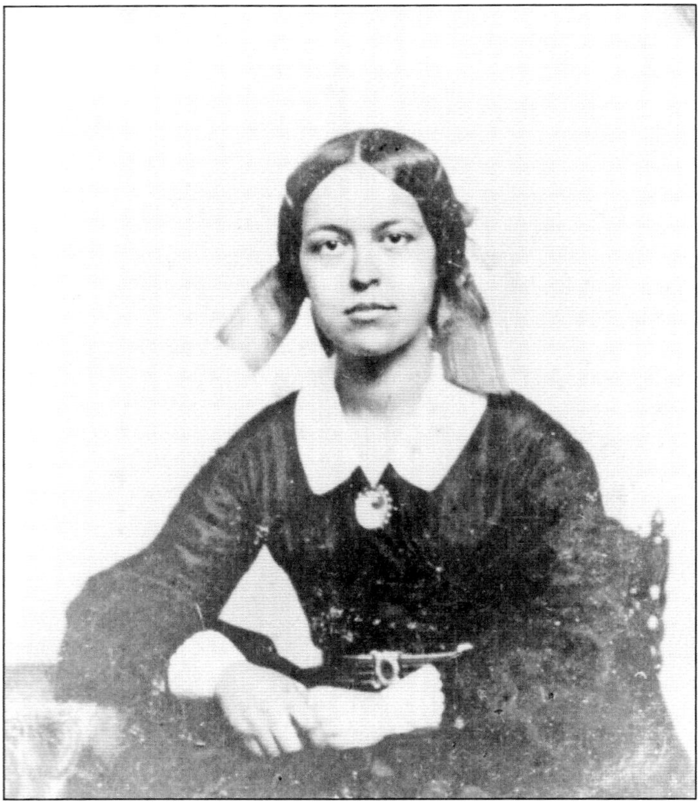

The LeBaron family came by oxen to Union Center from Connecticut in 1792 and 1793. They brought an oxbow plow and a bag of gold with which to buy land. These early settlers were ancestors of George LeBaron, who had a 70-acre farm in Union Center around 1856 and married Mary Andrews (pictured at left) in 1861.

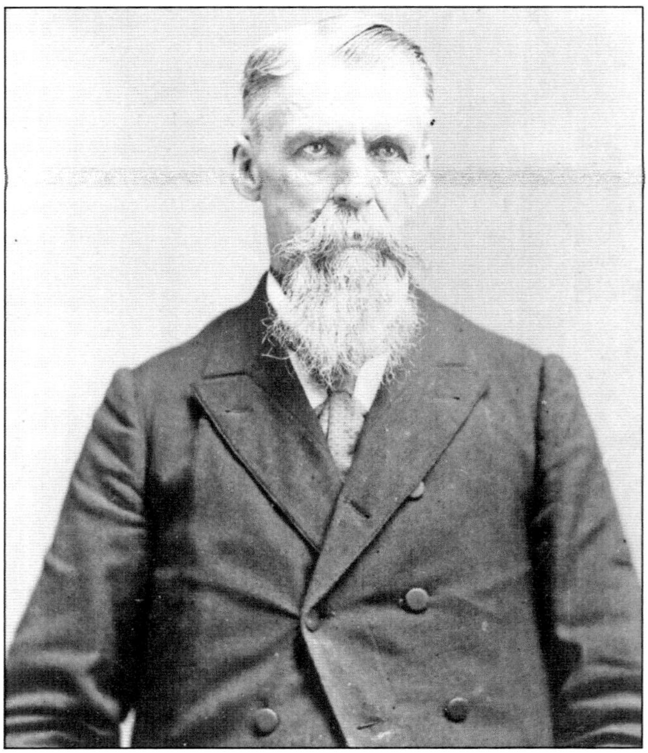

Keeping the farm, they moved to Union, where George (pictured at right) served as a trustee of the Union Methodist Episcopal Church, as well as a village trustee. He later became president of the village of Union. In a 1956 interview in the *Endicott Daily Bulletin*, the 86-year-old Julia LeBaron Smith, George and Mary's daughter, told of her father building several homes in Endicott with lumber that came from their farm in Union Center.

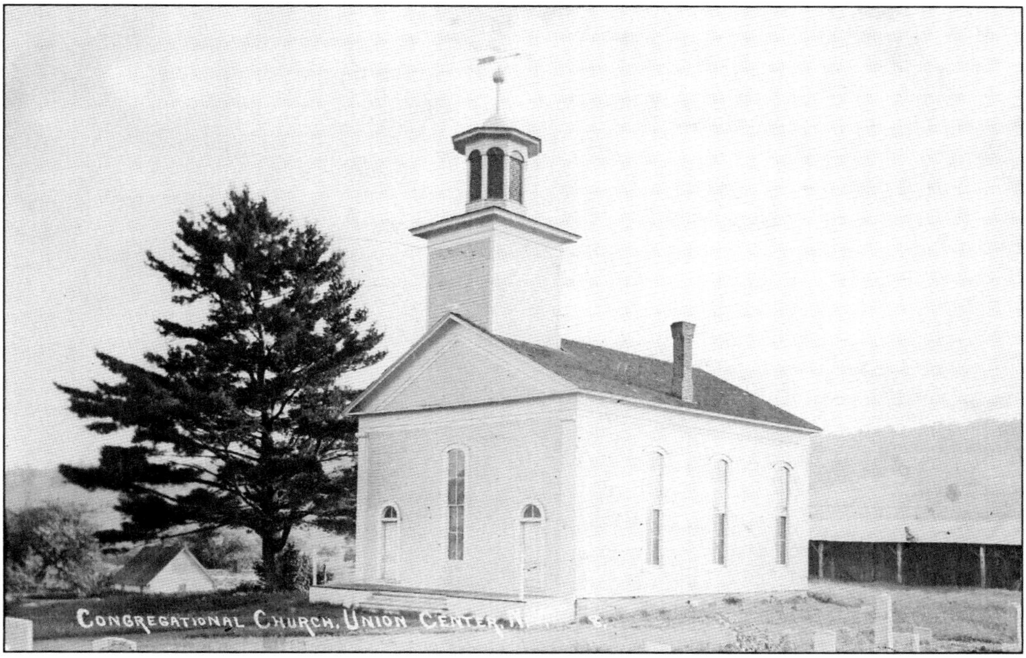

The photograph above shows the Union Center Congregational Church in 1908, before it was renovated. Located on Route 26, the church was built in 1841 and has been a large part of the religious and civic life of the town. It is still standing, with Union Center Cemetery nearby.

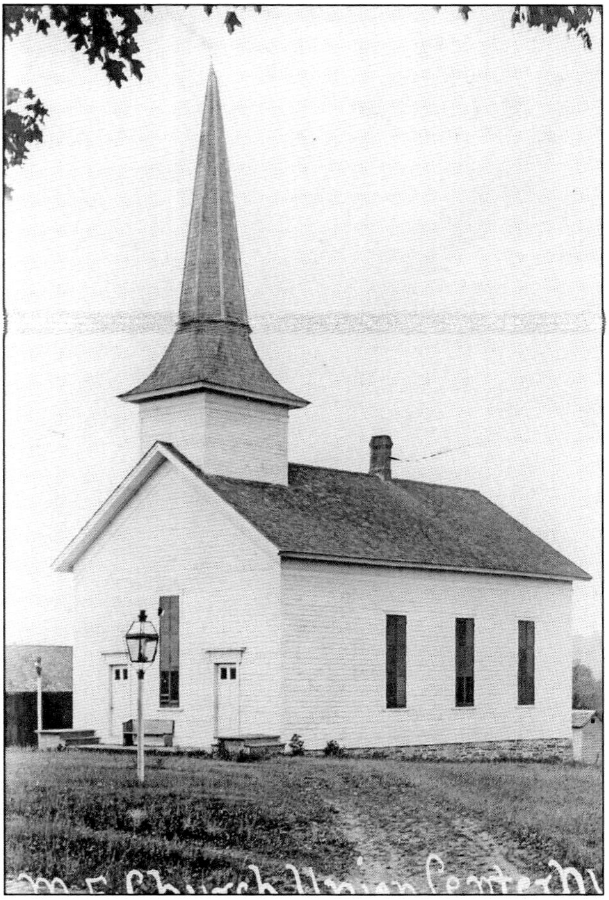

The Union Center United Methodist Church was built on Maple Drive in 1852 and was dedicated in 1853. Rev. S. Stocking was the first pastor. Before this church was built, Union Center was served by circuit riders on the Broome circuit, which was formed in 1812.

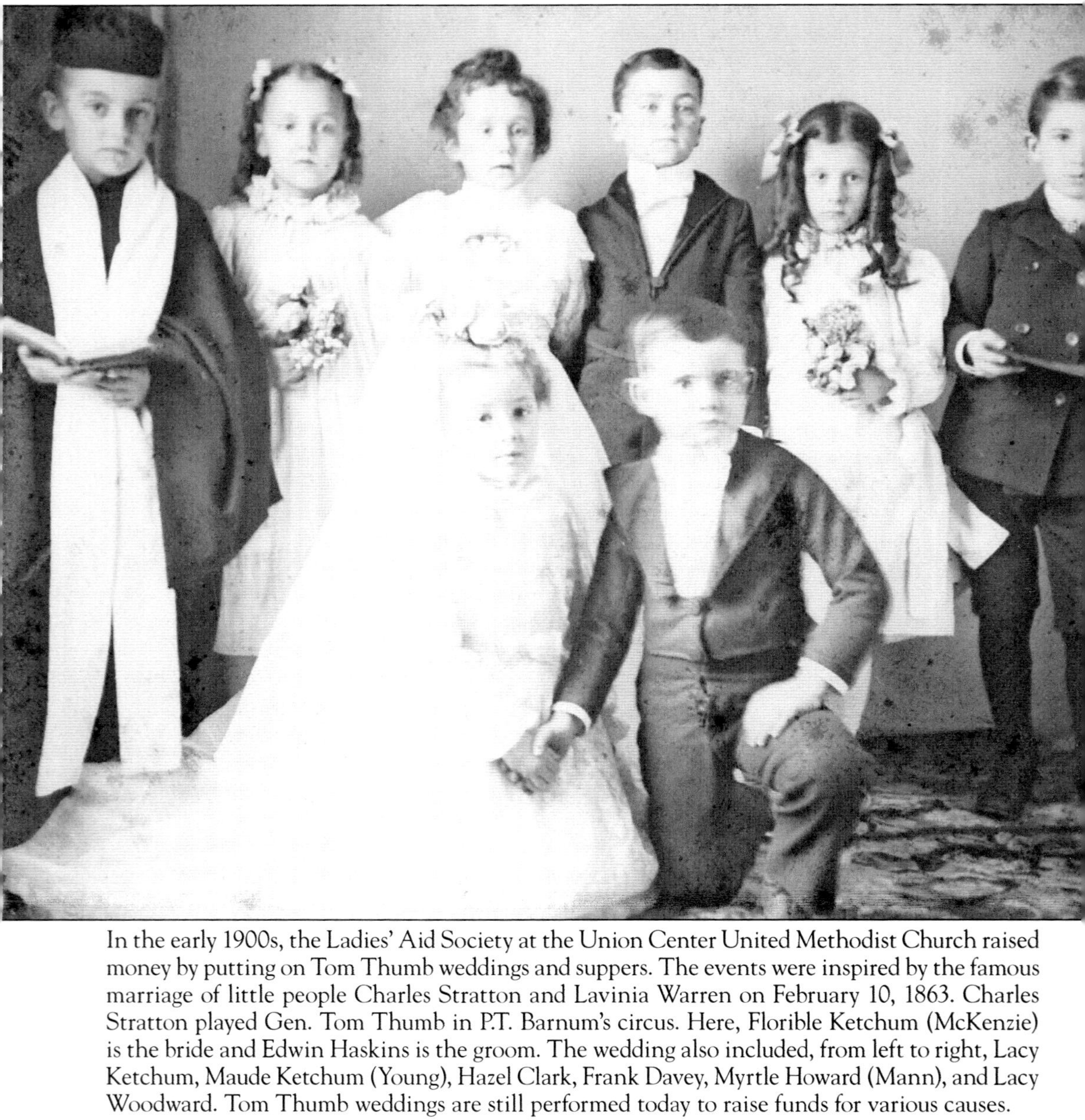

In the early 1900s, the Ladies' Aid Society at the Union Center United Methodist Church raised money by putting on Tom Thumb weddings and suppers. The events were inspired by the famous marriage of little people Charles Stratton and Lavinia Warren on February 10, 1863. Charles Stratton played Gen. Tom Thumb in P.T. Barnum's circus. Here, Floribel Ketchum (McKenzie) is the bride and Edwin Haskins is the groom. The wedding also included, from left to right, Lacy Ketchum, Maude Ketchum (Young), Hazel Clark, Frank Davey, Myrtle Howard (Mann), and Lacy Woodward. Tom Thumb weddings are still performed today to raise funds for various causes.

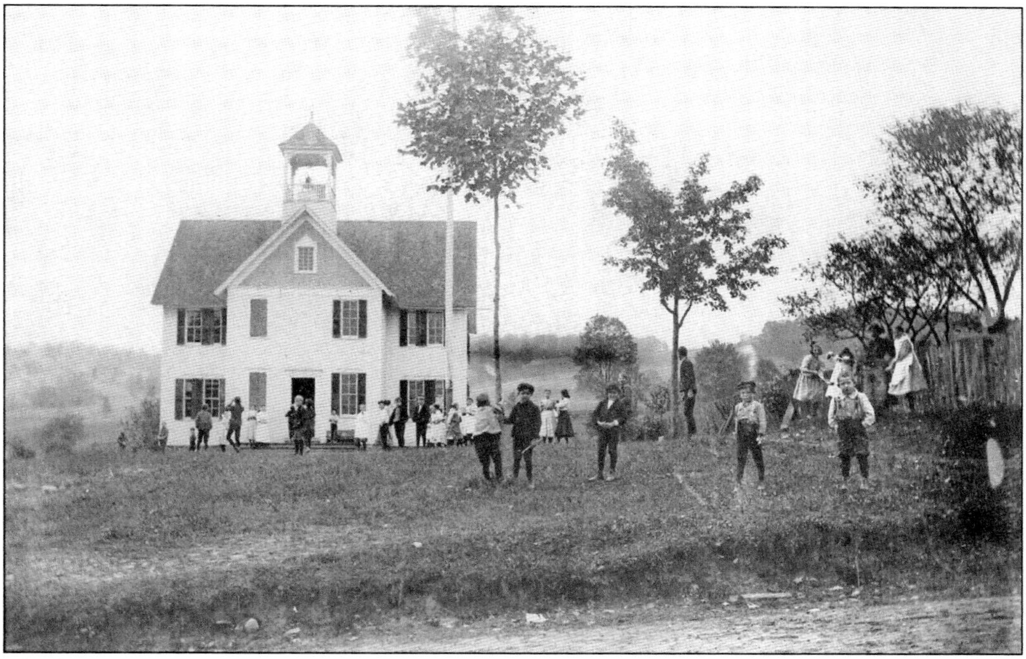

The first Union Center School on Maple Drive burned down in the 1890s. In 1897, Barzilla Howard built this school on the same spot. An itemized report listed the cost as $1,600, including the new bell and new desks. This property was once part of the Rhuben Decker farm. This photograph was taken in 1908.

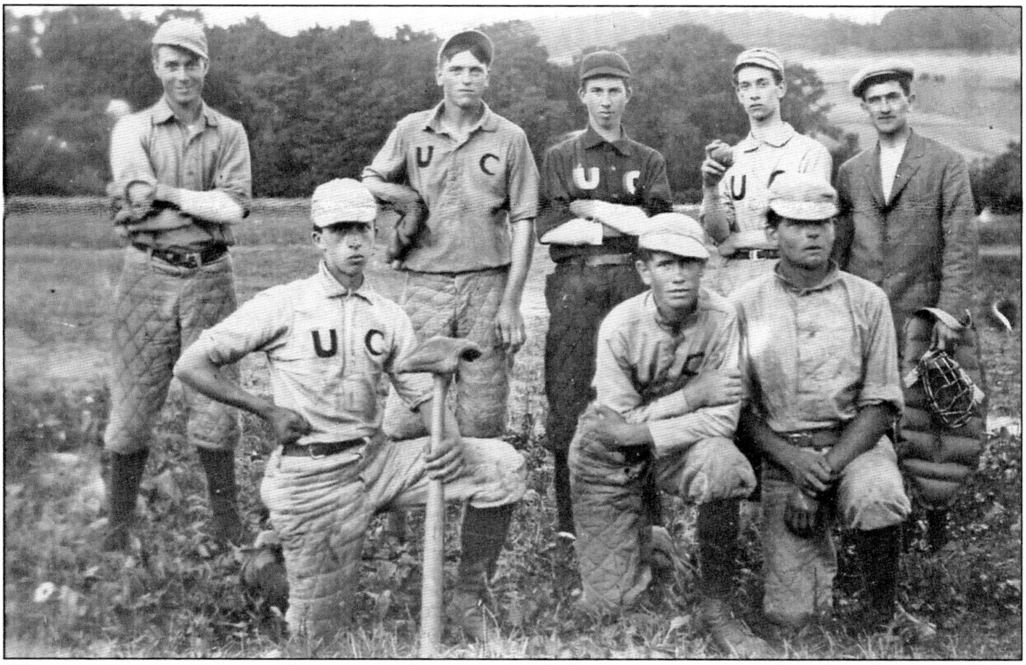

The 1908 Union Center Village baseball team included, from left to right, (first row) Nick Tappen, Fred Haight, and Harry Woodward; (second row) Fay Pitkin, Clay Harrison, Earl Knapp, Joe Cornell, and Ralph Howard. They sometimes played the Maine Village team in a friendly game after the morning chores were done.

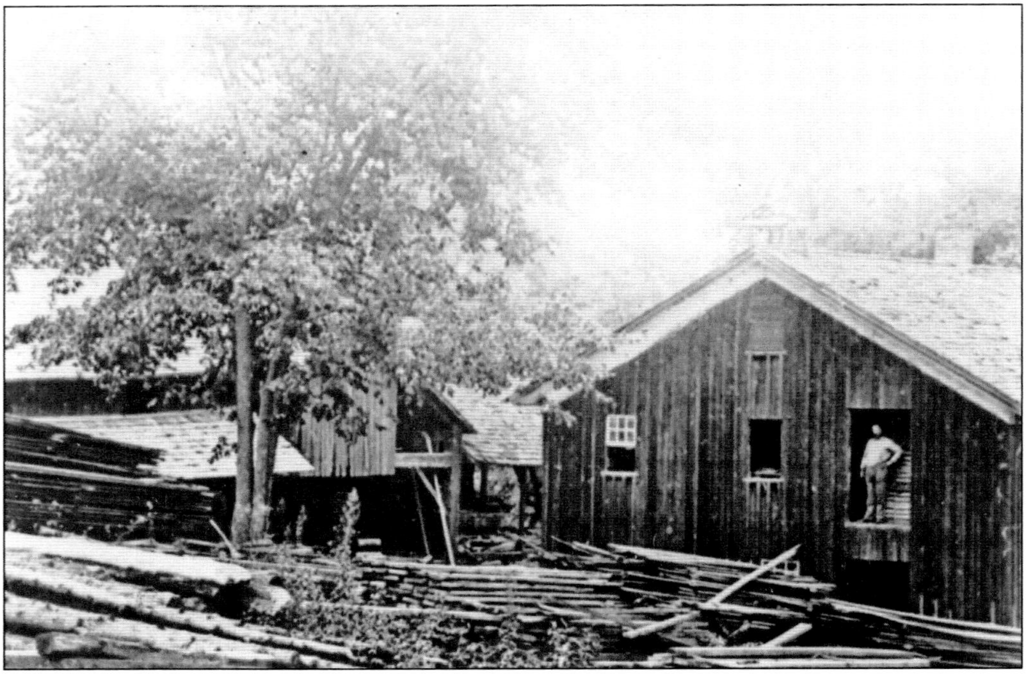

The sawmill on Nanticoke Creek in Union Center was built from 1812 to 1814 by Richard Bradley and a Mr. Doud. The rake factory (pictured below) that sat in front of the mill was built by Jonathan and Aaron Heath in 1839. At one time, the sawmill and rake factory were owned by William Edson, but they were eventually acquired by Barzilla Howard. The dense timber on the hills supplied the materials for the lumber, and the mill initially ran day and night to keep up with demand. By 1814, with most of the heavy timber gone, the mill was only running one month per year. The mill supplied lumber and decorative spindles for construction of local homes, among other things. When the logs arrived, they were dropped off at the top of the hill and then rolled down the hill into the millpond. Morgan Howard, who is standing in the doorway of the mill in the image above, was struck by a piece of flying wood and died of internal injuries. In 1920, the Union Center Grange started meeting at the rake factory and eventually voted to buy the rake factory and move it.

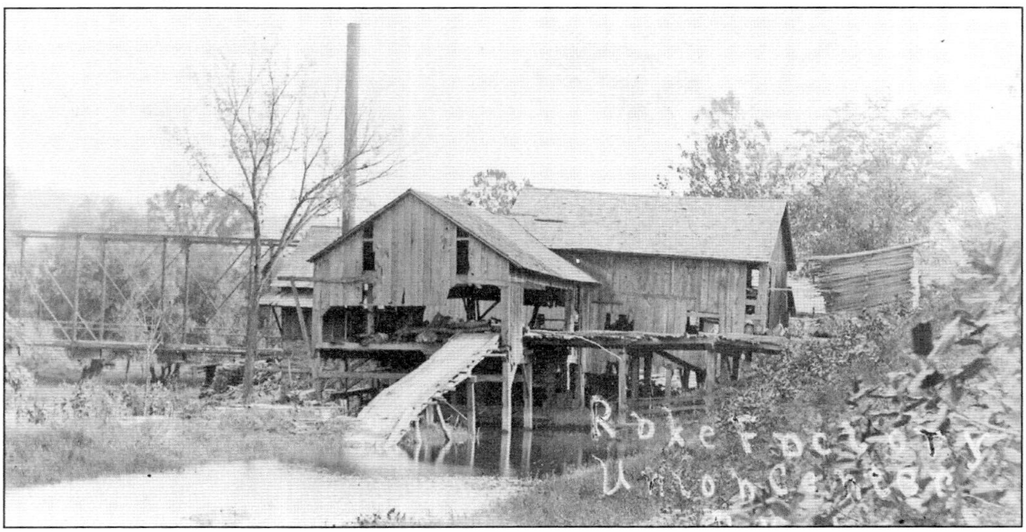

Charles L. Pitkin (right) owned the Pitkin store (below) in Union Center. The store was built in 1872 by James Howard. For a time, Westly Brooks owned the store while Eugene Edwards clerked there. In 1875, a Mr. Andrews and Charles Sholes purchased it, and in 1880, Sholes sold out to Pitkin. Around 1890, there was a burglary in Union Center, the safe at the Andrews and Pitkin store was blown open, and the thieves got away with $400. The Brougham and Willis store was also robbed. Soon after, Andrews sold out his interest to Pitkin. In the late 1920s, Wellington Tymeson bought the store and refurbished it, spending $4,500. Unfortunately, the store burned down in 1930 before Tymeson could reopen it.

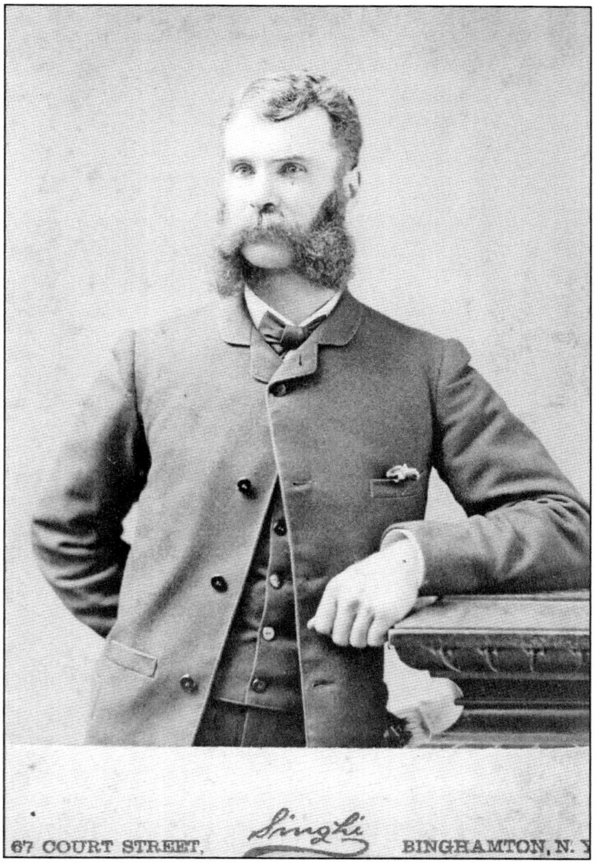

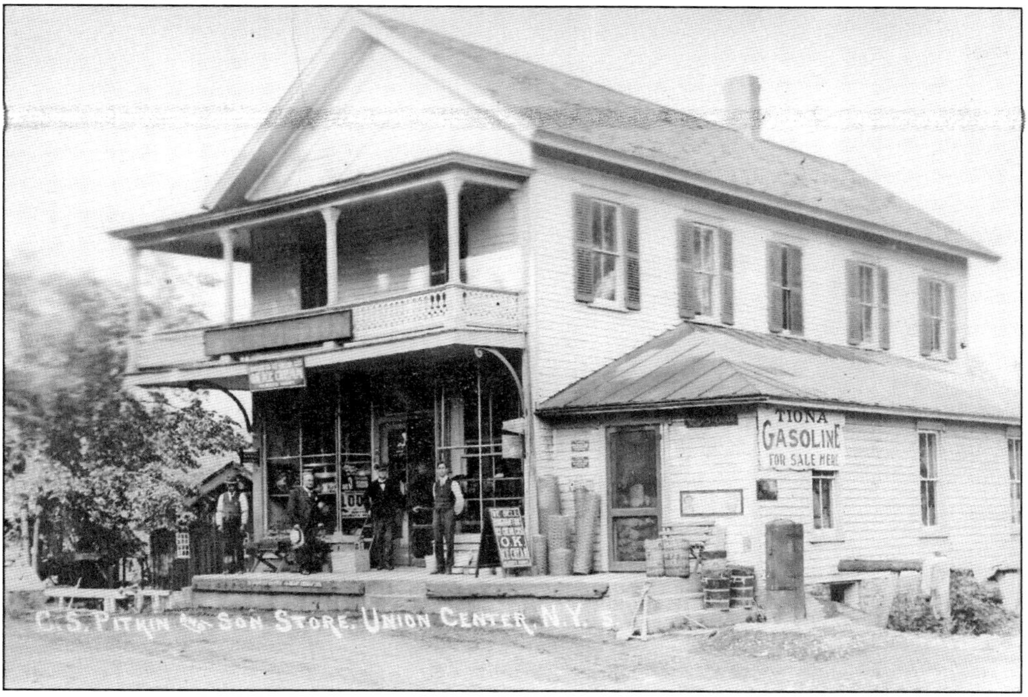

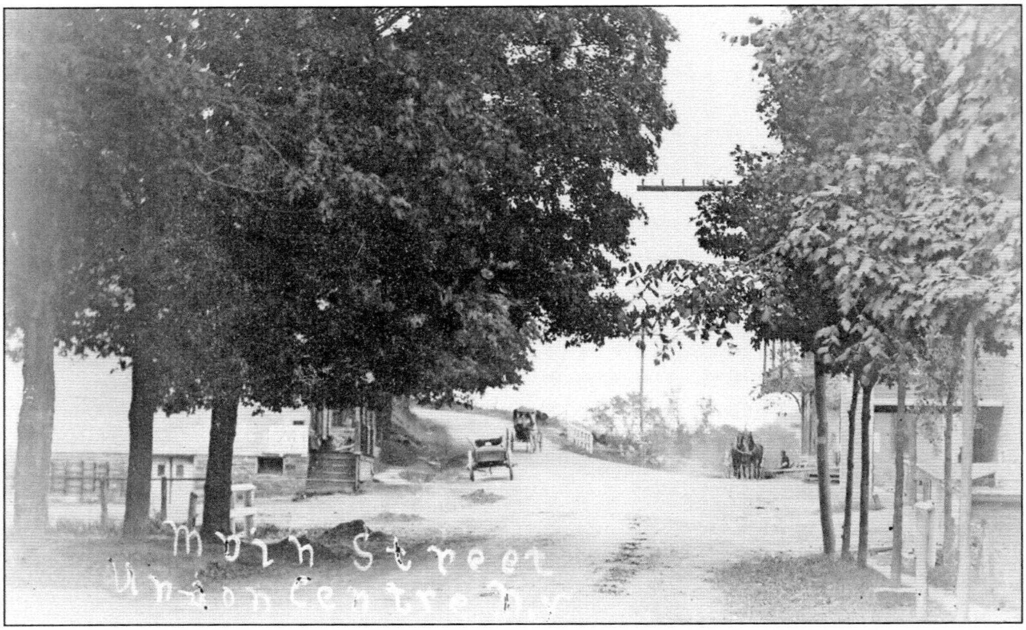

Lewis Brougham's store was across the street (present-day State Route 26) from Pitkin's store and the Crystal Creamery. It had many owners (and names) over the years, including Brougham and Son, (Irving, son of Lewis) Brougham and (George) Buffum, Brougham and (Clarence) Stevens, Stevens and (Fred) Rockwell, Rockwell and (William) Mann, Mann and Edson, and (Guy and Elmer) Smith. Ray Ketchum owned the store in 1934, and it burned down in 1938. In 1897, the post office was moved to Brougham's store, and—depending on who was president of the United States—it would move back and forth between Brougham's store, which was Republican, and Pitkin's store, which was Democratic. The Brougham family—Irving, Anna May (center), and Hattie (Ketchum)—is pictured below.

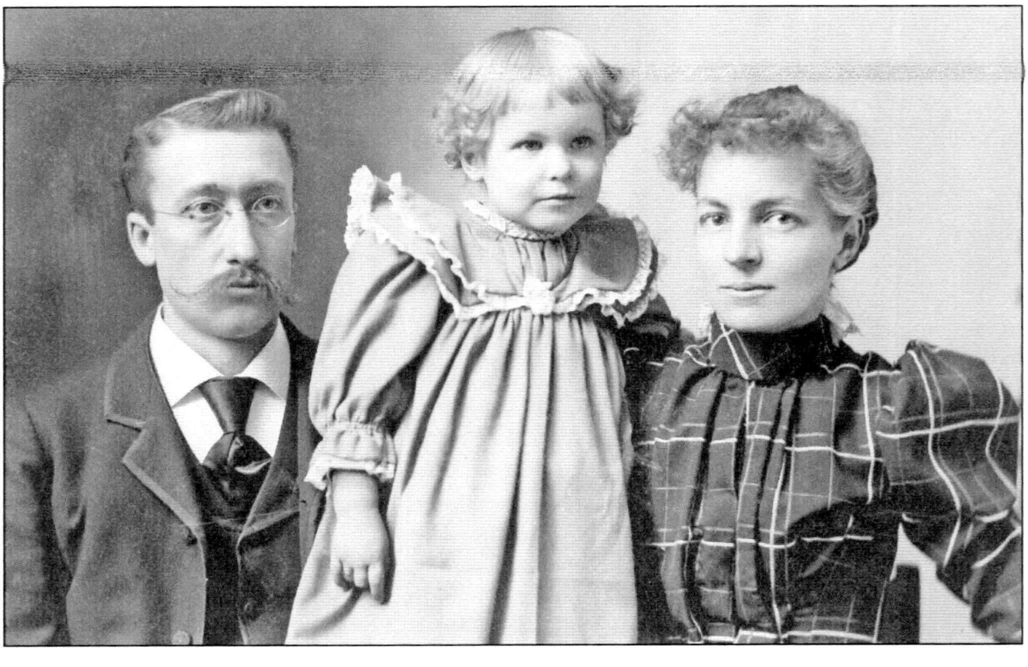

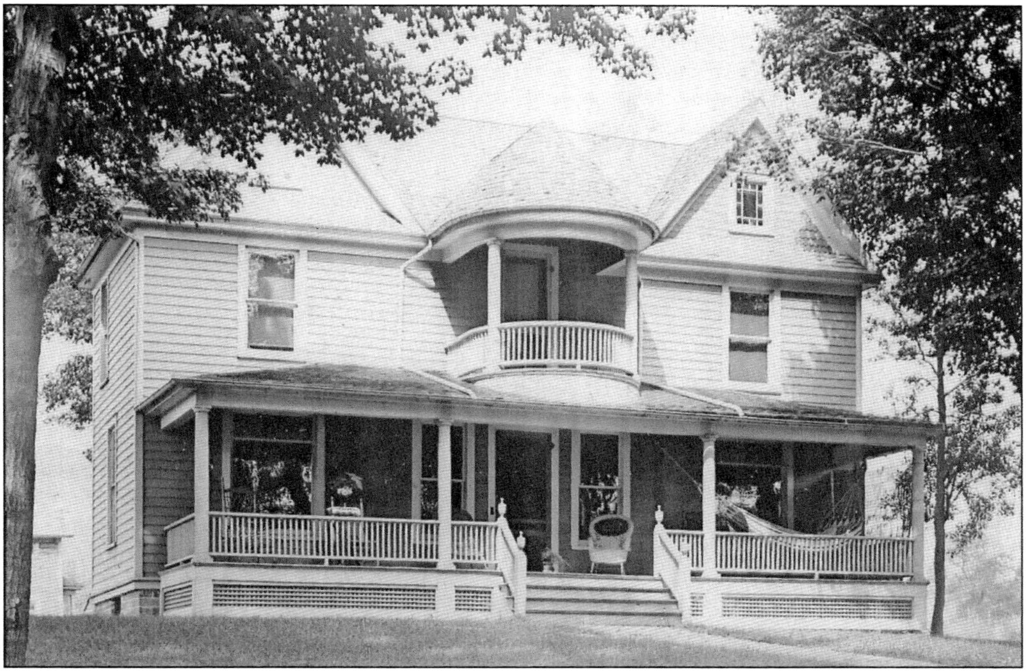

While he was running the store in Union Center, Lewis Brougham built this beautiful home next door to the store and lived there with his second wife, Georgia. The house has had many owners over the years and is still standing.

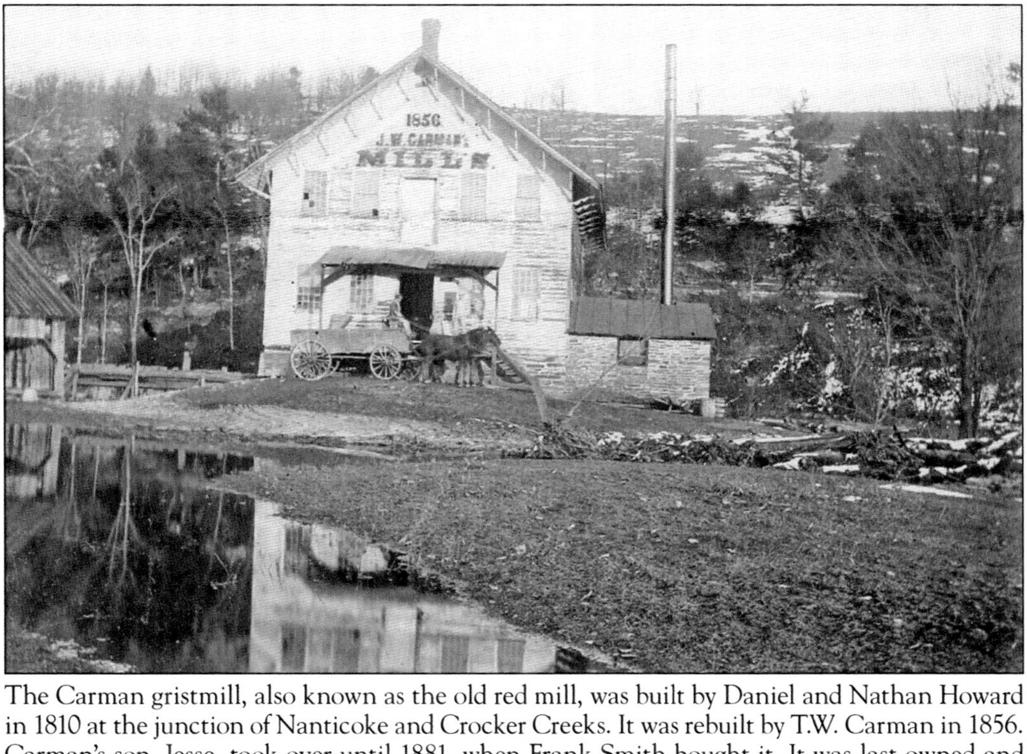

The Carman gristmill, also known as the old red mill, was built by Daniel and Nathan Howard in 1810 at the junction of Nanticoke and Crocker Creeks. It was rebuilt by T.W. Carman in 1856. Carman's son, Jesse, took over until 1881, when Frank Smith bought it. It was last owned and operated by Wayne Woodward and was torn down in 1939.

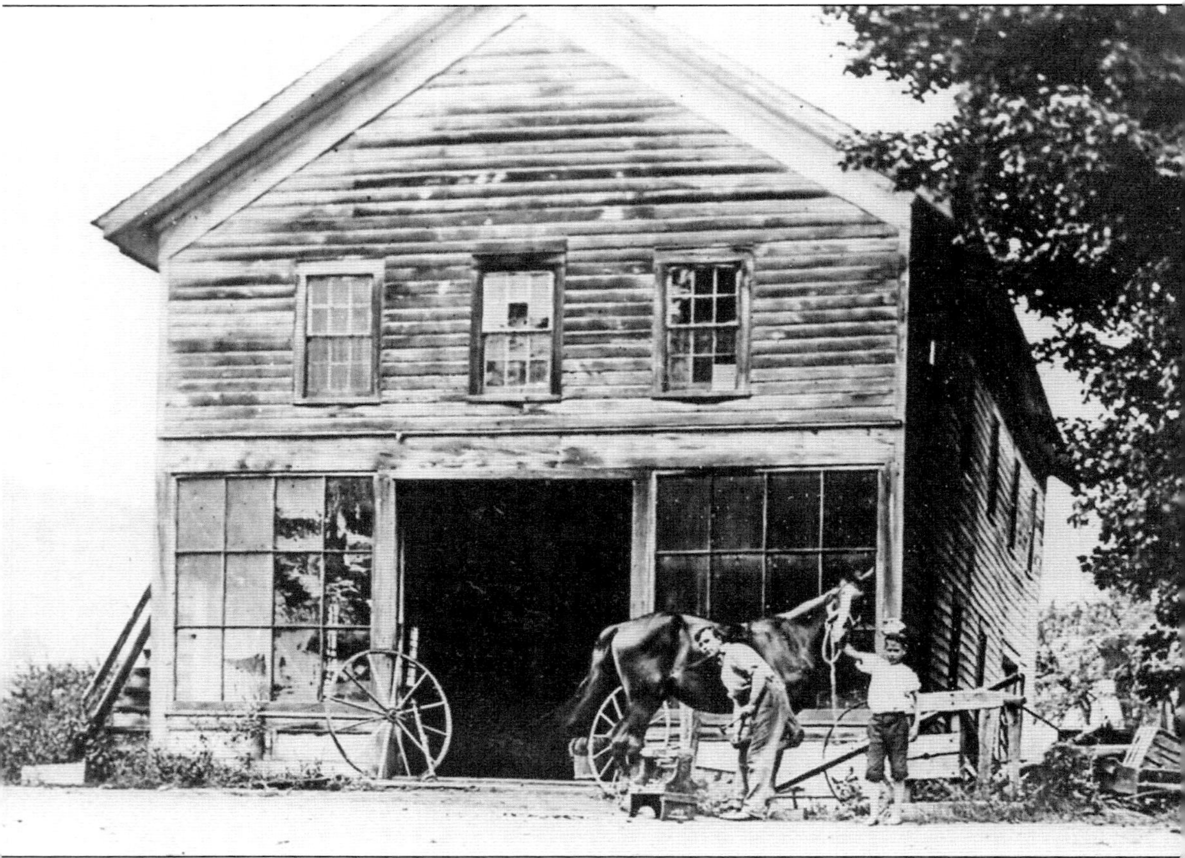

The first blacksmith shop in this section of the Town of Maine was in Broughamtown, next to the Toby Mill, and was owned by Albert White. He specialized in shoeing oxen, using a canvas sling to raise oxen off the floor; early farmers preferred oxen to horses. The first blacksmith in Union Center was a Mr. Bingham, whose son, Josiah, followed the trade until 1881. Atwell Rogers, pictured above, then ran the shop for more than 30 years, with his son (holding the horse's bridle in the picture) eventually doing the blacksmith work. The shop was located on Maple Drive, north of Union Center Cemetery. Smith Lyon also had a blacksmith shop across the Union Center Bridge, just before the Bradley Creek Bridge.

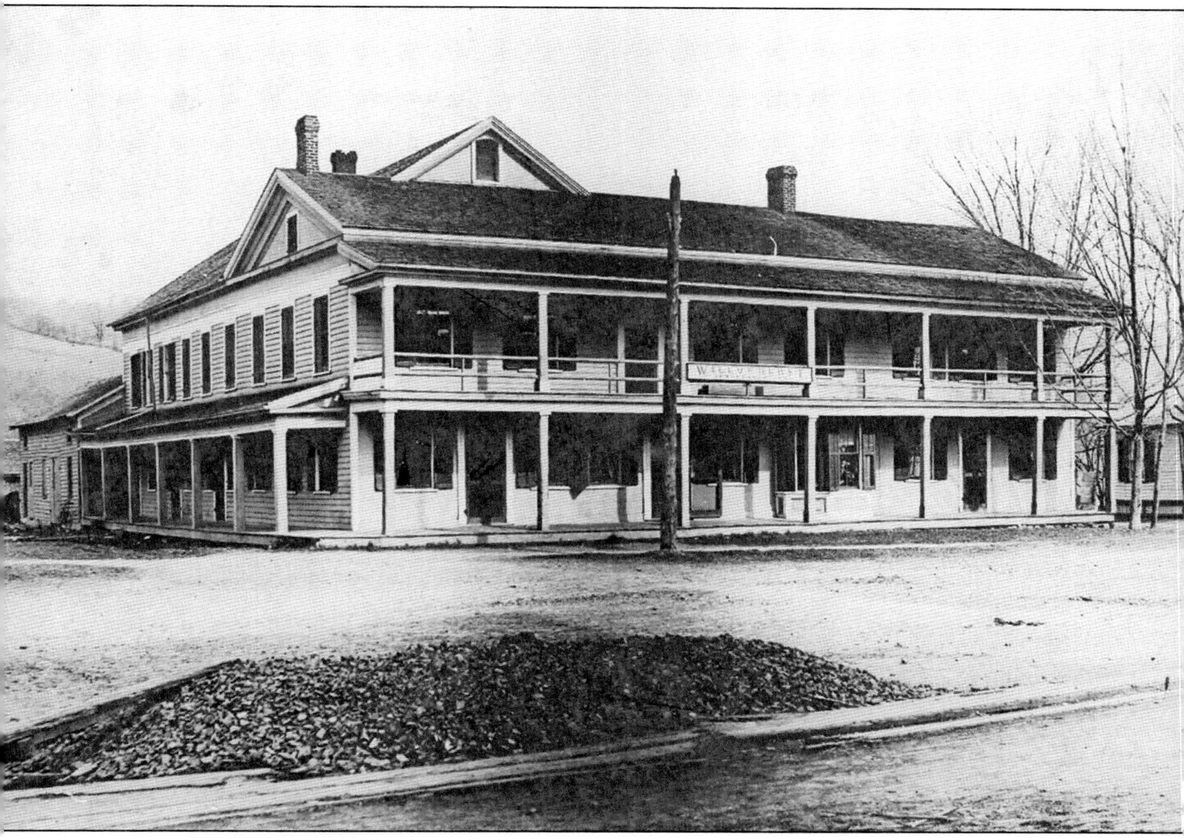

From 1860 through 1876, when the Willowhurst hotel (pictured) in Maine Village was called the Ketchum Inn, it was famous for being a horse-dealing center run by Ephraim Ketchum and his brother-in-law H.E. Hathaway. After the Civil War, there was a serious shortage of horses, so Ketchum went back and forth to Canada and Missouri to purchase quality animals, once making 100 horses available at the Ketchum stables behind the inn. It was called the Willowhurst hotel from the early 1900s until 1942, when it was sold to the Catholic church.

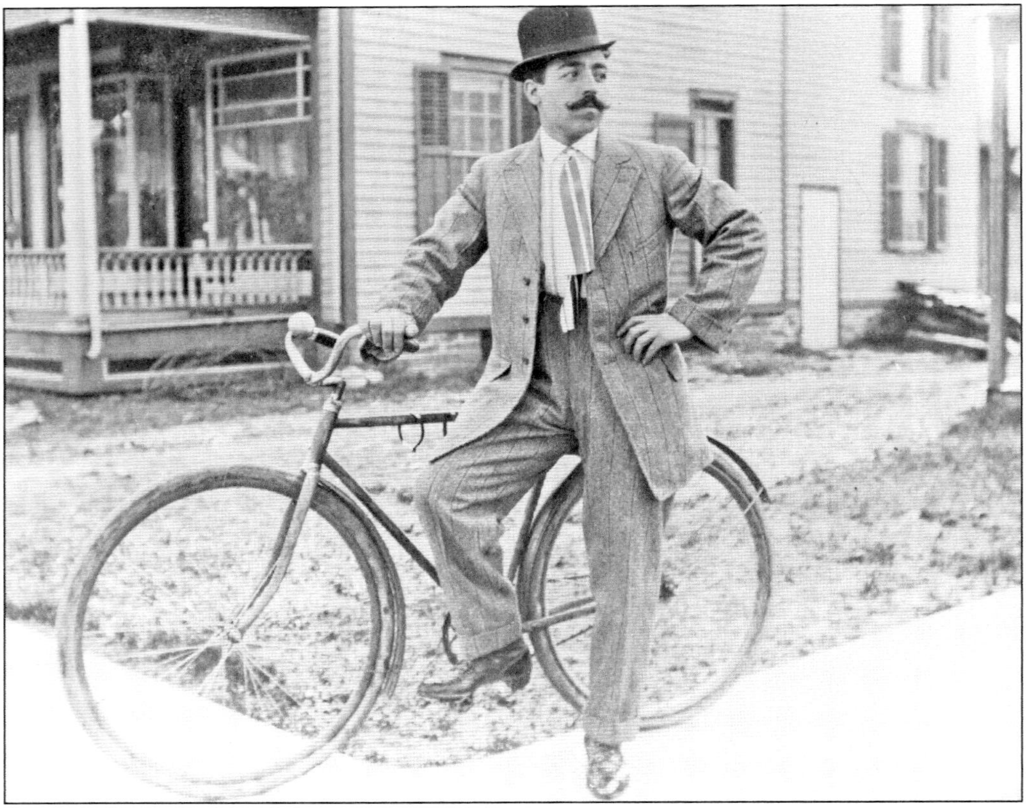

During the late 1800s and early 1900s, bicycles were all the rage. In the early 1920s, one of the first macadam roads in southern New York was built from Union to Maine. That, along with the introduction of the balloon bicycle tire, made riding more enjoyable. Jimmy Cacciala, pictured above, was an Italian immigrant who came to work on the road. He is standing with his bicycle in front of the house at 2590 Main Street. The photograph below, taken by Lee Loomis, shows Ina Tymeson (left) and her mother, Minnie Ellis, with their bicycle.

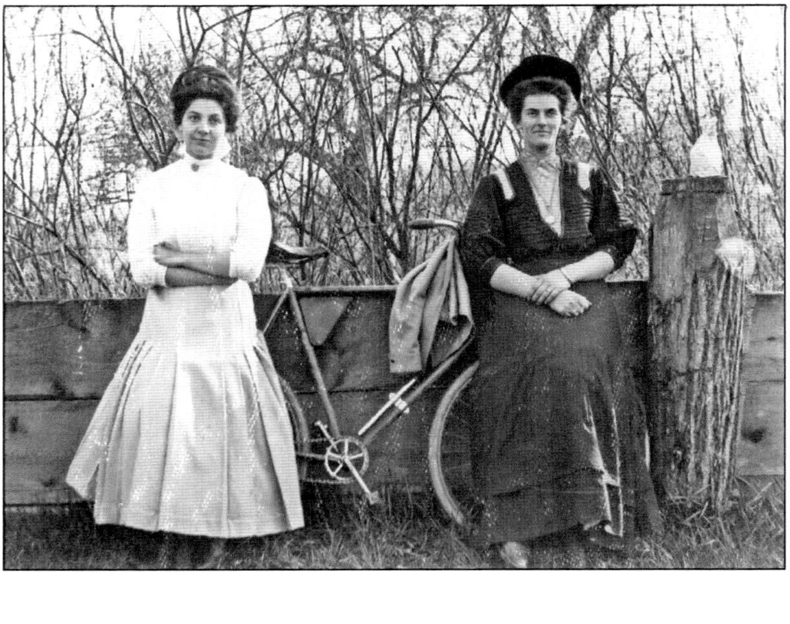

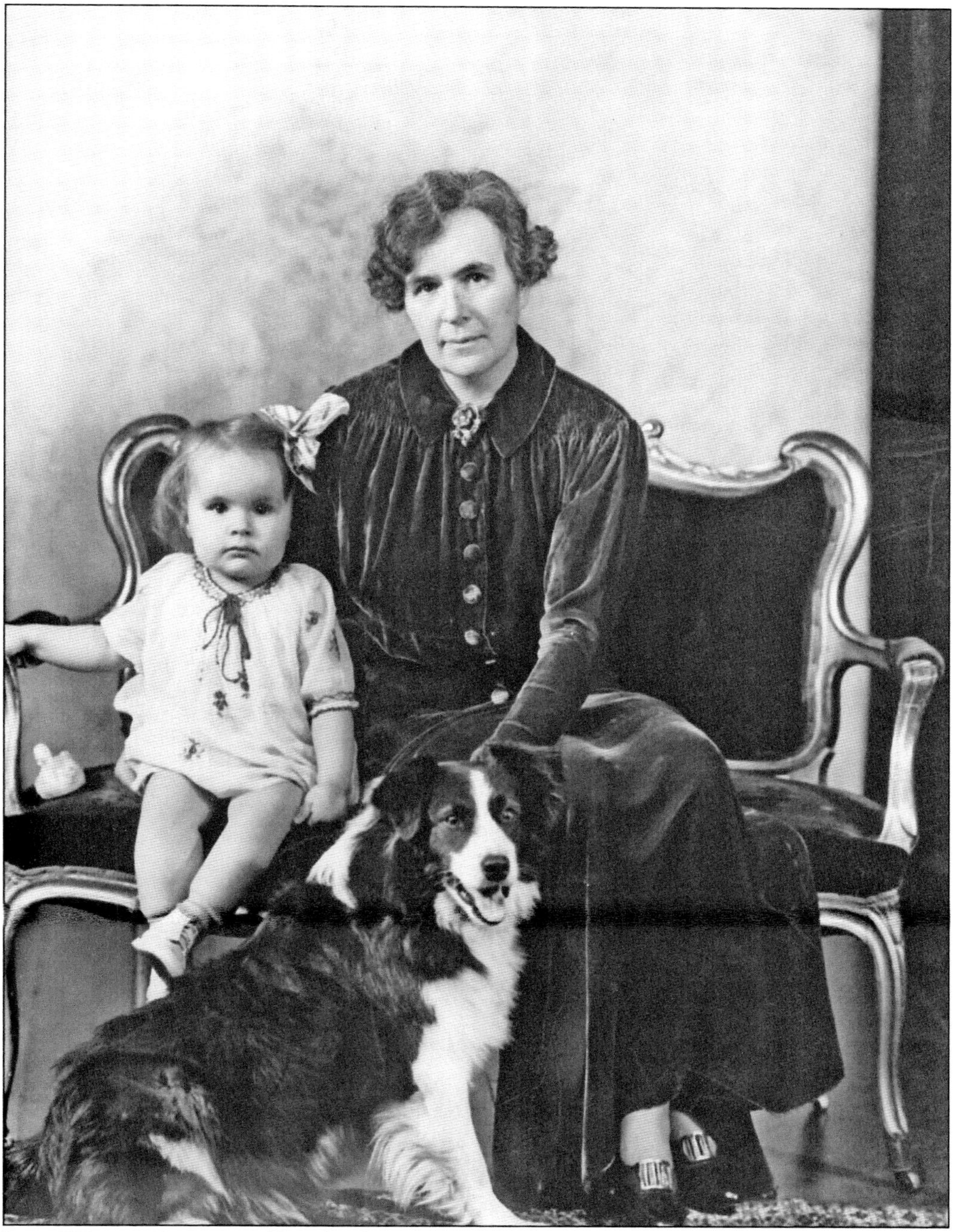

Janet Whitney Bowers and her daughter, Janet, posed for this photograph in 1936. Young Janet was born in 1935 and grew up in Bowers' Corners, just north of Maine Village. She attended Vassar College in Poughkeepsie, New York, and Union Seminary College in New York City. She married Lawrence Bothwell, established the Bowers Foundation, and was an advocate for the historic preservation of the Nanticoke Valley. In 2000, the Preservation League of New York State honored her for her efforts in historic preservation.

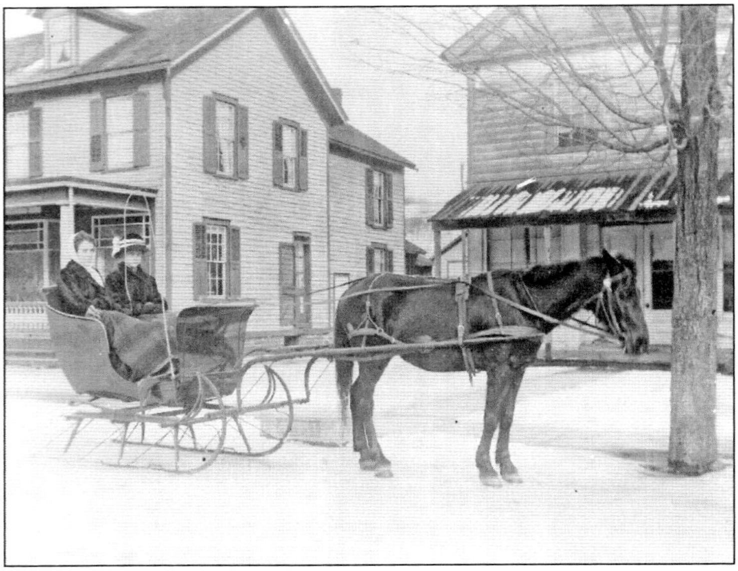

When the roads became covered with snow in the winter, people got out sleighs and cutters—light sleighs pulled by one horse featuring high, curved dashes in front to deflect the snow and ice being thrown up by the horse's hooves. Even though cars were gaining popularity when this photograph was taken in 1908, many people left them at home and traveled on sleighs and cutters instead when it snowed.

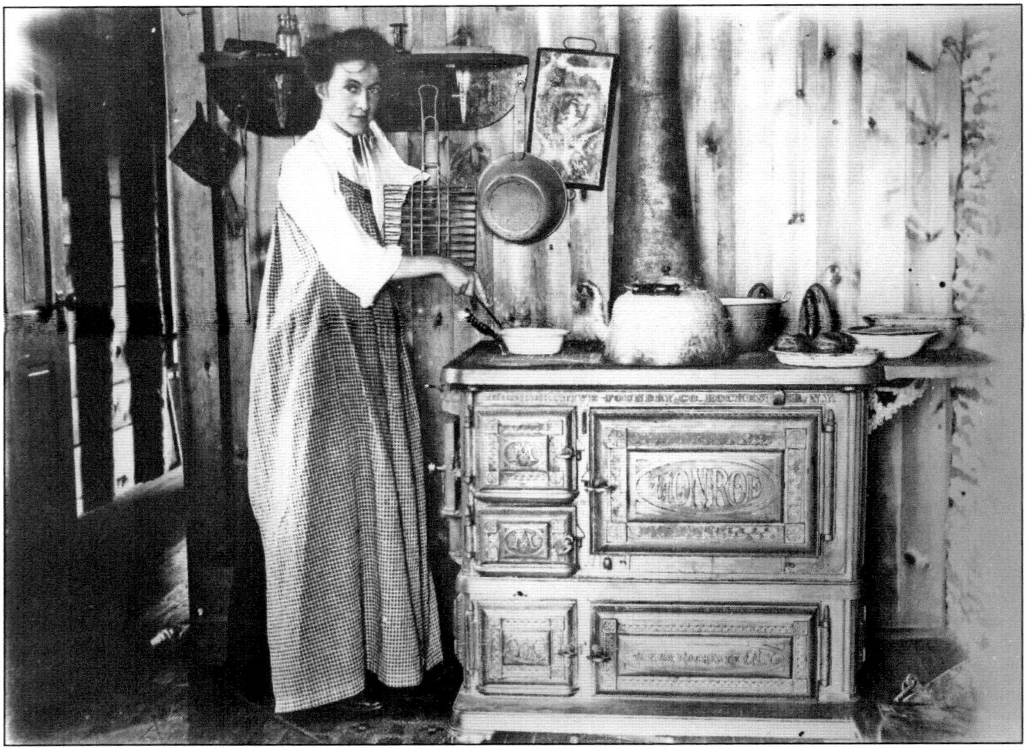

Cooking was a strenuous part of a woman's work day, with most cooking implements made of cast iron. Wood and water had to be carried in, making for hot, exhausting work in the summer. Most women learned to cook by observing their mothers in the kitchen. Janet Whitney Bowers (pictured) was the wife of Dr. Clement G. Bowers of Bowers' Corners. The photograph was taken by Dr. Bowers's brother, Franck Taylor Bowers, who was a professional artist.

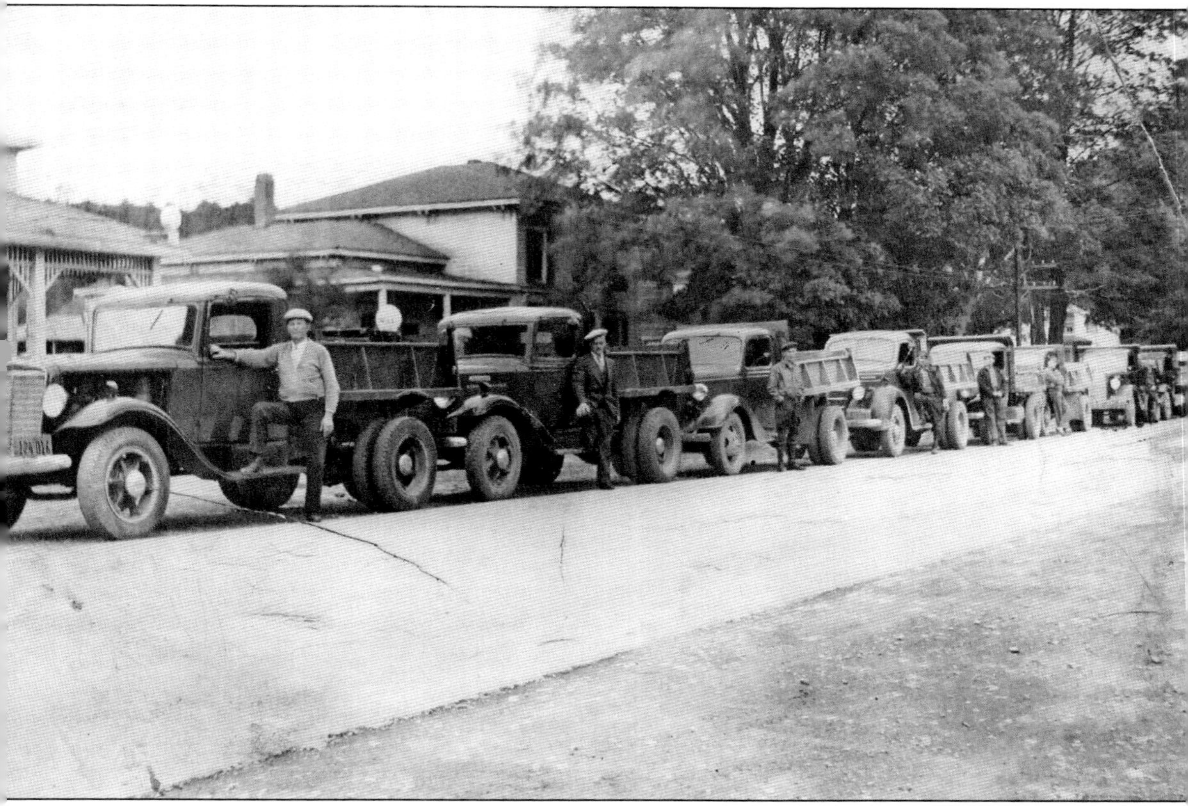

These trucks lined up in front of Padbury's store in 1939 or 1940. The fleet was headed for Bath, New York, to work on a road job for the state. The men standing in front of the trucks are, from left to right, Roscoe Jones, Ray Hart, Lawrence Walters, unidentified, Louis Zimmer, Harold Corson, and Bob Zimmer. (Courtesy of Betty Welch.)

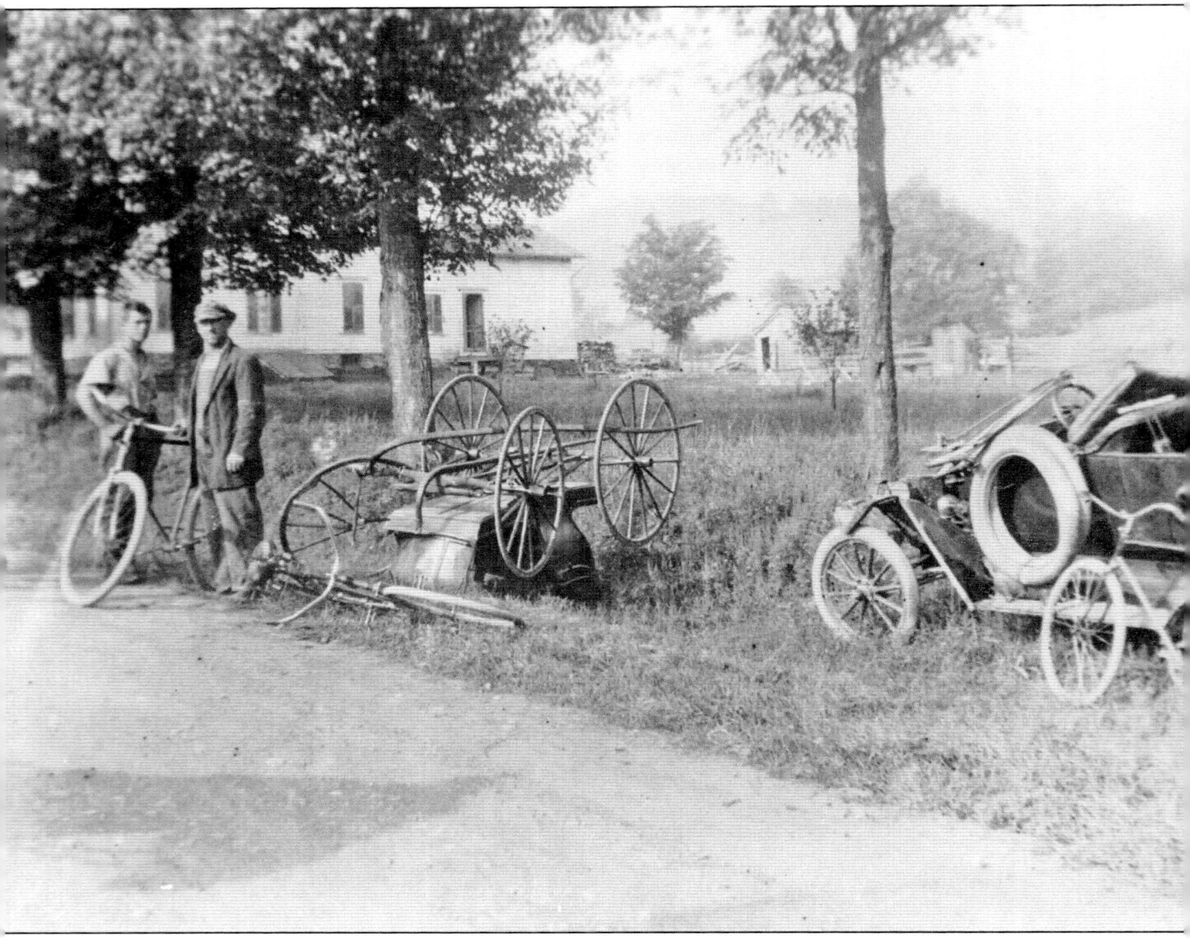

Accidents like this were common when the automobile was first introduced. This automobile was probably heading south on Nanticoke Road when it frightened the horse pulling the buggy, causing it to overturn. The horse's shadow is visible on the road in the lower left corner of the image. Three bicyclists were apparently on the scene. Note the two spare tires tied to the side of the automobile.

Two
NANTICOKE

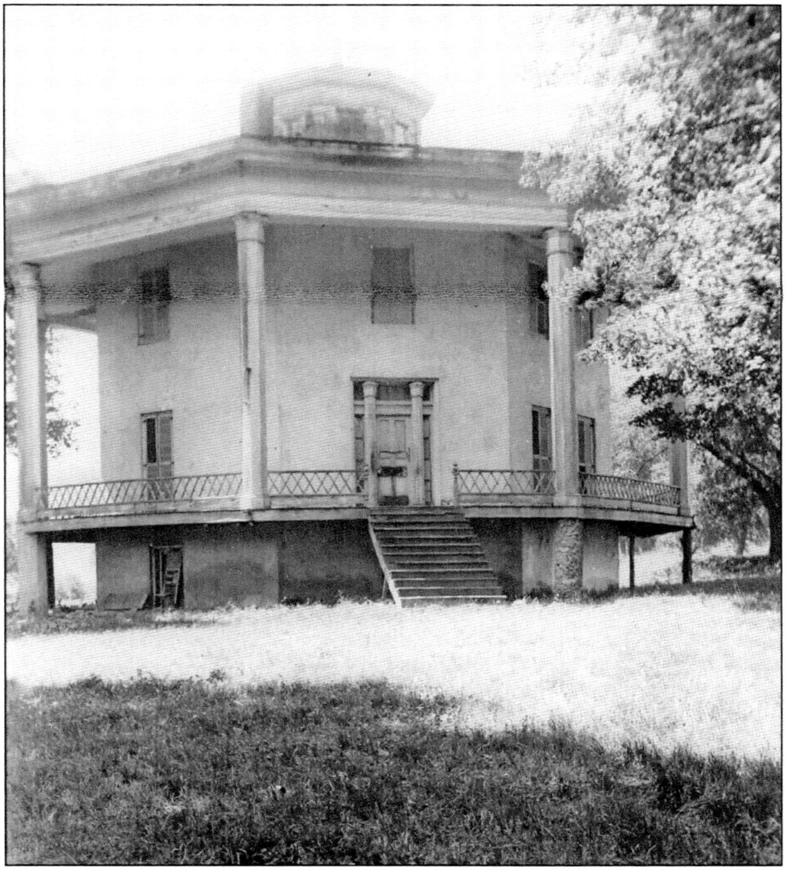

The Octagon Inn in Glen Aubrey was built between 1835 and 1850 by a Mr. Smith, who owned and operated the nearby tannery. He could go into the cupola of this unique building to keep an eye on his workers felling trees in the surrounding woods. The Octagon Inn started out as a personal residence before becoming an inn, a grocery store, and, finally, a tavern. It burned down in 1996.

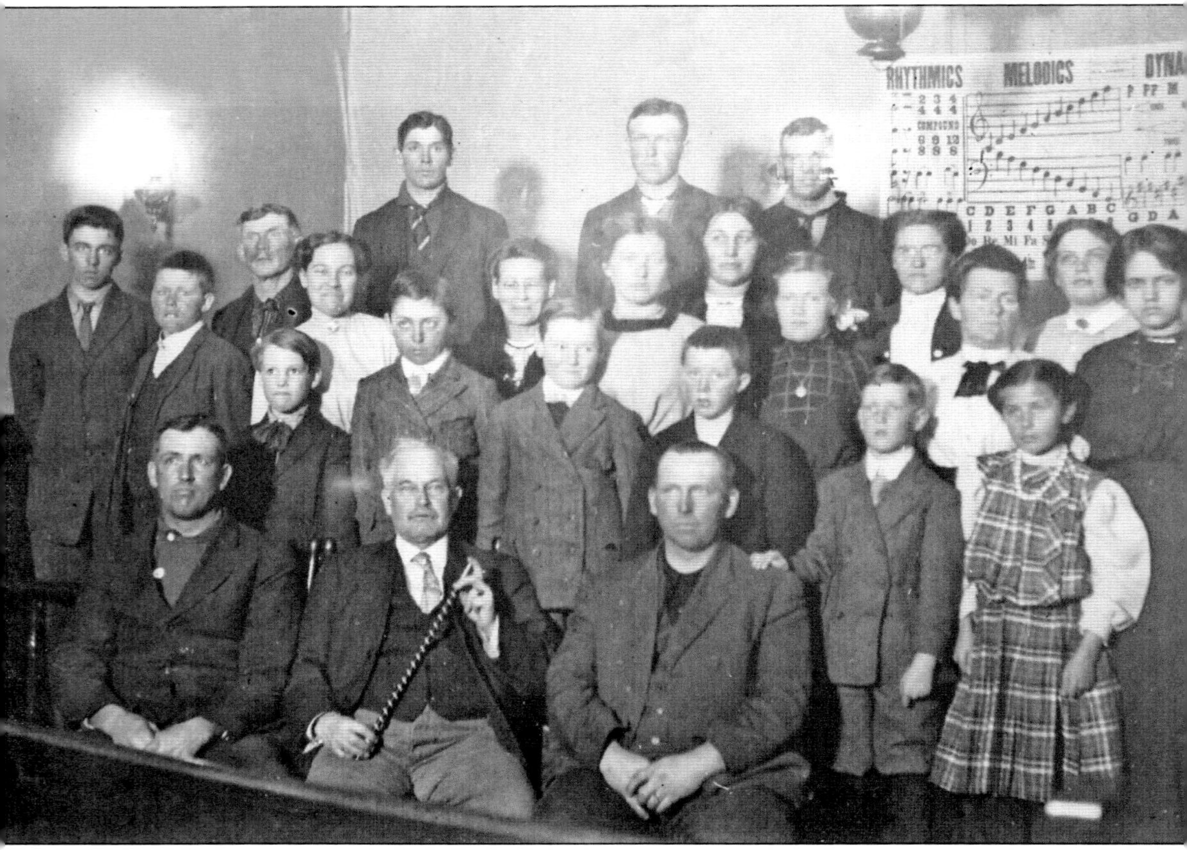

Around 1910, these students attended a singing school in Nanticoke. It was a great way to socialize and was something to look forward to on a monthly basis. The participants are, from left to right, (first row) Ralph Carley, teacher Mr. Thayer, and John Marean; (second row) Earl Vandeburg, Bill Wade, Clyde Millard, Arthur Bailey, Herman Ames, unidentified, Byron Riley, and Vera Bailey; (third row) Arthur Riley, Alice Tappan, Mary Bailey, Mabel Riley, Ina Marean, Viva Riley, Nellie Millard, Etta Riley, Ollie Riley, and Ethel Vandeburg; (fourth row) Bruce Millard, Clarence Allen, and Vere Riley. (Courtesy of Joyce Jackson.)

This 1915 photograph shows a sugar bush on the Martha and Fred Marean farm in Allentown. It is on Flint Road, east of Route 26 from Allentown Cemetery. Note the sugar shack with the firewood pile. The top of the hemlock tree was a bee tree. The first 16-foot log produced 800 board feet of lumber, which was sawed at the Barnes and Whittaker sawmill. (Courtesy of Joyce Jackson.)

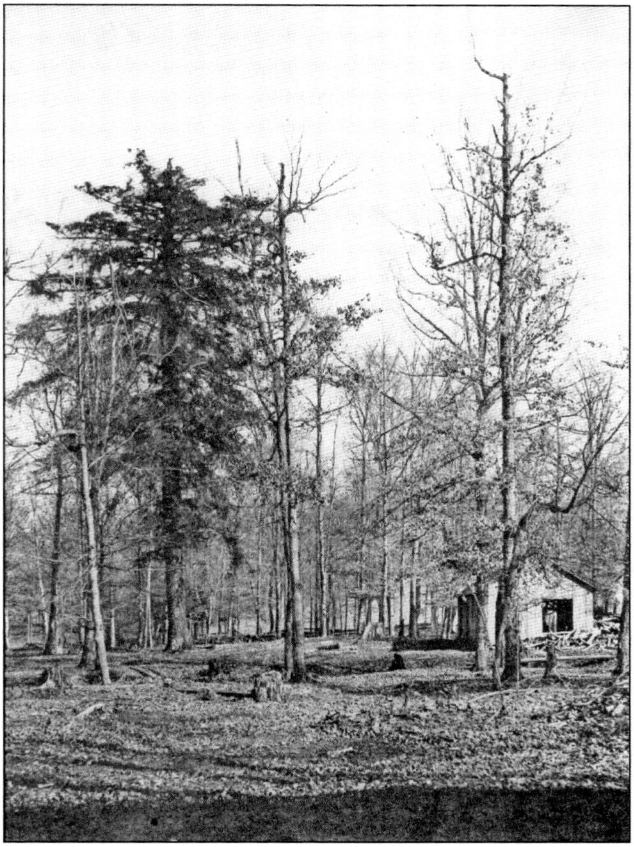

Below, Lewis Whittaker makes butter at the Barnes and Whittaker Creamery. The creamery was on the Barnes farm on the east side of Route 26. Whittaker and his brother-in-law, Duane Barnes, made butter and cheese to sell in Binghamton twice a week; the quality was so superior that they got top price for their products. The creamery equipment was delivered to Whitney Point by train, then carried over the roads by wagon. (Courtesy of Joyce Jackson.)

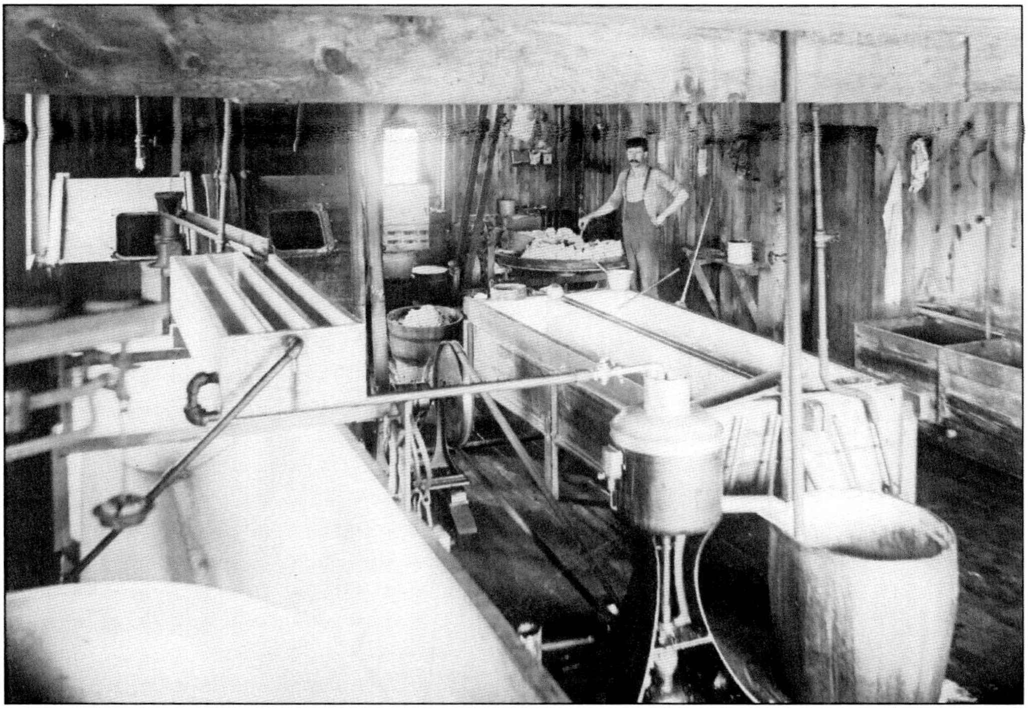

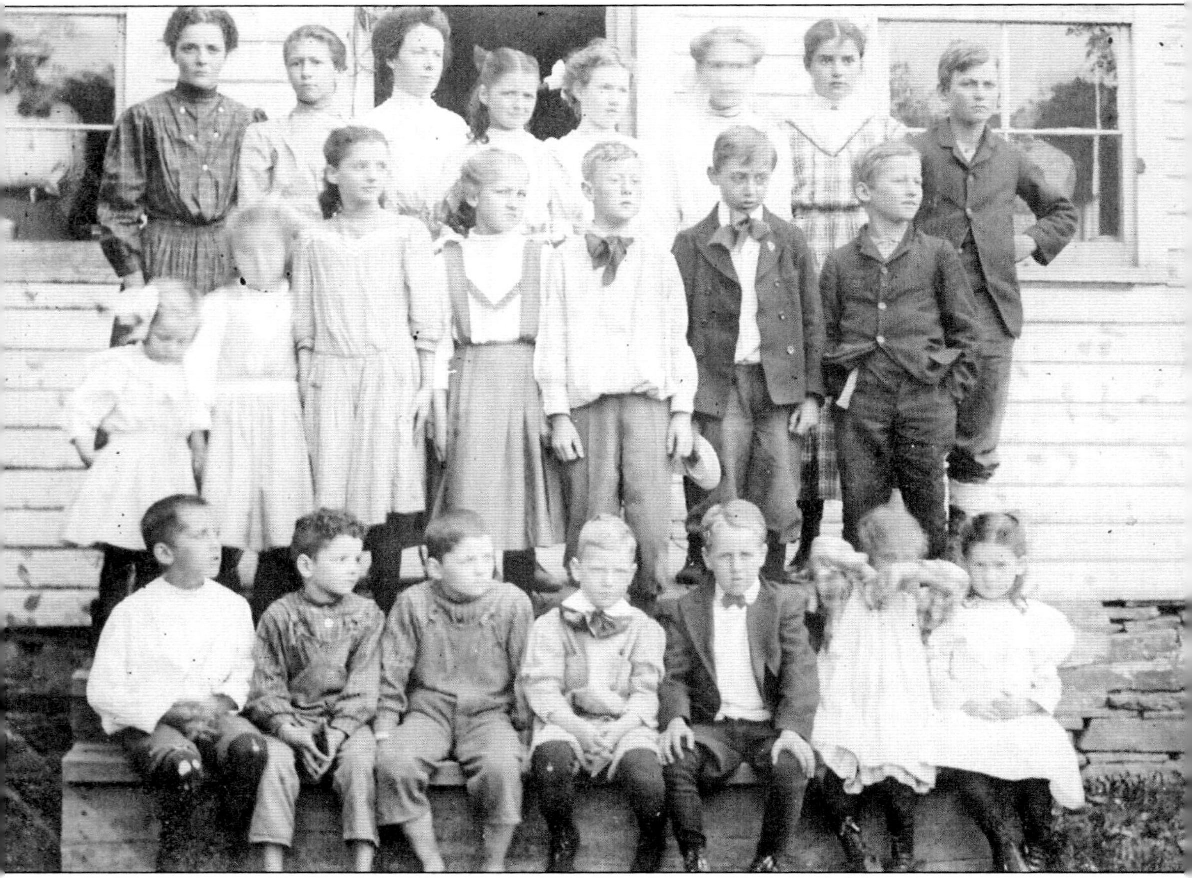

Students at Glen Aubrey School posed for this photograph in 1910. They are, from left to right, (first row) Ray Councilman, Eddie McGinnis, Robert McGinnis, Byron Riley, Lawrence Hodges, Ada Vandermark, and Viola Smith; (second row) Gladys Hodges, Vera Bailey, Katherine McGinnis, Hazel Vandermark, Herbert Meade, Arthur Bailey, and Guy Vandermark; (third row) Mary McGinnis, Mildred Swan, Anna Bradley, ? McGinnis, Veva Riley, Edith Councilman, Rose McGinnis, and Leo Vandermark.

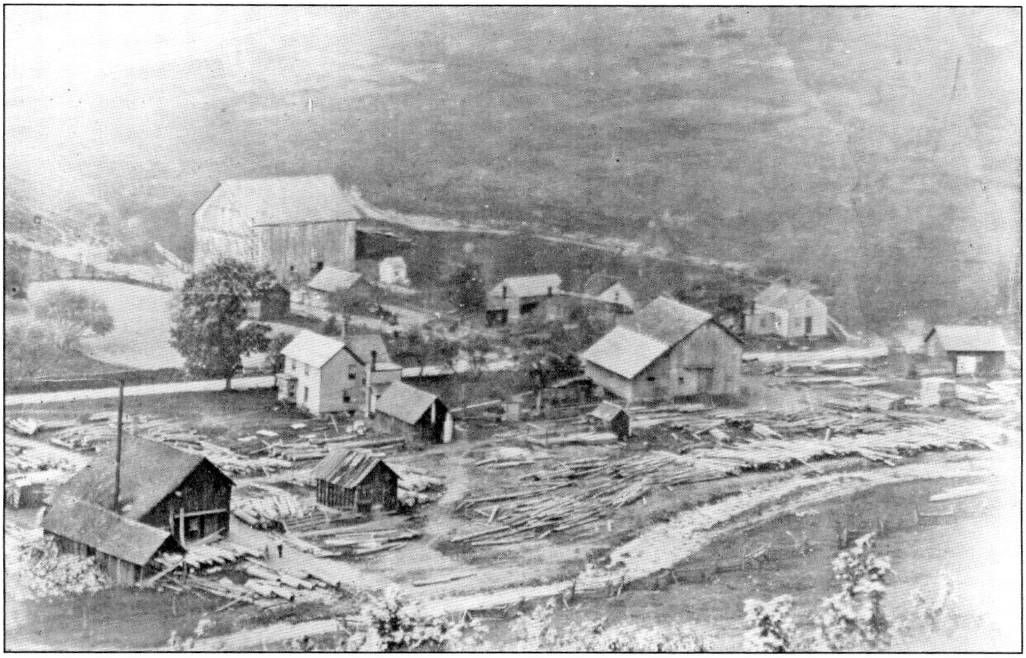

In February 1865, Nathan Barnes and Polly Carley moved from Lapeer, New York, to Nanticoke with a team of oxen and horses. In 1906, Nathan's grandson, Duane Barnes, and his brother–in-law, Lewis Whittaker, started a large sawmill by the creek, located behind where the old Barnes store building is today.

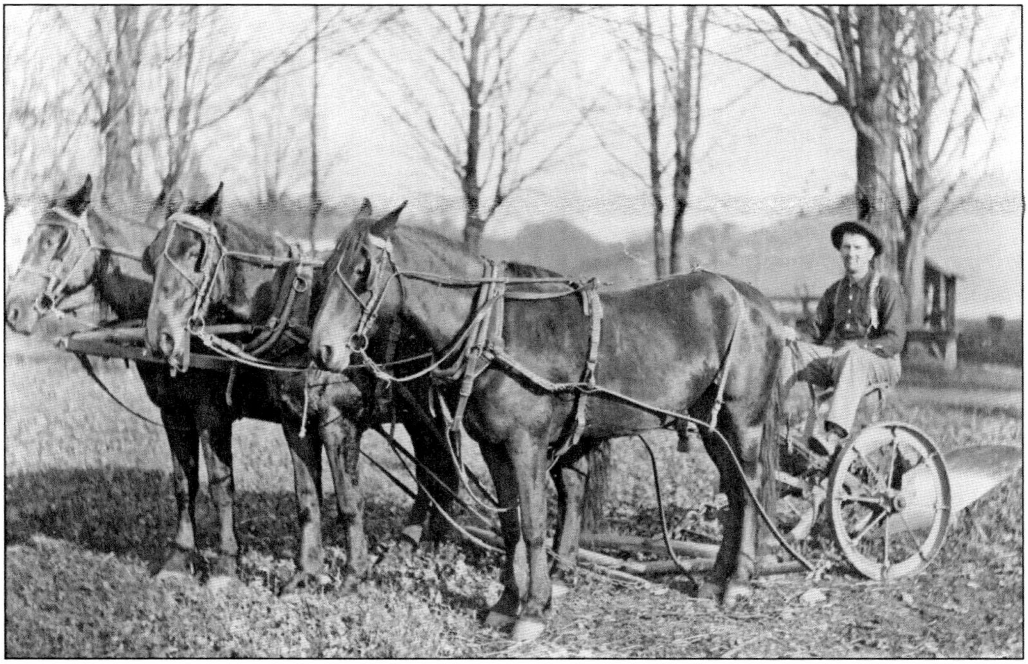

Ralph Carley uses his three-horse team and moldboard plow on his farm near Allentown and Glen Aubrey. He was the son of Wellington Carley and is buried in Allentown Cemetery with his first wife, Cora. His second wife, Nell, was from Canada and eventually returned there for a time. (Courtesy of Joyce Jackson.)

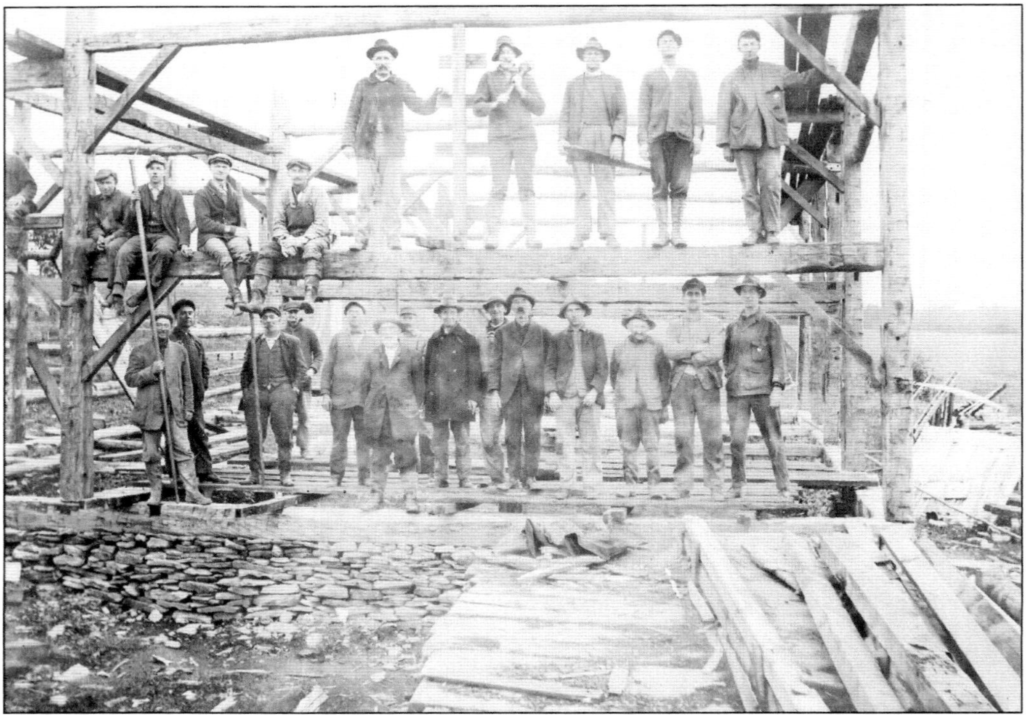

In the 1920s, there was a barn raising in Glen Aubrey at the Flook farm. Those who helped included, from left to right, (first row) Bill Flook, Edgar Flook, Alson Smith, unidentified, Wellie Tymeson, Duane Barnes, unidentified, E.J. Swan, Andrew Stork, Mont Walter, Dick Swan, Charles Slack, Nate Barnes, and Joseph Thompson; (second row) Bill Dingman, Byron Riley, Harry Wade, Morris Councilman, Herman Kenyon, Herbert Meade, Loren Hodges, Leon Vandermark, and Elmer Frink.

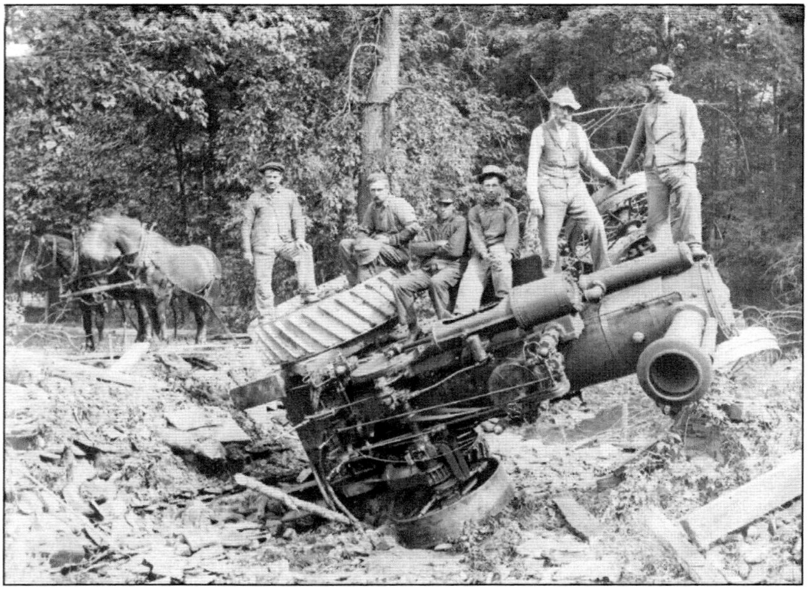

Nathan Barnes told his daughter, Joyce Barnes Jackson, that this accident happened on Dunham Hill Road when the steam engine tipped over while working on the road. The team of horses stands ready to upright the engine. (Courtesy of Joyce Jackson.)

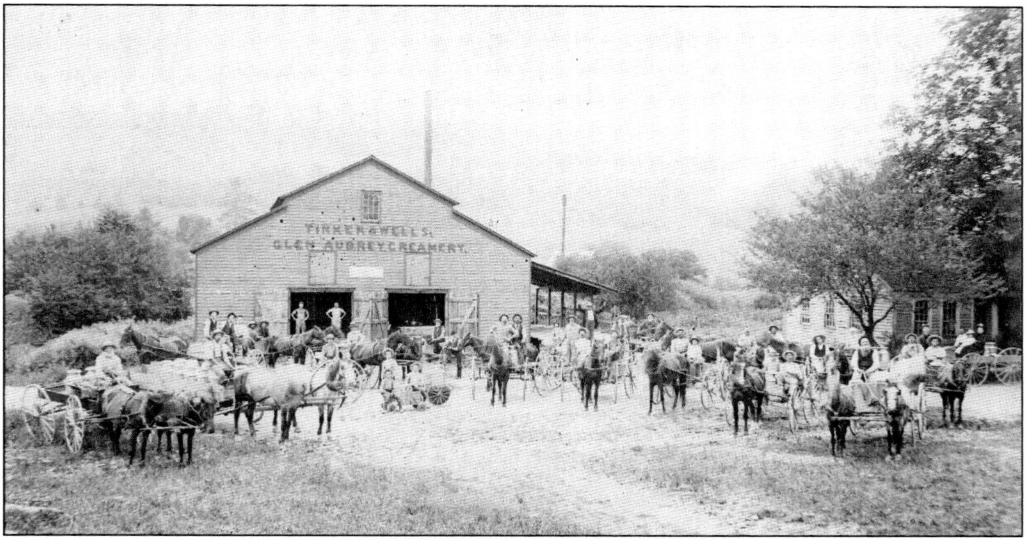

Tinker & Wells Glen Aubrey Creamery was built in the 1800s. The roof was changed in the early 1900s, but it was still a creamery. In the 1930s, the building was used as a repair shop and garage by Vede and Harold Croft. A home and store are visible at right. Some of the people pictured here include, in no particular order, Arthur and William Riley, John Marean, Henry Swan, Loren and Lena Hodges, James Wood, and a Mr. Munson.

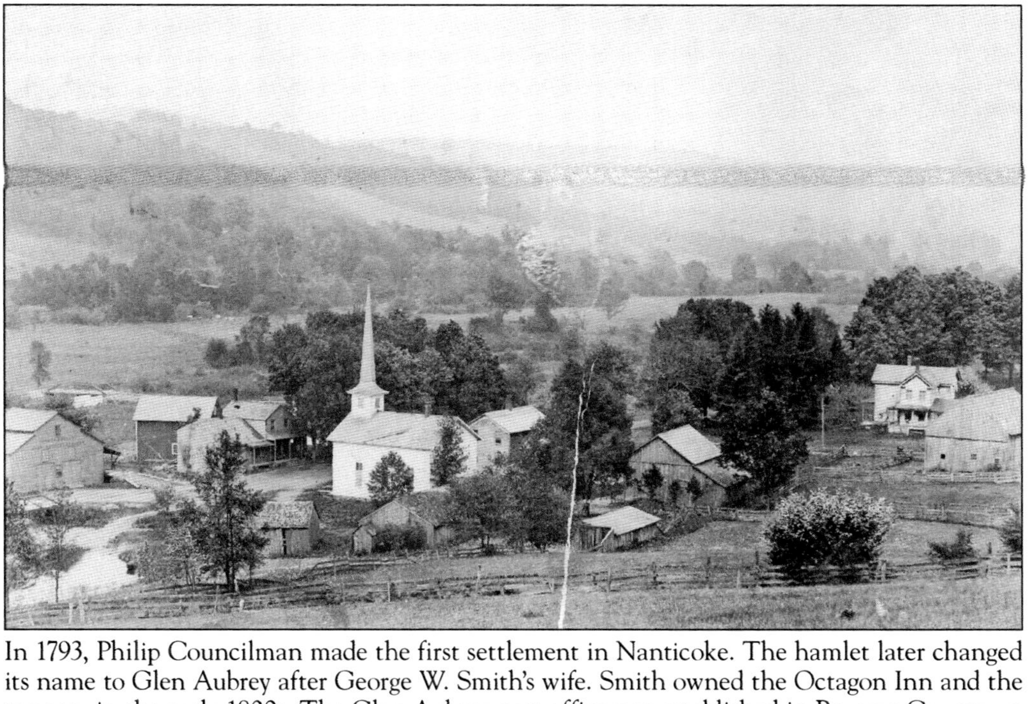

In 1793, Philip Councilman made the first settlement in Nanticoke. The hamlet later changed its name to Glen Aubrey after George W. Smith's wife. Smith owned the Octagon Inn and the tannery in the early 1800s. The Glen Aubrey post office was established in Broome County on July 10, 1855, with Smith serving as the first postmaster.

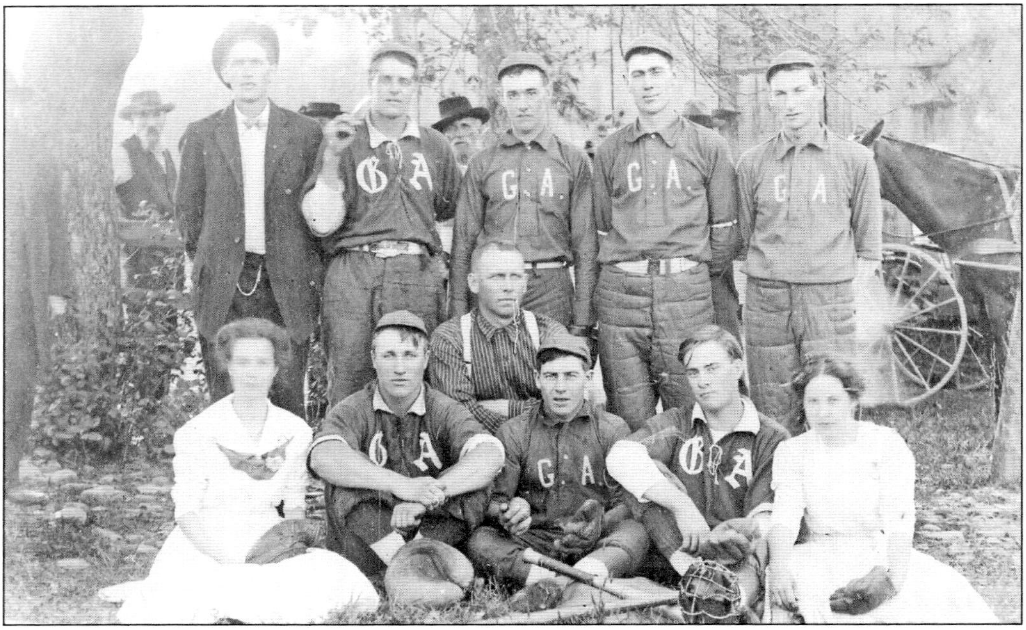

The Glen Aubrey baseball team and assorted others are pictured here in 1908. They are, from left to right, (first row) unidentified, Murel Pope, John Marean, Henry Smith, Nick Tappin, and Alice Tappin; (second row) an unidentified bewhiskered man, Dan Marean, Loren Hodge, Lige Smith (also bewhiskered), James Slack, Frank Smith, and Kern Smith.

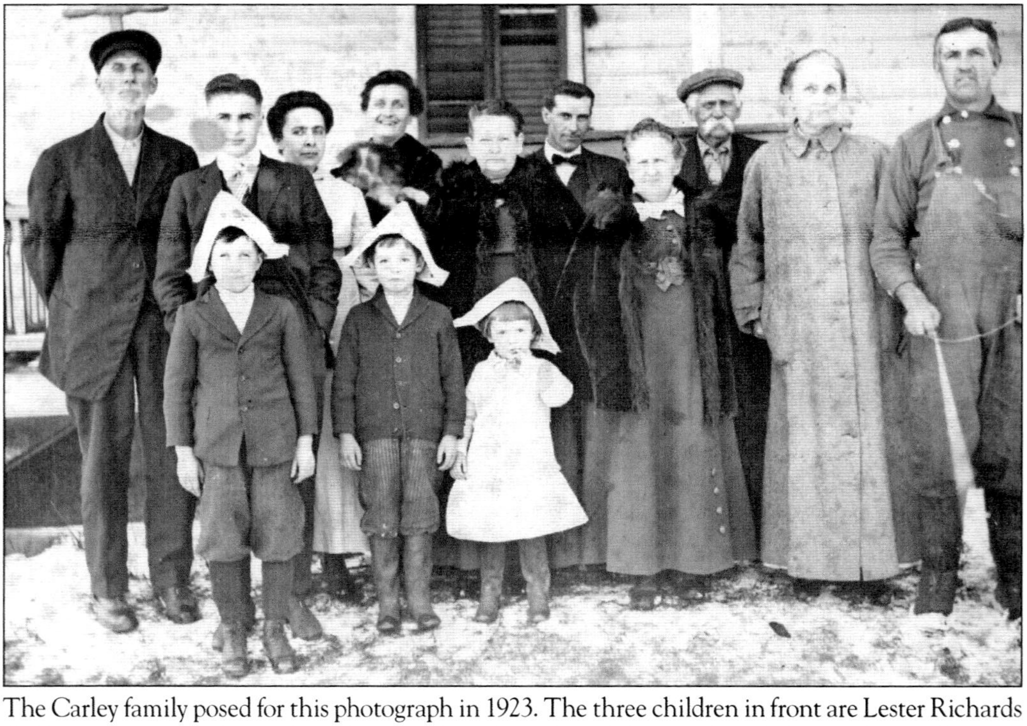

The Carley family posed for this photograph in 1923. The three children in front are Lester Richards (left), Roger Carley (center), and Howard Carley. The adults are, from left to right, Wellington Carley, Elwin Richards, Cora Carley, Florence Richards, Fannie Atwater, unidentified, Matilda Atwater, Chas Atwater, Fannie Carley, and Ralph Carley. (Courtesy of Joyce Jackson.)

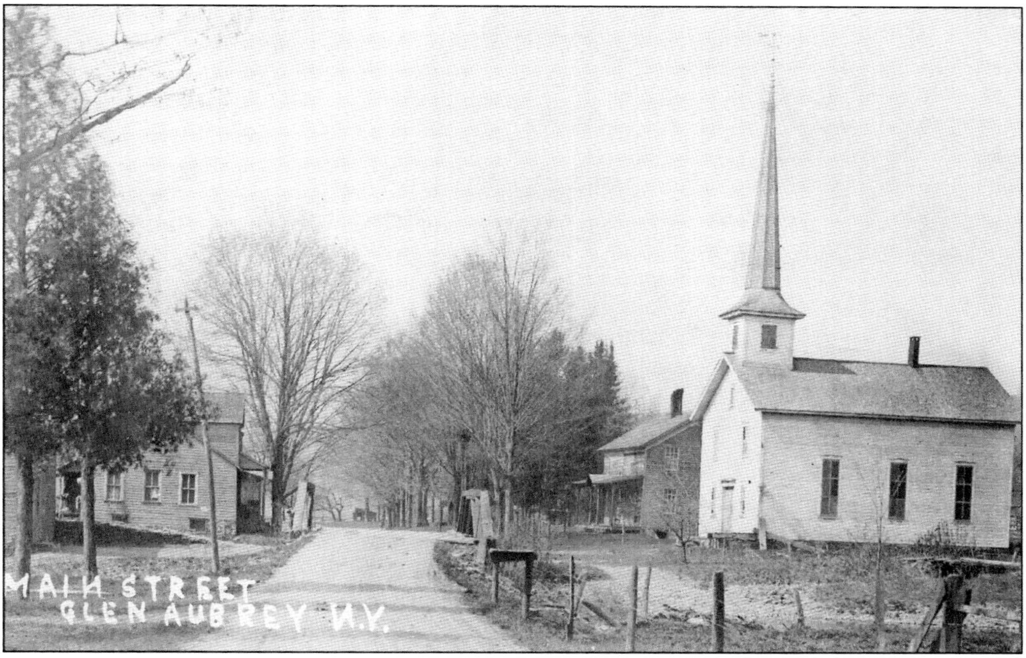

The Community Baptist Church in Glen Aubrey started out as a Methodist church in 1867, housing a large congregation full of familiar Glen Aubrey names like Councilman, Hawver, Walter, Lewis, Swan, Allen, Riley, and Tappen. In the 1920s and 1930s, membership dropped off, and there was no longer a pastor there. In the late 1930s or early 1940s, the Baptist Conference asked to use the church and leased the building for 99 years, a period which has not yet expired. The current name of the church is the Community Baptist Church.

Charles Stoddard built this Glen Aubrey home for himself in 1877. Boyd Thompson recalls Morris Councilman telling him that a 14-year-old Councilman dug the cellar for this house using a team of oxen. The house burned down in 1977, and the barn burned in 1979. An older house once stood near the road just south of this house. The women pictured here are unidentified.

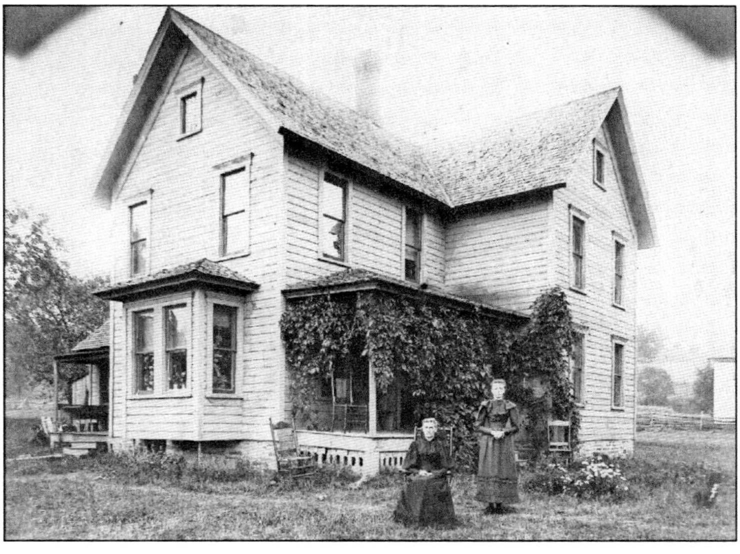

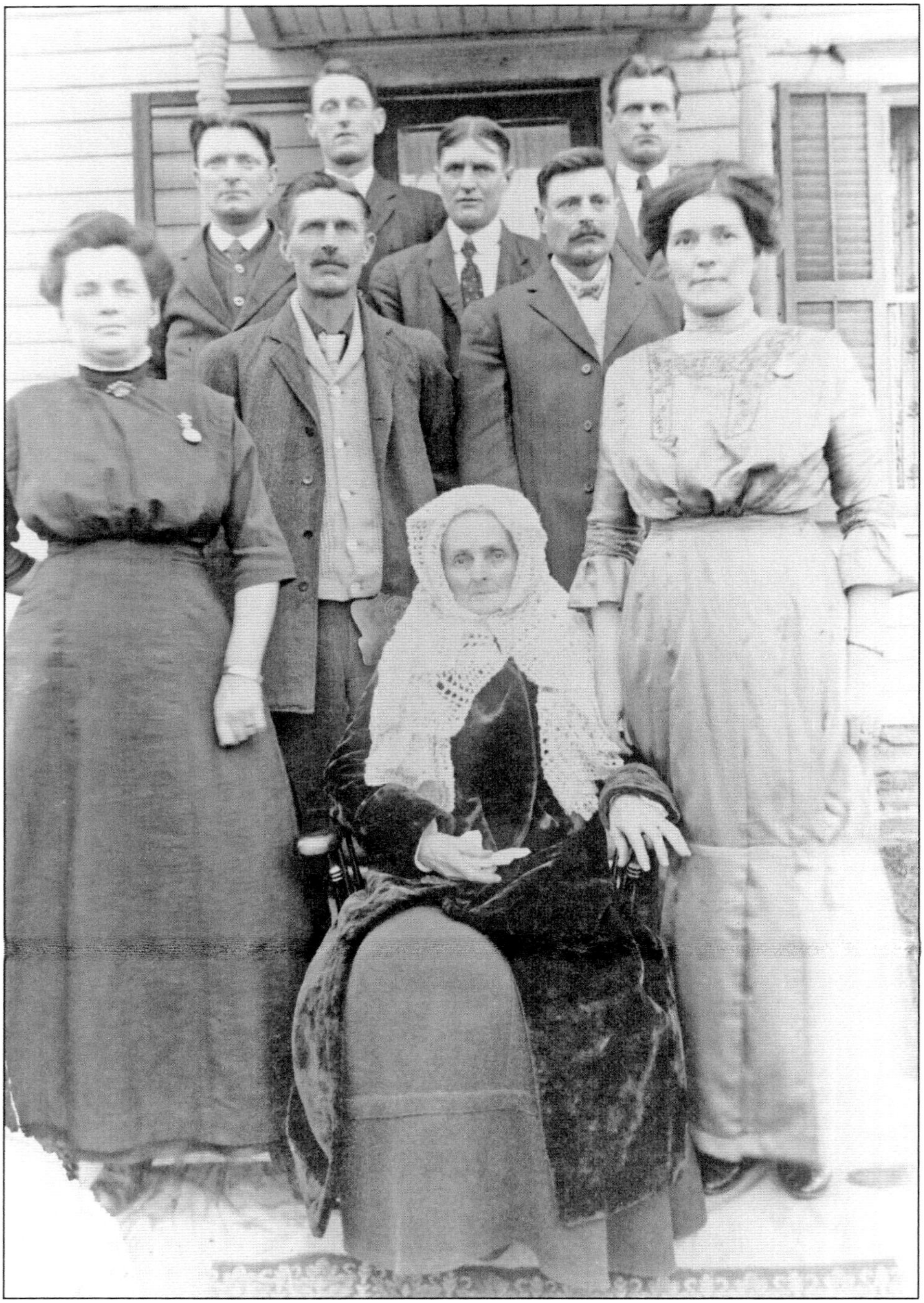

On March 4, 1911, the Ames family, of Nanticoke, posed for this photograph at a family gathering in Glen Aubrey. Laura Ames gave birth to all of her children at home except for Myron H. Ames, who lived in Fresno, California, at the time this picture was taken. Pictured here are, from left to right, (first row) Hattie Ames Strong, Laura Deitz Ames (seated), and Maggie Ames Audibert; (second row) Fred Ames and George Ames; (third row) Clarence Ames, Hiram Ames, Arthur Ames, and Clayton Ames. They were a large, hardworking family. (Courtesy of the late Leigh and Dorothy Ames.)

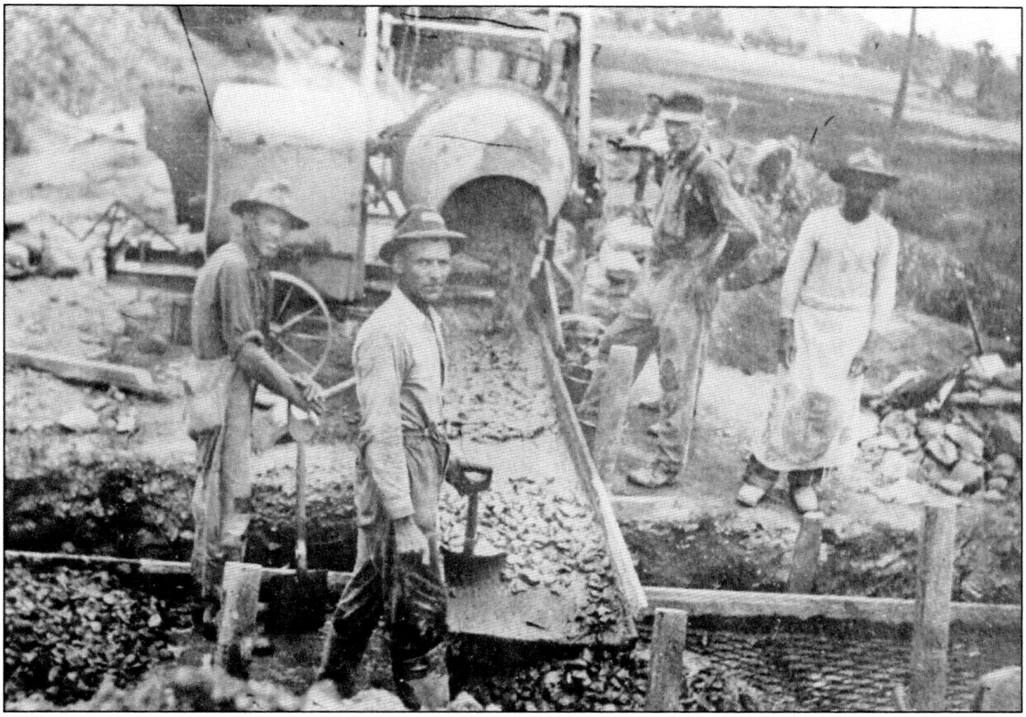

Nanticoke put down its first stone and tar road in 1911 and 1912. It ran from the Lisle town line to the Maine town line and cost the state $64,000. The road was built by T.H. Gill Company of Boston. Four steel bridges were built for the road. Above, men work on the road in front of the Croft property. The photograph below shows the steam engine and the road crew, with Frank Smith in the center. Two twin-cylinder Frick steam traction engines hauled rock for the project from the Whitney Point railroad. Del Barrows and Will Smith ran the steamrollers to finish the surface.

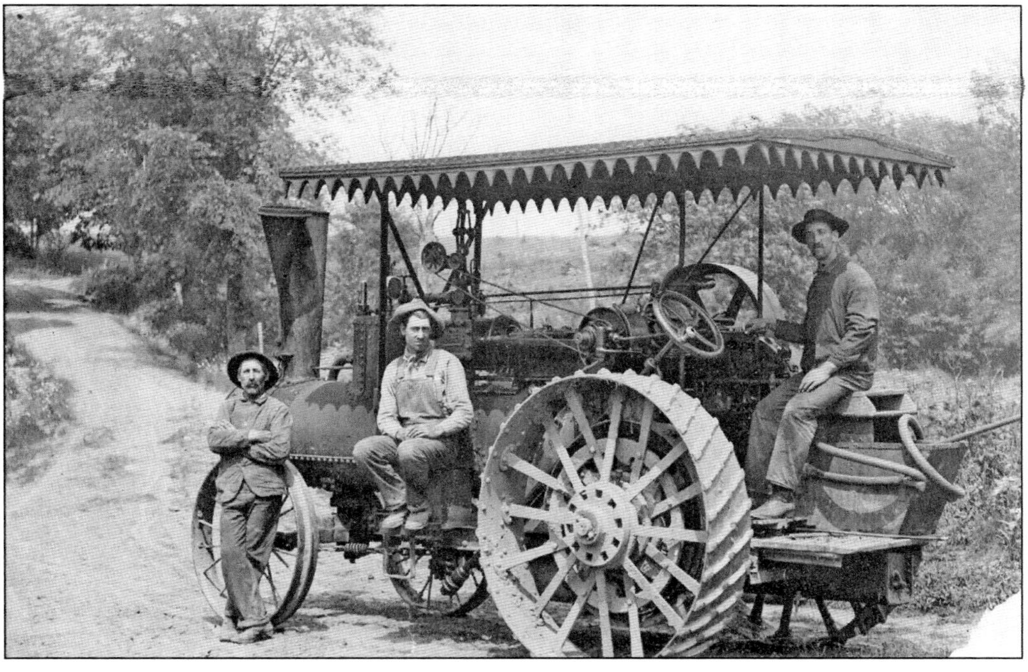

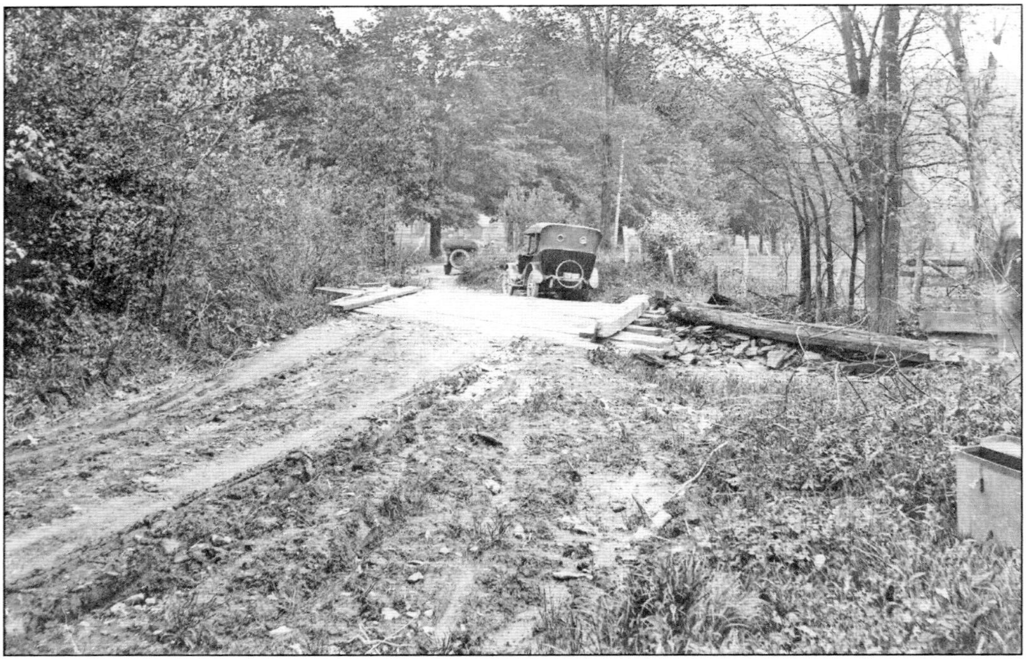

This photograph shows the first bridge on Dunham Hill Road. The car nearest to the bridge is a Dodge, owned by Vernie Allen, and the second car is a Ford. Dunham Hill Road was first called Chestnut Hill Road and was later named for the Dunham family, who lived there. The first sawmill in the county was built on Dunham Hill Road in 1853. (Courtesy of Joyce Jackson.)

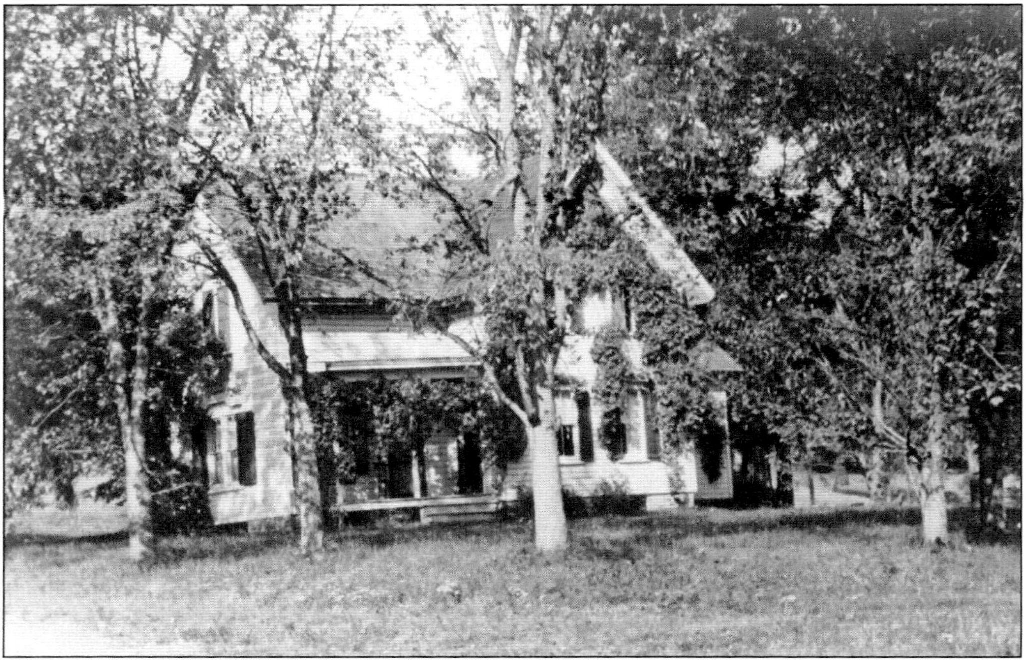

Elmhurst Cottage in Nanticoke was built in 1882 by Warren and Dethulia Johnson Gee; a log cabin was previously on the site. Before the house was built, Warren erected a chicken house in which the family lived until the log cabin was torn down and the new house was constructed. Warren was a blacksmith in Nanticoke for many years. (Courtesy of Jane and Gerald Youngs.)

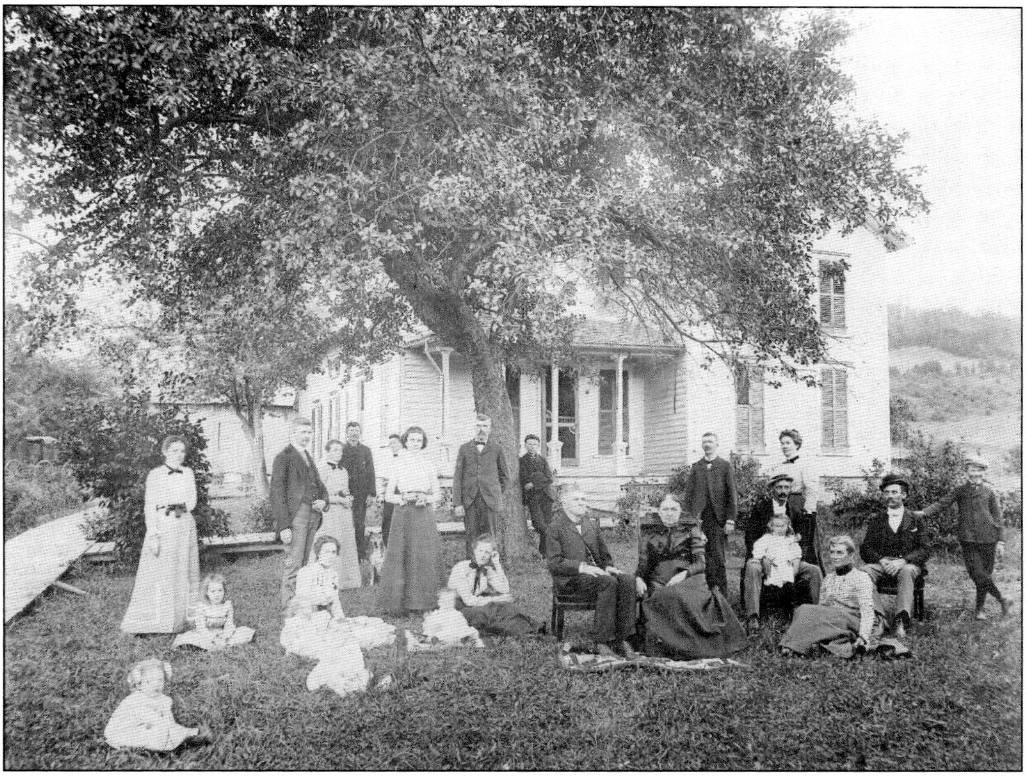

This is the William Riley homestead in Glen Aubrey with several generations of the family posing out front. Riley was a blacksmith with a shop in Glen Aubrey and also owned the Tinker and Wells Creamery for a time. (Courtesy of Laura Riley.)

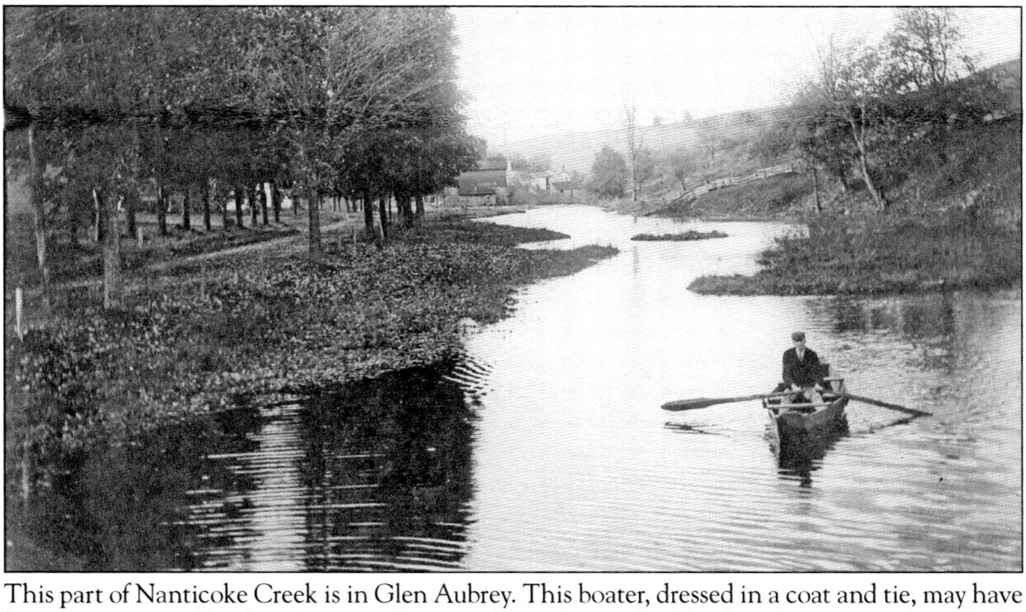

This part of Nanticoke Creek is in Glen Aubrey. This boater, dressed in a coat and tie, may have been rowing on a Sunday afternoon. Rowing down the creek offered a relaxing trip through the pasturelands. The water is low on this summer trip, showing quite a contrast to how the creek looks during the floods that occur from time to time.

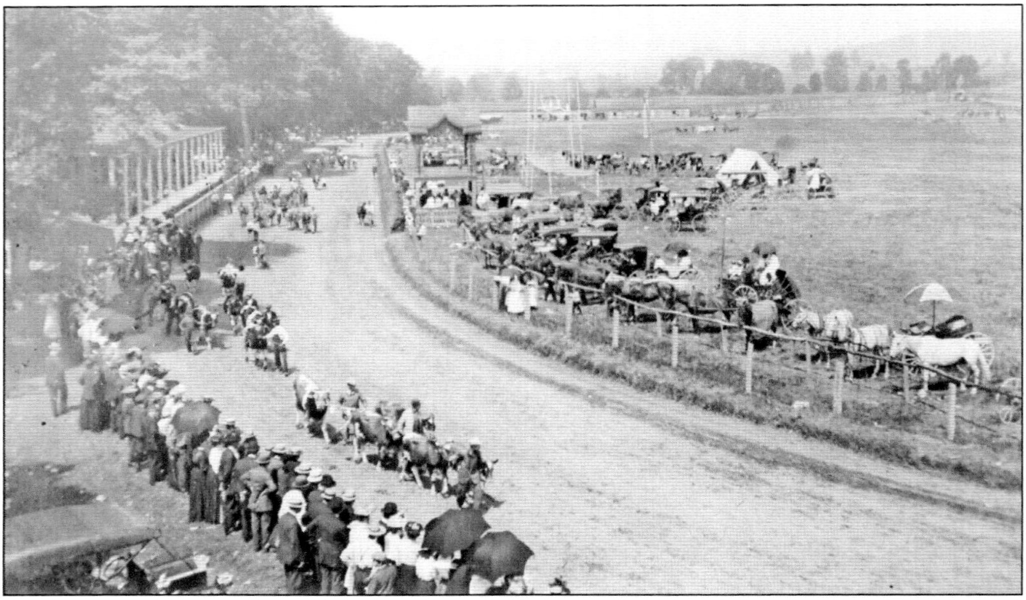

The Whitney Point Fairgrounds is pictured here, probably in the early 1900s, judging by the number of horse-drawn wagons and the relative lack of automobiles. People from Nanticoke and Maine would attend the fair to participate in the celebration of local agriculture. This photographer was just in time to record the cattle judging.

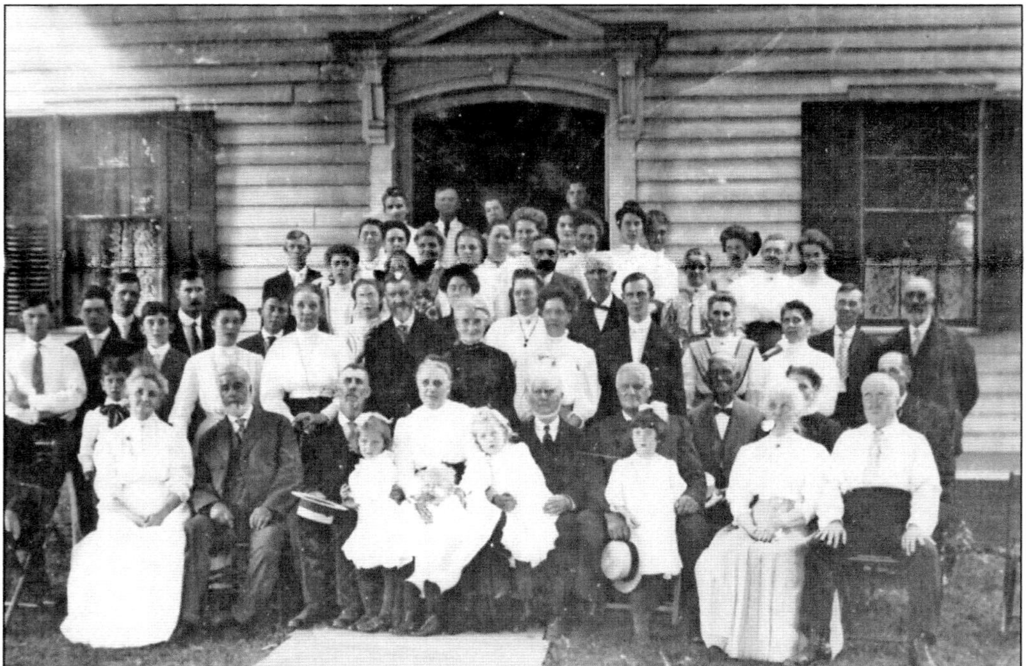

Ebenezer Carley was a Revolutionary War veteran who came to the Nanticoke area from Vermont in 1800. Carley reunions started before 1900. The Allens and Whittakers were also related to the Carleys. Neighbors often married into each other's families, creating strong ties and associations.

Three
150 Years of the Maine Community Band

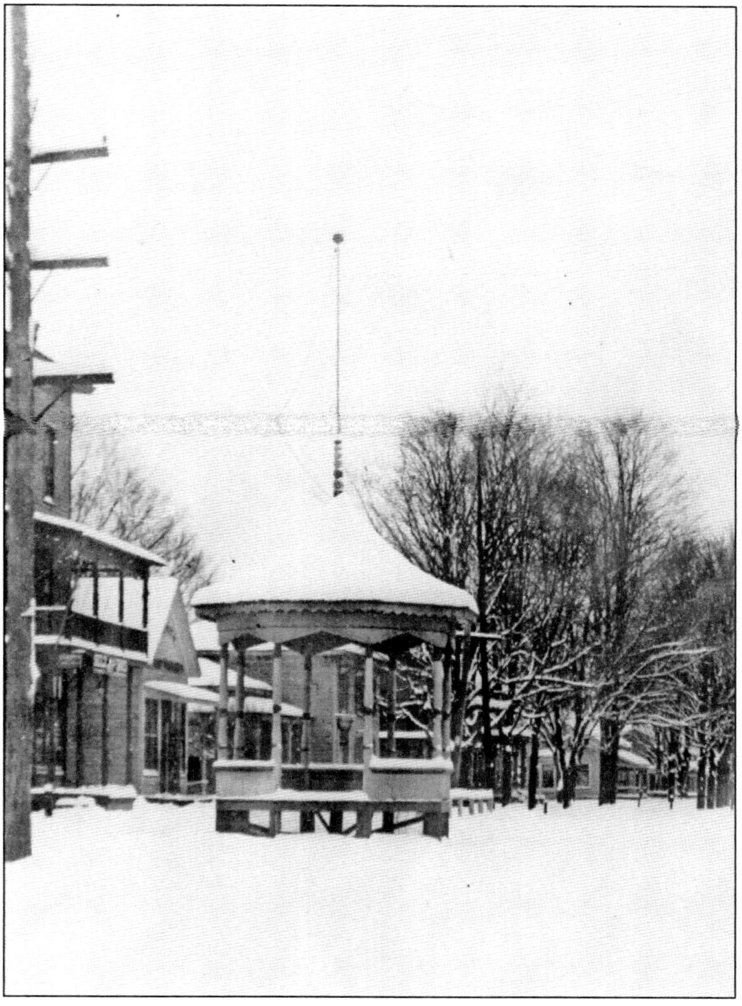

One of the landmarks in Maine Village was the band pagoda, which stood in the middle of the road at Main and Church Streets. Thinking back to 1914, George Dudley remembers, "When I was a boy we had a large band known as the Maine Progressive Band. I used to play the tuba. We serenaded the villagers in the pagoda on Saturday nights."

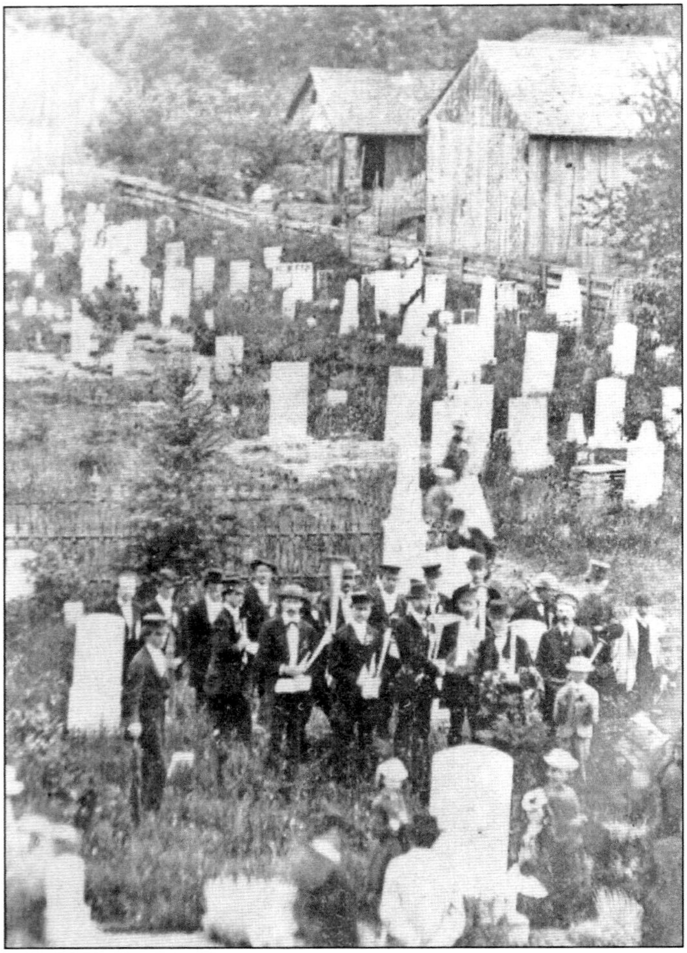

Members of the first Maine community band, pictured here in 1861, included N.B. Wright, George Hathaway, E.E. Todd, Henry Marean, F.W. Hovey, Orin Holden, Ed B. Harmon, Dwight Dudley, Myron Lewis, and W.O. Lincoln. This band, consisting mostly of brass and percussion instruments, contained several over-the-shoulder horns. These particular instruments were only popular during the Civil War, when the band needed to be heard by the army following behind.

Local historian Al Parr says that around 1900 the Maine town band hosted this picnic on Baseball Island with families of the players. Baseball Island was in the creek behind where the large plaza is located today. It was rented out to the baseball team because it flooded on occasion and was not useful for more permanent purposes.

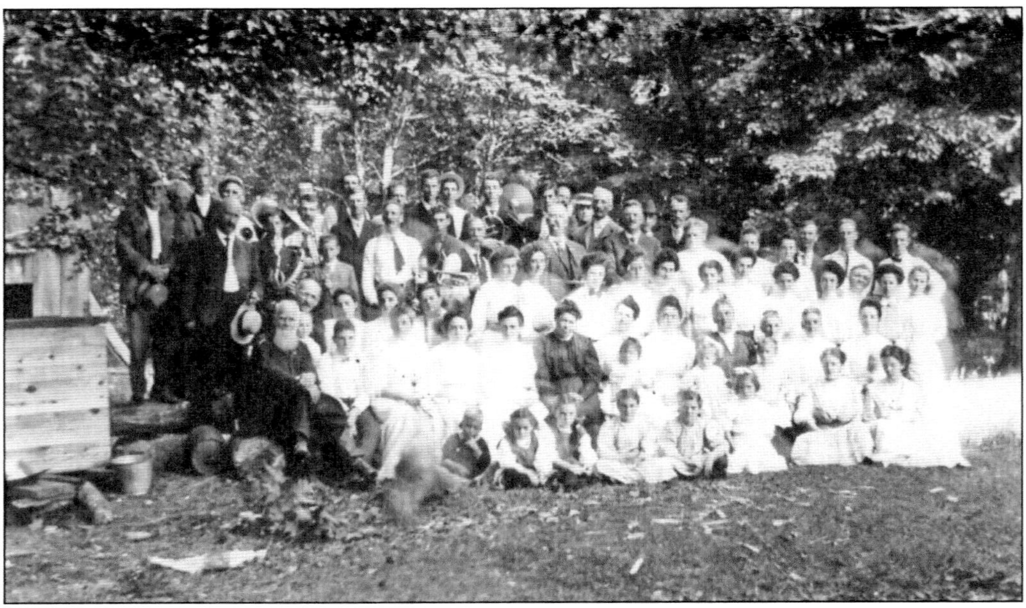

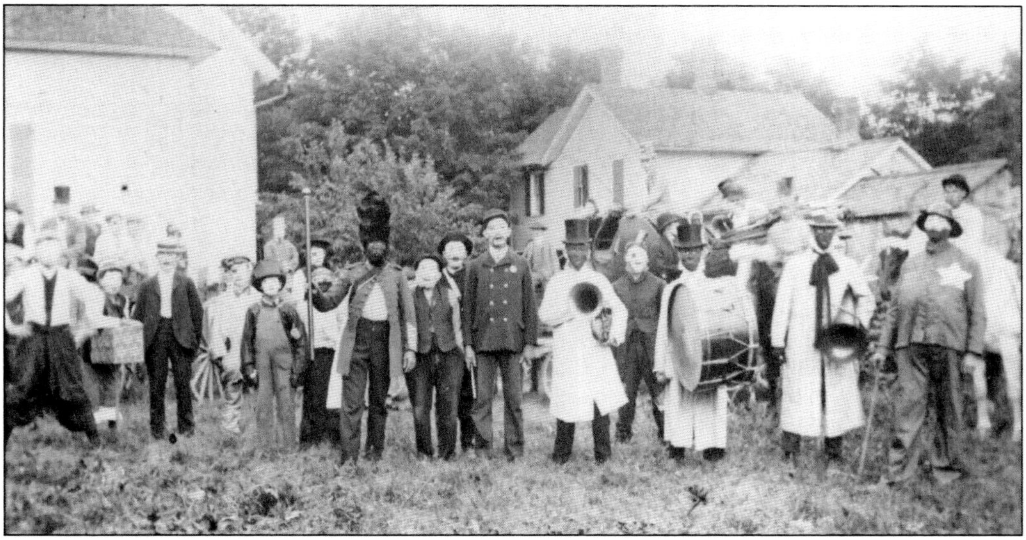

In 1905, there was a parade in Maine Village for the Fourth of July. The town band led the parade in a wagon and carriage and were dressed in costume. The first in line was the drum major, leading the band. The costumes added to the festivity of the occasion.

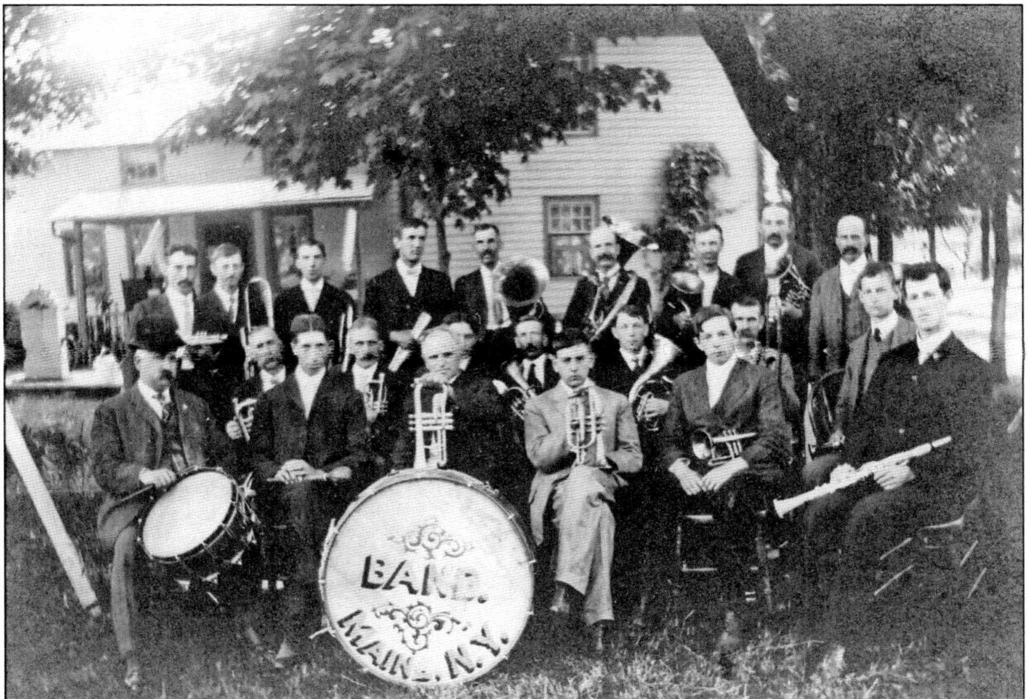

In 1907, the band played at Joe Hathaway's on Main Street in Maine Village. A lot of the names are familiar from their involvement in local music, including Lincoln, Bean, Allen, Bronk, Dyer, Holden, Dudley, and Delano. Charles Lincoln (first row, far left) holds a drum that is now in the Nanticoke Valley Historical Museum collection. It was donated by the Padbury family, who received it from Lincoln. Fred Ingalls played clarinet until he lost his fingers at work, at which point he switched to trombone. The band practiced at various places in town, including Hinaman's blacksmith shop and the four-room schoolhouse in Maine.

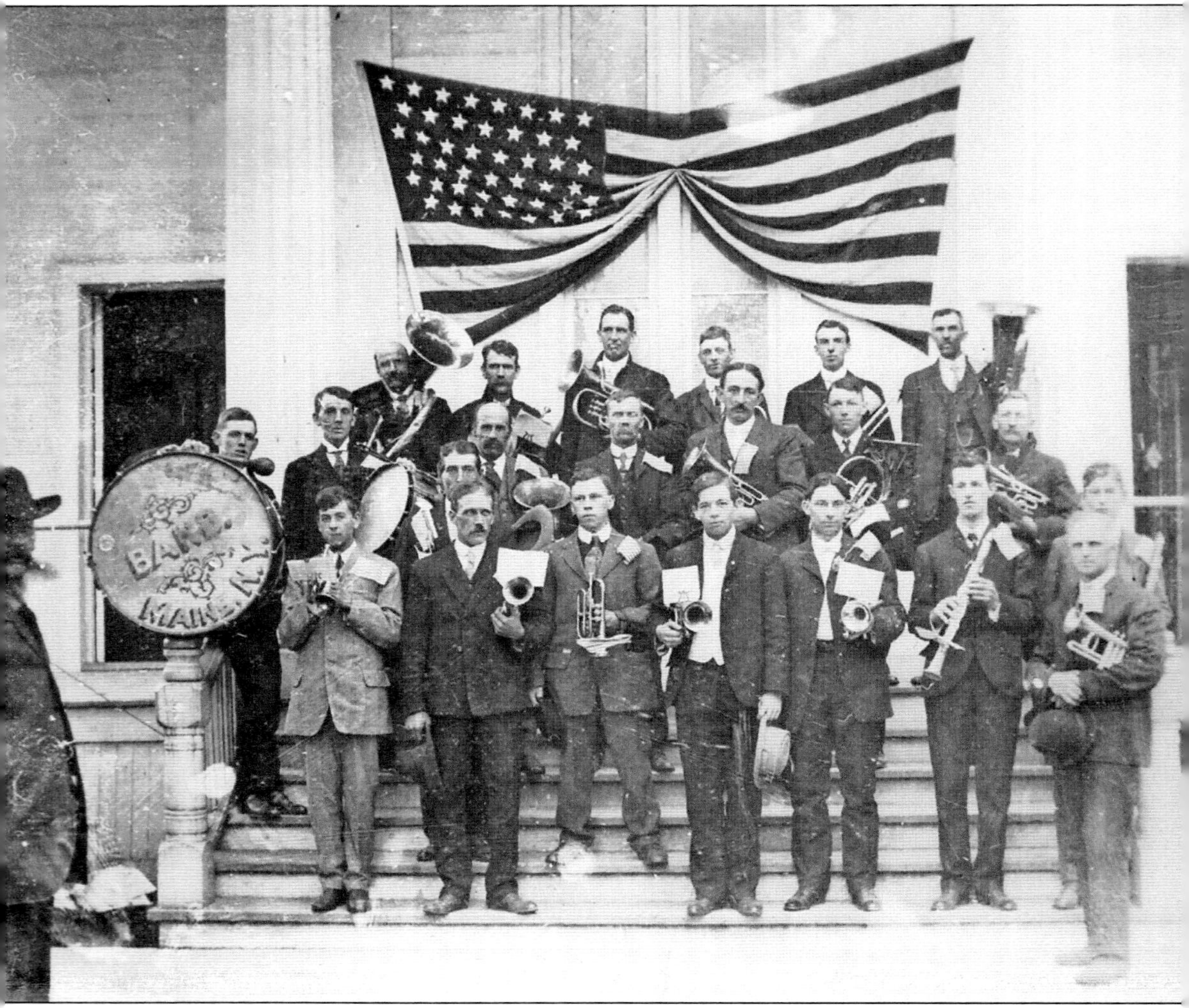

The Maine band poses at the Congregational church in 1905. They are, from left to right, (first row) J.R. Allen, drum; Fay Bronk, coronet; Clem Green; Wellington McIntyre; Guilford Dudley; Ray Moulton; Lynn Delano; and band leader Frank Bean; (second row) Earl Hineman, snare drum; John Allen; Henry Ingalls; Chauncey McIntyre; Earl Lewis; Rev. Ralph Gould; Dee Crandall; and Fred Ingalls; (third row) Fred Davey; Brom Green; Ralph Carley; William Frost; Roy Ellis; and Leroy Benton. Henry Hineman is in the lower left corner of this image.

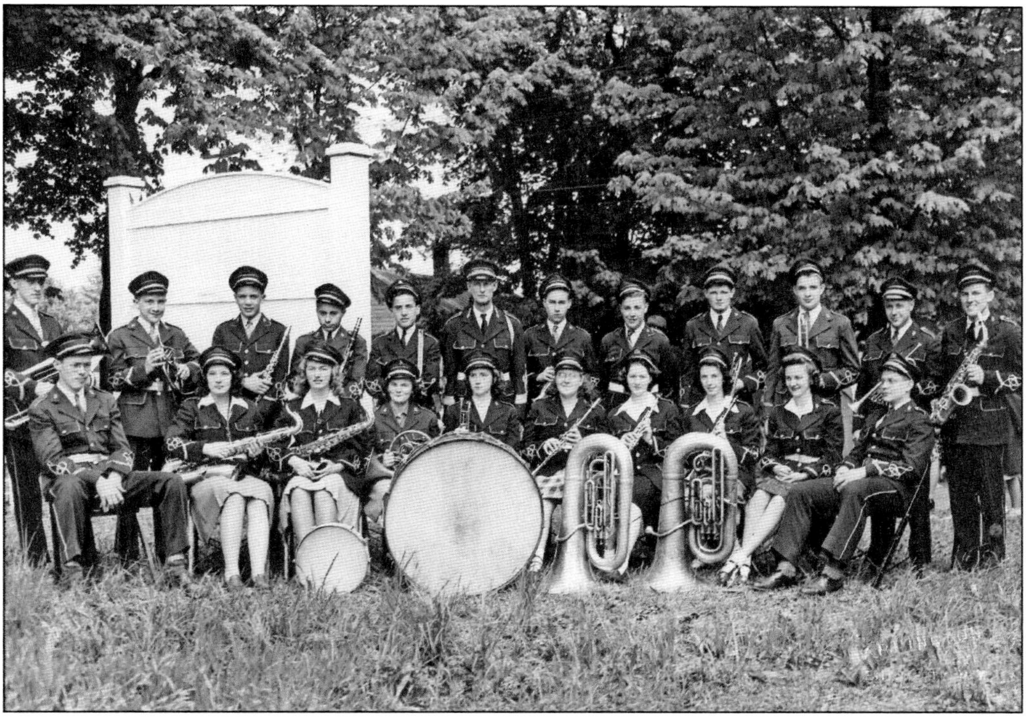

World War II meant that many from the all-male band had to leave town to join the effort, so a number of women were in the 1943 band. Pictured here are, from left to right, (first row) Allen Townsend, Marjorie Woodward, Virginia Wheeler, Ruth Ludington, Mildred Jordon, Alice D.E. Anjou, Winifred Ryder, Betty Welch, Maxine Holden, and Gale Tymeson; (second row) Donald Hess, Creighdon Ward, Lewis Dougherty, Richard Rude, Robert Barnes, Fred Ingalls, Norman Rude, Alan Payne, Donald Young, Trever Gamble, Edward Herendeen, and Guilford Woodward.

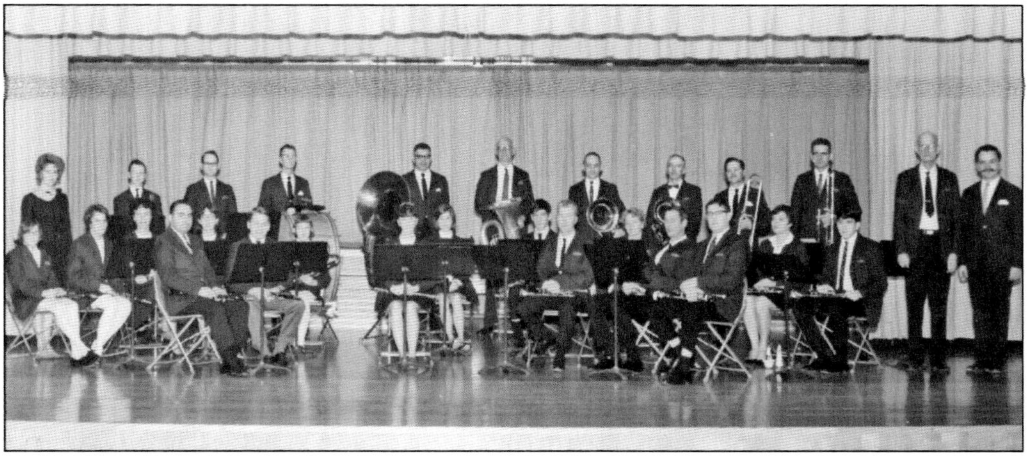

This February 9, 1969, concert was held in the Maine Memorial School. The band included, in no particular order, Sally Boettger, Lois Standish, Lynne Richardson, Douglas Welch, Betty Welch, Richard Rude, Charles Mydette, ? Jackson, Robert Babbitt, Earl Ingalls, ? Jackson, Elaine Welch, Robert Boettger, Cindy Moody, George Latell, Wayne Chadwick, William Moody, George Weisert, Eleanor Moody, Robert Ingalls, Newton Greenwood, Laurel Fry, Robert Zizzi, Jean Babbitt, Russell Clark, Stephen Boettger, Fred Ingalls, (conductor) and James Babbitt (assistant conductor, standing at far right).

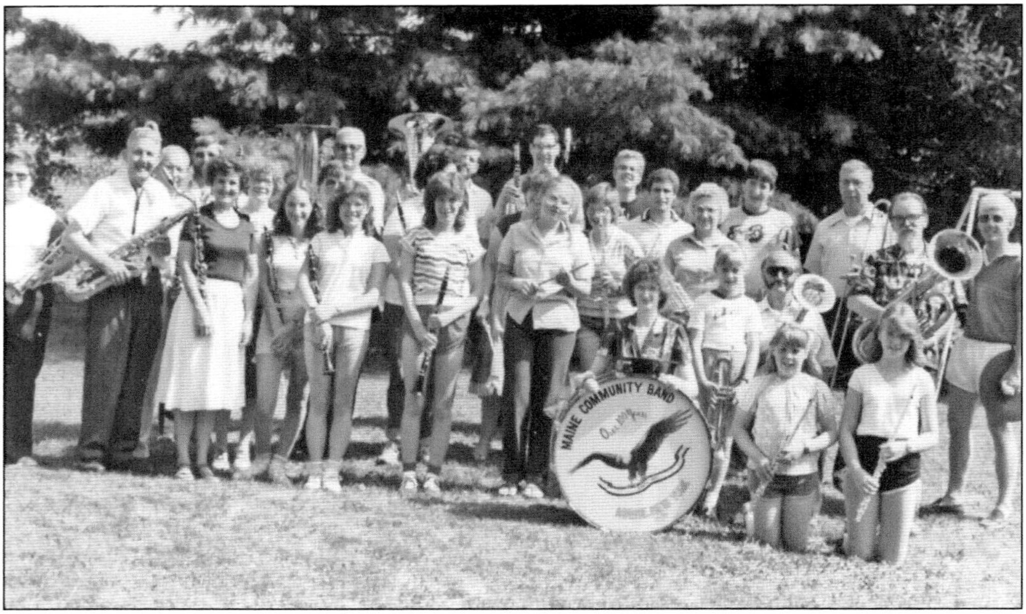

On August 15, 1982, the band met at Jim Babbitt's home in Allentown, New York, for the annual clambake. The band included, in no particular order, Bonnie Babbitt, Lyle Naylor, John Engstrom, Jan Kliewer, Gertrude Campbell, Mildred Brady, Lisa Halperin, Georgia Gall, Richard Shipway, Elaine Campbell, Janise Hanus, Jean Farley, Gage Stermensky, Gay Stannard, Scott Eddy, Edlyn Shipway, Anne Austin, Earl Raney, Kathleen Babbitt, Robert Rizzi, Dorothy Engstrom, Hillary Rozek, Kurt Eschbach, Joseph Hickey, Kassandra Rozek, William Eschbach, Sonya Babbitt, and Kenneth Rozek. (Courtesy of the Maine Community Band.)

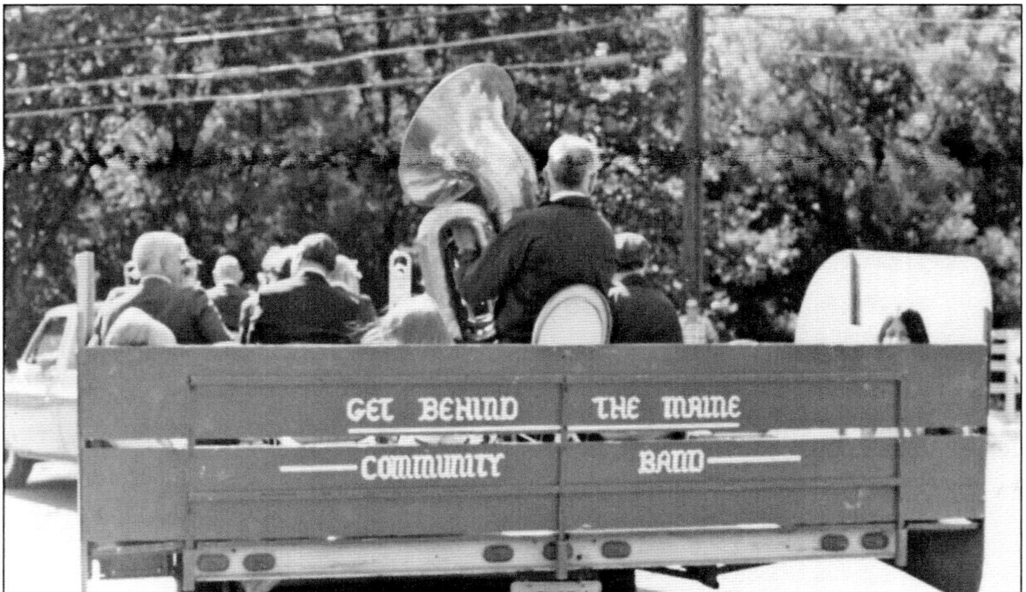

In 1973, band member Joe Hickey built a bandwagon for the group to ride on during parades. This red one was quite wide and had trouble turning corners when there was a large crowd. The later version of the bandwagon was somewhat smaller and narrower.

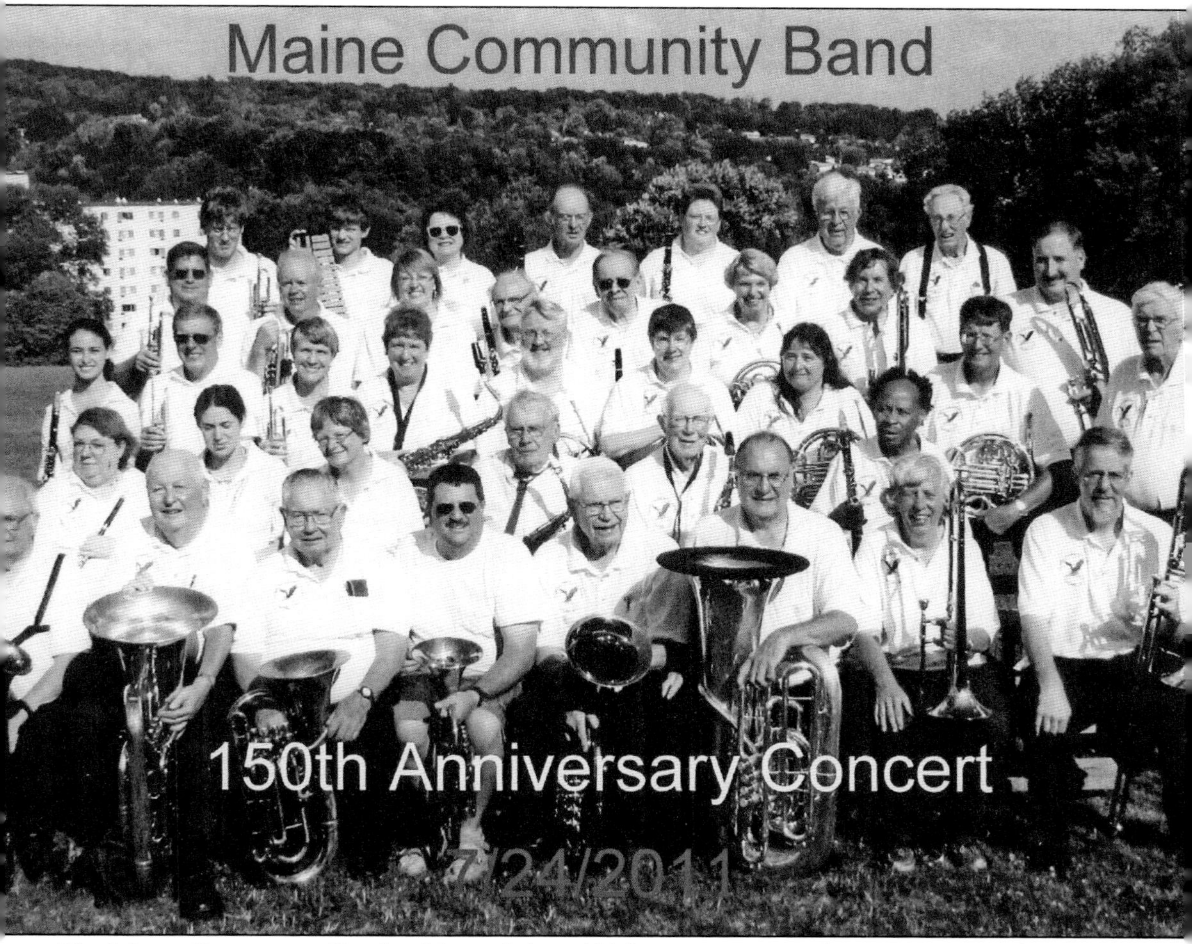

The Maine Community Band celebrated their 150th anniversary with a concert on July 24, 2011. The band included, from left to right, (first row) Wayne Rockwell, Richard Shipway, Carl Larson, Steve Robinson, Robert Boettger, Jack Moulton, Diane Wickman, and Glenn Fausel; (second row) Lyla Vinning-Wolford, Judy Kahn, Anne Austin, Jerry Heiss, William Garrett, and Chuck Pettus; (third row) Laura Jones, William Prinz, Ann Lowdermilk, Laurie Holdridge, David Banner, Donna Frye, Tama Mann, Jay Kosta, and Vern Hockenberry; (fourth row) Brian Miller, John Ruth, Edlyn Dutton, Pete Bolan, Maynard Koplin, Jane Scheibner, Nathan Raboy, and Kurt Eschback; (fifth row) Christopher Underwood, Charles Dutton, Sue Lisk, William Clark, Sheila Dodge-Davies, John Hiza, and Paul Smith. (Courtesy of the Maine Community Band; photograph by Tom Scheibner.)

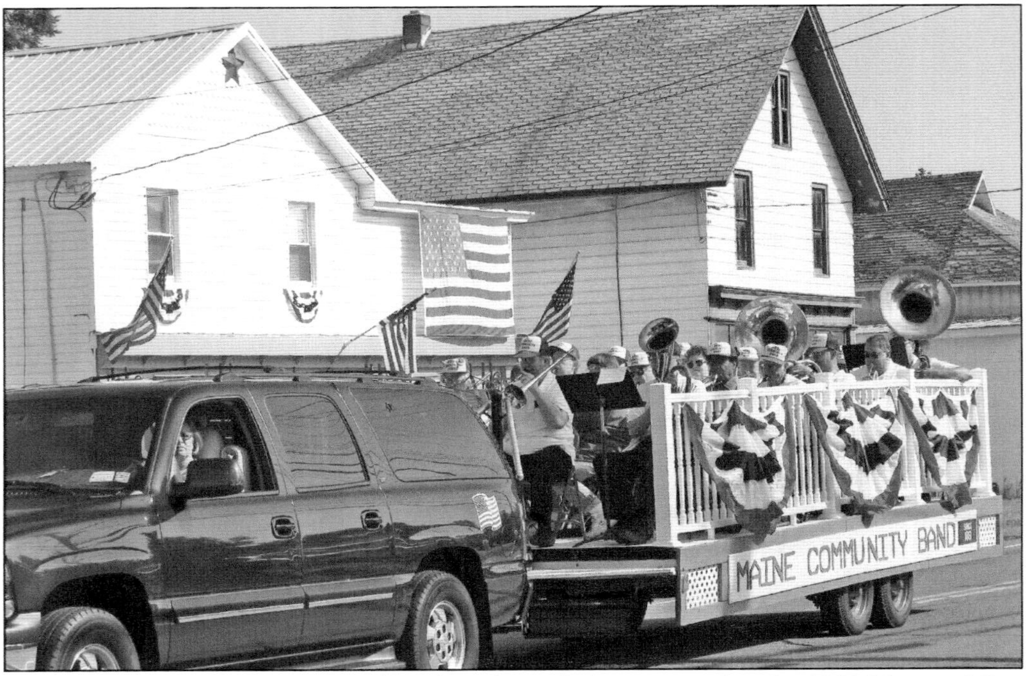

The new bandwagon, redone by Bill and Nathan Clark, is pictured at the 2009 Memorial Day parade in the hamlet of Maine. The parade is sponsored by the American Legion and always begins at Maine Memorial School at 9:00 a.m. sharp. It stops at the Maine Cemetery, where a ceremony is accompanied by two selections played by the band.

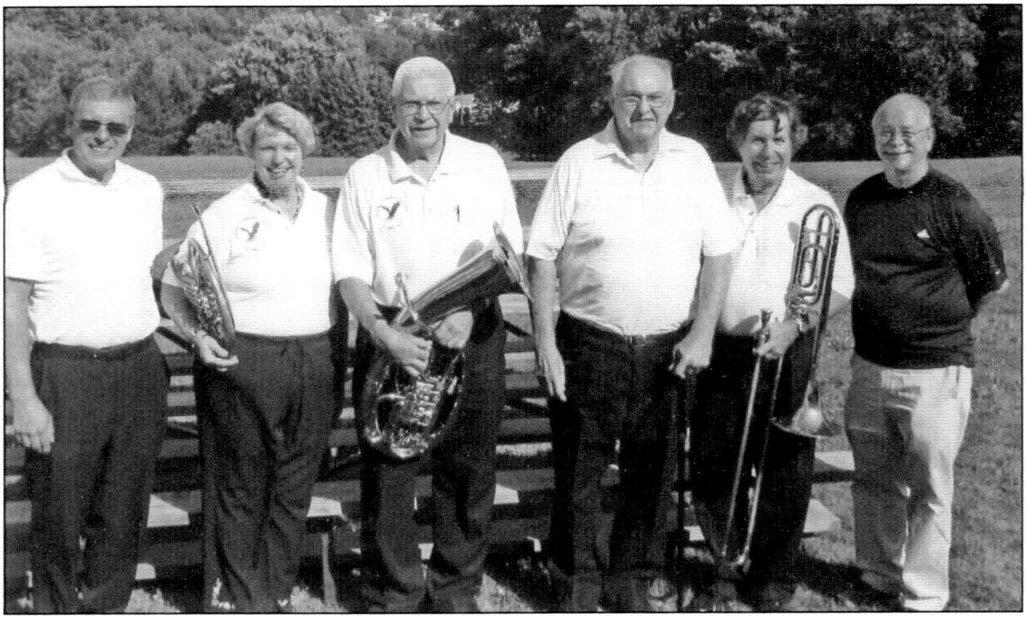

This photograph, taken at the 150th anniversary concert, includes, from left to right, William Prinz, Jane Scheibner, Robert Boettger, Thomas Mann, Nathan Raboy, and Robert Smith. All except Raboy were conductors of the band at one time. However, Raboy, with his brother Asher, composed the Maine Community Band March in 1973, when they were both students at Maine Endwell High School. (Courtesy of Maine Community Band, photograph by Tom Scheibner.)

Four

THE NANTICOKE VALLEY HISTORICAL SOCIETY

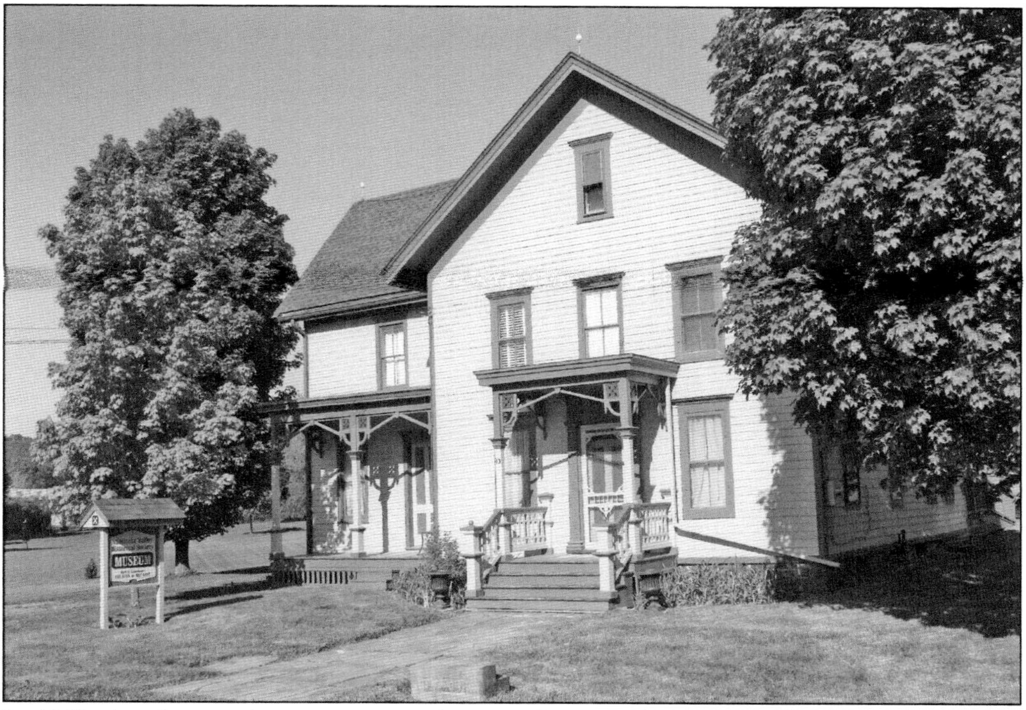

In 1969, the idea was born to create a historical society focusing on the Nanticoke Valley. The charter was signed in 1973, and the Nanticoke Valley Historical Society came into being. The museum is located at 13 Nanticoke Road, just north of Maine Village, and houses various exhibits and the community archives. The museum is open for meetings, school tours, to groups or individuals on Sundays in the summer, and by appointment. (Photograph by Stan Lisk.)

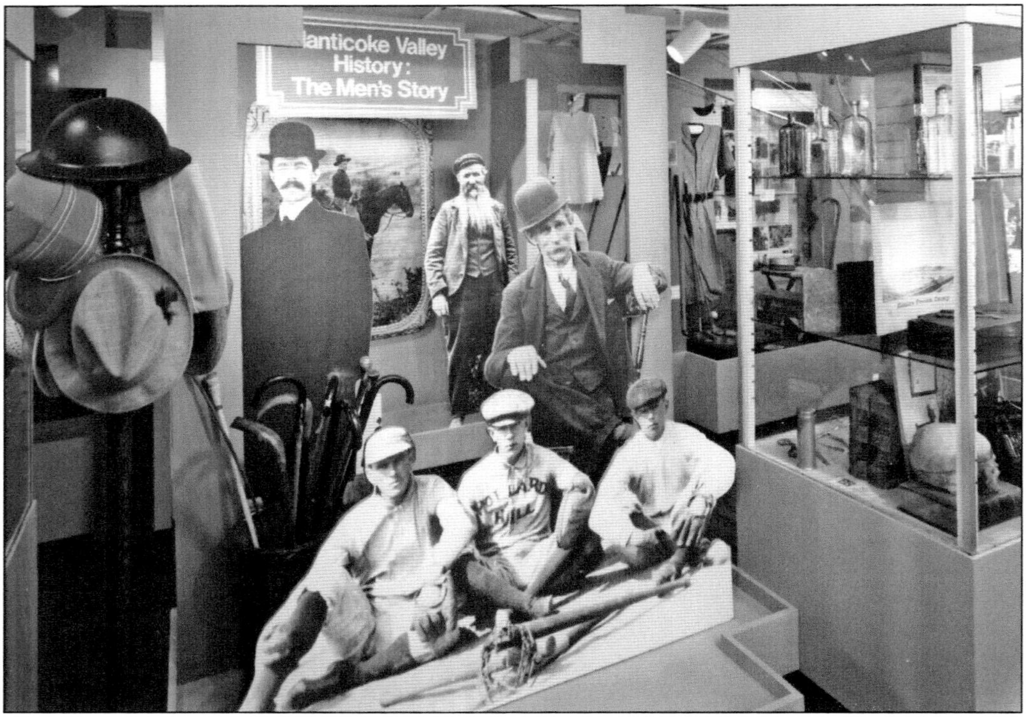

"The Men's Story" exhibit at the museum covers the history of the Nanticoke Valley from its earliest settlement in 1790 into the early 1900s. The exhibit also features doctors, lumbermen, farmers, architects, and various other tradesmen, plus a section focusing on leisure pursuits.

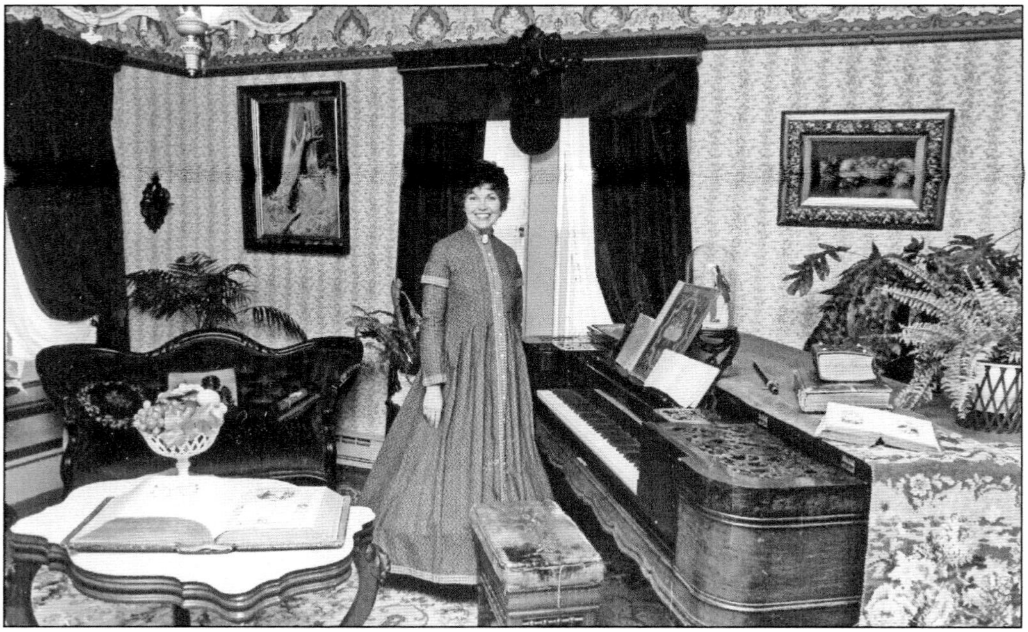

The 1870 parlor is the only period room in the museum. It is furnished as it might have been when the ell of the building was added after an 1870 fire. The piano was made in Syracuse in 1855 and is enjoyed by many children during school tours. In this photograph, Joyce Smith poses in a 1860s antique gown.

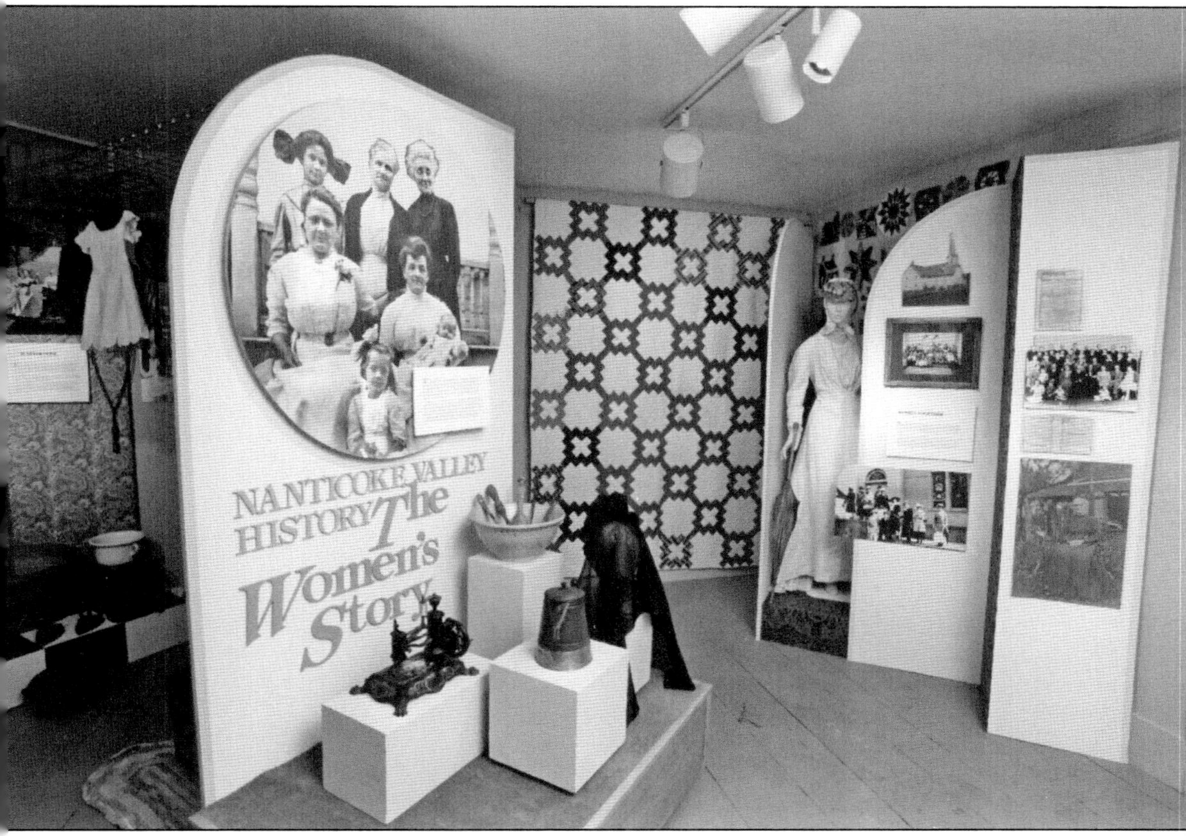

"The Women's Story" is told in this exhibit on the second floor of the museum. The display includes artifacts pertaining to women's work inside and outside the home and also covers family and social life in the Nanticoke Valley. There is a child's coffin to demonstrate the harsh reality of the times before modern medicine.

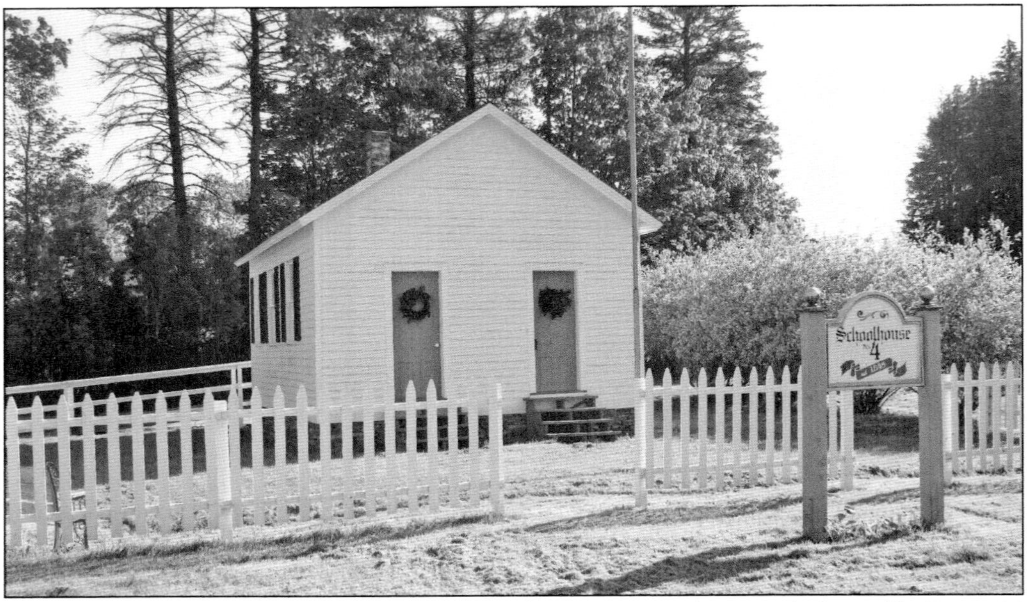

Schoolhouse number four is located across from the museum on the triangle formed by Route 26 and Nanticoke Road. It was once part of the joint school district of Owego and Union and was moved here and restored in 2000. The schoolhouse was built in 1845 and donated by Mr. and Mrs. Larry Thornton. The people of Nanticoke Valley donated part of the funds for the renovation. In 2010, the Maine Boy Scouts repainted and repaired the schoolhouse so that children of all ages could enjoy a trip back in time when they enter it. (Photograph by Philip Childs.)

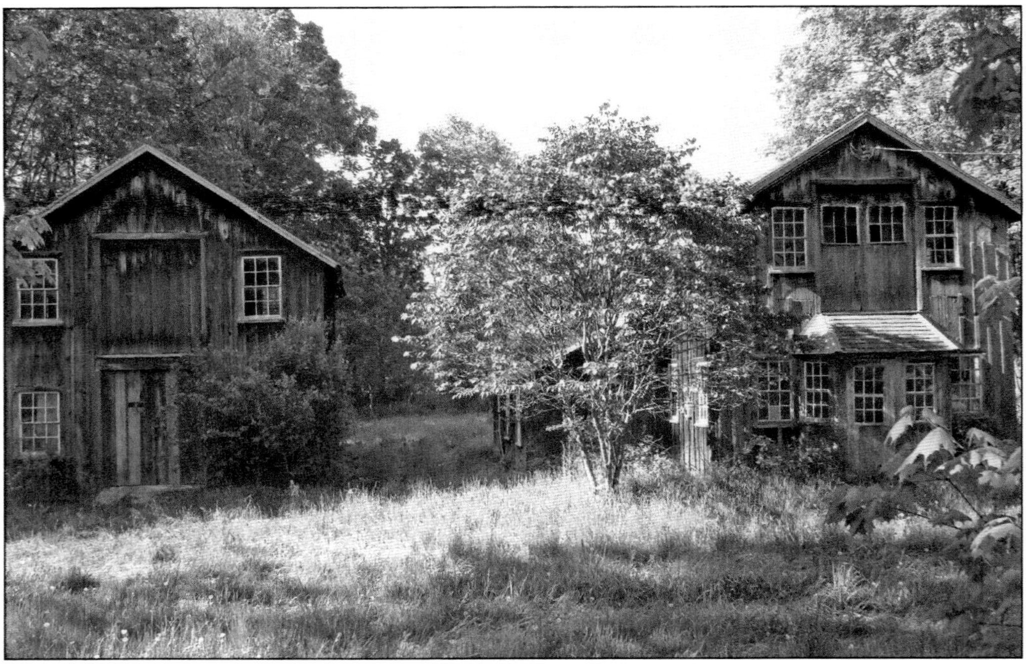

The old Norton Wagon Shops are on Nanticoke Road, across from Tiona Road. These buildings were owned by Janet Bothwell and were deeded to Nanticoke Valley Historical Society in 1978. Various repairs have been made and both roofs have been replaced. Plans are being considered for displaying various horse-drawn vehicles and agricultural items. (Photograph by Philip Childs.)

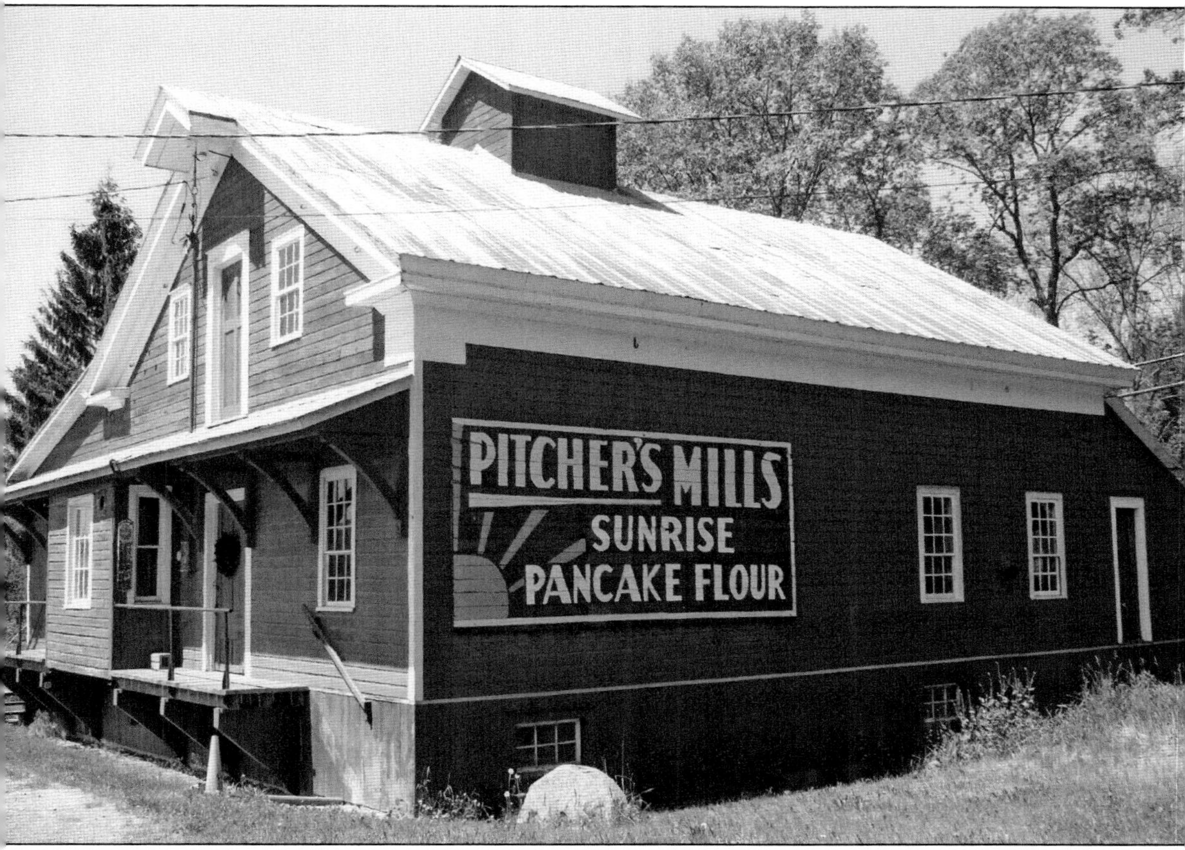

Pitcher's Mill, at 2819 Route 26, just north of Maine Village, was purchased by the Bowers Foundation in 1985 and donated to the Nanticoke Valley Historical Society in 1988. Maine Village residents launched a large restoration effort in 1993, led by Tom Kotasek and his assistant, Bob Griffin. Pitcher's Mill opened for tours in time for the 1998 Sesquicentennial of the Town of Maine. Tours of the mill are given on Sundays in the summer.

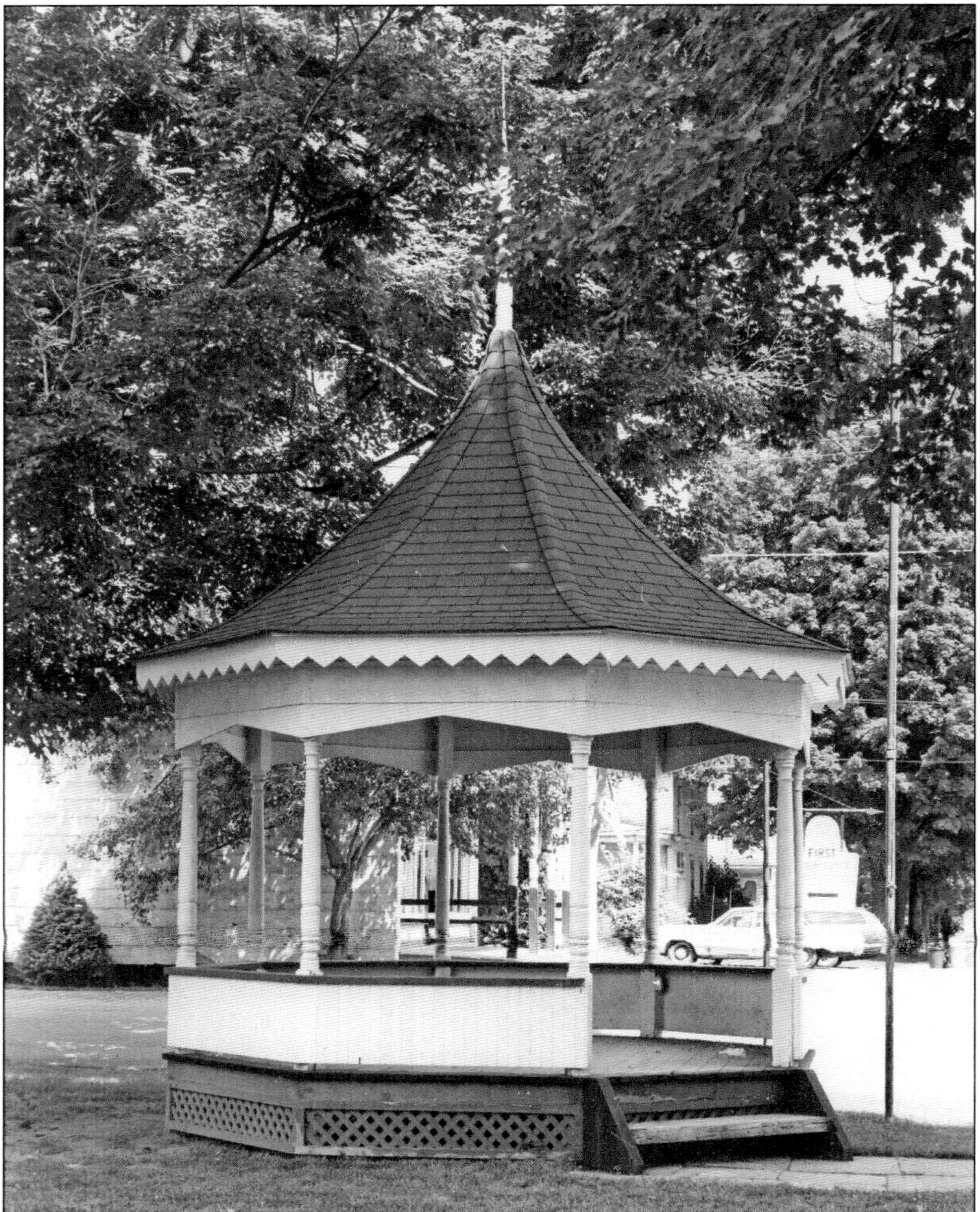

This pagoda was built in 1973 as part of the 125th anniversary celebration of the founding of the Town of Maine. It is a small-scale replica of the original pagoda that was located in the middle of Main Street and Church Street and was torn down in 1928. Built by Clarence Ames and his friends and family during a very mild winter, it was recently donated to the town by Clarence's wife, Lily Ames.

Bibliography

Bowers, Janet Whitney. *Cooking up the Creek: Recipes from a Rural New York Valley*. Maine, NY: Bowers' Corners Press, 1994.

Lewis, Ann Page. *Then and Now: A Pictorial History of the Town of Maine*. Maine, NY: self-published, 1998.

Osterud, Nancy Grey. *Bonds of Community: The Lives of Farm Women in Nineteenth-Century New York*. Ithaca, NY: Cornell University Press, 1991.

Platt Book of Broome County, New York, 1908. Des Moines, IA: North West Publishing Company, 1908.

Seward, William Foote. *Binghamton and Broome County, New York*. New York, NY, and Chicago: Lewis Historical Publishing Company, Inc., 1924.

Smith, H.P. *History of Broome County, New York*. Syracuse, NY: Mason Publishing Company, 1885.

Swan, Eleanor Brown. *Story of the Valleys: Towns of Nanticoke*. New York, NY: self-published, 1981.

Woodward, Shirley L. *A Short History of Maine, New York*. Maine, New York, NY: self-published, 1973.